THE HEART OF GLASGOW

THE HEART OF GLASGOW

JACK HOUSE

NWP

First published by Hutchinson & Co, 1965

This edition published by:

Neil Wilson Publishing
303 The Pentagon Centre
36 Washington Street
Glasgow G3 8AZ

Tel: 0141 221 1117
Fax: 0141 221 5363
E-mail: info@nwp.co.uk
www.nwp.co.uk

A catalogue record for this book is available
from the British Library.

ISBN 1-903238-85-4

Typeset in Aldine
Designed by Sallie Moffat

Produced in Poland by Polskabook

CONTENTS

EDITOR'S NOTE

W hen Jack House revised *The Heart of Glasgow* in 1972 he acknowledged that the city had altered considerably in the seven years since the book's first publication. He wrote, with some concern, of the threat of demolition work and motorway construction to the centre of the city, but hoped that architectural heritage would become more of a priority to the people of Glasgow than blind progress.

In the 21st century his concerns are as valid. Although preservation work and façade maintenance go on all over the city, Glasgow continues to lose buildings of historic interest and redevelopment is as common now as it was then.

In the forty years which have passed since the book's first appearance, some of the landmarks that Jack House describes have been converted – or have vanished entirely – and some of the streets have been renamed.

In keeping with the spirit of the revisions he made to the second edition, to account for topographical differences and for the sake of clarity, I have cut or amended his references to reflect the current situation. Stirling's Library on Royal Exchange Square, for example, has become The Gallery of Modern Art; St Enoch's Square no longer has a hotel and station platforms and St Mary's Place is now better known as Nelson Mandela Place.

'Perhaps,' he wrote in his Preface to the second edition, 'Glasgow is in danger of losing the cosy feeling it once had of a city state. In that case, I feel it's all the more important that I should keep *The Heart of Glasgow* abreast of the times.'

Graham Watson 2005

INTRODUCTION

The Dunrobin in George Street was a small public house to which was attached an even smaller restaurant. This was unusual in the Glasgow of the early 1950s but not unique. I mean, restaurants were unusual, and certainly ones that were part of public houses. There was of course Danny Brown's and the One O One and Guys and the famous Shandon Buttery. But in those days few people went to restaurants, ever. They went to chip shops if they ate out at all.

Even more unusual was that my mother and father went out to dine. It'd be 1955 I think. My father proudly took my mother to the Dunrobin which, though it was situated in an especially dingy slum district – the oldest area of Glasgow, Townhead – was in fact rather smart, with a trim exterior, and the restaurant tables had snowy napery and refulgent silver cutlery. My father summoned the waiter and ordered a steak for my mother. 'I'll have the Welsh rarebit,' he said. My mother looked up. 'No, David,' she said, 'I'd like the Welsh rarebit. Why don't you have the steak?' They began to discuss the matter. My father insisting that he preferred Welsh rarebit to steak, my mother demanding that *he* had the steak. The conundrum was soon settled however because the next thing they knew two bloody great plates of fillet steak with sautéd potatoes, mushrooms, sauce Bearnaise and a bottle of excellent burgundy arrived. My father was appalled. He could scarcely afford the Welsh rarebit, even if it *was* their 15th wedding anniversary. 'We didn't order this,' he cried. At this point a familiar pawky face appeared, a smiling face with two large rabbity teeth and a bald dome of a pate surmounting it. 'I hope you don't mind,' said the face, 'I couldn't help overhearing your conversation and I've always wanted to say this.' The buck-toothed smile shone again. 'This,' the benefactor said, 'is on The House.' It was, of course, Jack House – writer, journalist, broadcaster and, at that time, one of the most famous men in Scotland.

The entire story was typical of Jack House, all of the story. First, he loved to eariwig, and enjoyed, throughout his long life, observing other people. He was very good at that, and the practice made him *the* writer for newspapers, rather than a mere journalist, which he was. Secondly, he was a very generous man, generous in more than money, for he was more likely to praise than criticise. Thirdly, this was just the sort of eatery where you would find Jack House. Good, solid, unpretentious, in a poor district, but with distinction. And in Glasgow.

Jack used to, sort of, boast that he was not an aborigine of his beloved Glasgow. He was born in Tollcross in 1906, then not a part of Glasgow (it amalgamated with the city in 1922). Jack liked to make a point of another fact. The writer of perhaps the most vivid urban chauvinistic song of all – and we can include *Maybe it's Because I'm a Londoner, New York, New York* and *I Left my Heart in San Francisco* – the greatest paean of praise to a city, *I Belong to Glasgow*, was written by Will Fyffe; and as Jack House was ever telling us, the writer of this anthem hailed from Dundee. He relished the irony of this, just as he wallowed in his tale of being an incomer. For that Jack House became known as 'Mr Glasgow'.

There have been two others since who have aspired to the title. One was wee Cliff Hanley, another pawky and talented writer. The other is, I suppose, me. Luckily, like Will Fyffe and Jack, I am not a native-born Glaswegian either: I was born in Irvine, Ayrshire. I took less time than Jack to adopt my city though. My father, a Gorbalian of Highland parentage, moved our family to Glasgow when I was six months old.

We moved to Cathcart, then as now a small douce village on the edge of the city. When I was seven we moved to a dreadful part of the city, and the oldest part, the very Heart of Glasgow, a stone's throw from the Cathedral, at the bottom of Rottenrow, whose primary school was where my father, a school janitor, held office and majesty.

So far I have talked a great deal – too much – about myself. But there is a reason for this. When I rang up *The Herald* to check on the date of Jack's death, the nice lassie in the library had never even heard of Jack House. I have a suspicion she had never heard of me either. She turned to the Internet and typed in his name on Google. The closest entry it threw up was as follows: Jack's House – a seven piece Soul Band playing a selection of classic and present-day soul music hits.

Jack would have loved that.

When he died in 1991 he was 84, much loved and revered by older Glaswegians, but almost forgotten by younger ones, few of whom knew what he had done for the city they lived in. For in House's heyday, and it was a long day too, he oversaw one of the darkest periods in Glasgow's history, when the very name of what was once known as the Second City of Empire was a by-word throughout the world for violence, deprivation, slums, drunkenness and decay: Sodom and Gomorrah rolled into one. Novels such as *No Mean City* and plays like *The Gorbals Story* had seen to that. House recalled that a young American woman had asked him, seriously, if Glasgow had any gardens (Glasgow still has more parkland per square mile than any other city in Europe), but, he reported, she knew all about the razor slashers. As a young boy of 12 on a visit to my great aunt in Weston-Super-Mare I was asked by a shopkeeper where in Scotland I lived, and when I answered, 'Glasgow', was rewarded by the astounding outburst: 'What a terrible place to come from!' This was the Glasgow which Jack House defended, promoted, and eventually even got politicians to do the same.

Jack was a proselytiser, an evangelist, for Glasgow and although he wrote about and around Glasgow all of his long life, *The Heart of Glasgow* was his most famous. And it is only about the *heart* of it, a spare few streets in the old city, where I was brought up.

He wrote the book over a three-year period and it was published first in 1965 as a hardback. I was living in London then; the Beatles were triumphant, London was about to start swinging, flower power was just around the corner, the Vietnam war was raging and the world was changing. Youth flourished, but not Glasgow. The city, whose motto is 'Let Glasgow Flourish', was doing nothing of the kind: it was rotting in front of our eyes. Jack brought out this book about the very origins of the city at an inauspicious time. Yet it became a bestseller throughout the UK and, I believe, gave a new heart to the heart of Glaswegians. They re-invented their spirit, that zeitgeist which had fuelled the confidence of their mid-Victorian forebears. Twenty-five years later Glasgow was the European City of Culture. In 1965, battered and worn, nobody could have possibly imagined such an accolade. *The Heart of Glasgow* told Glaswegians what they had been. It looked to the past and told the lieges what their history was, and what the present of that time had been. But it presaged another circumstance: what the future could be, and indeed what it became. Fourteen years after that European culture accolade Jack House's Glasgow is battered and worn again. It has somehow lost the plot.

Edinburgh is once more haughtily ascendant. There was no reason why the Glasgow City Chambers, that most magnificent municipal edifice, the most splendid in Northern Europe, should not have been the seat of a Scottish parliament, yet that went to Edinburgh. Jack House was a fighter for Glasgow and enjoyed eight decades of taunting the good folk of Edinburgh. It was a good-natured taunt though and he was respected in that city too. The book made Glasgow look as big as it is. It made Edinburgh look what it is as well, a wee bit small.

But in truth Jack's sojourn in the old city was limited to only a little stretch of his adopted burg. He says himself in his Envoi that he hadn't been able to write about the great and splendid suburbs of Glasgow, or of the East End or West End or my own South Side. This is a book about the origins and the originals of Glasgow. I grew up in that part, the old city, at a bad time in its history. I know and knew every street and mean alleyway. When Jack described Dobbies Loan in Townhead as a smart little spot, he was talking about a century before him. In my day it was a deposit for litter, raw sewage and prostitutes. The Cross Keys Inn at the top end of Rottenrow was a shebeen, and the Angel Closes were indeed closes. They were closed down when an outbreak of cholera occurred, unbelievably, in 1957.

There is a difference today. The Merchant City, which Jack House lived long enough to see, revitalised much of what he writes about in this book. Buchanan Street is still for toffs. The Argyle Arcade remains a centre for expensive jewellers. Sloan's still exists though those of us who recollect it as a pleasant little old-fashioned supper establishment are a little nonplussed at its present air of senility. Enough there is of the present Heart of Glasgow for Jack to have recognised.

And he would have recognised one particular aspect. No matter what, the Glaswegians themselves remain much the same as ever they were. The younger ones look dirtier and shabbier, to my mind, than those of old and the older ones look, to my mind as well, much the same. It is up to Glaswegians like myself to keep up standards. Smart, generous, and a little loud-mouthed with a drink in you. A guid conceit.

When this book first came out many Glaswegians were a little ashamed of their city but wanted to express their affection for their homeland, for, don't mistake this, Glasgow is a country: a city state more than any other in Britain. Indeed, like Buda and Pest, it is two cities and I know, for I live on the South Side. I am a Sou-Sider. But I am also, like Jack House, a Glaswegian. And both of us belong to Glasgow. The Heart of it.

Jack McLean 2005

1

THE NONSUCH OF SCOTLAND

The City of Glasgow is undoubtedly the greatest city in the world. This, of course, is the opinion of Glaswegians – and maybe not altogether the whole of the population of Glasgow. Purists, by the way, say that natives of this great city should be known as Glasgovians, but nobody in Glasgow recognises himself under that title. We are an irrational lot and we have been called Glaswegians for so long that we like the name.

The City of Glasgow is known for its ugliness, its dirt, its slums, its ships, its 'Red' Members of Parliament, its gangsters, its soldiers, its tramcars – gone, alas, like our youth, too soon – its Saturday nights, its journalists and its drinking.

When I refer to the City of Glasgow, incidentally, I should emphasise that I am talking about Glasgow, Scotland. Some time ago I made a visit to the United States of America to see the Glasgows there. There are ten towns called Glasgow in the USA, and one place called Glasgow Village. I found that in Glasgow, Kentucky – the largest of the American Glasgows, population seven thousand – they had heard of Glasgow, Scotland, because a letter addressed to *The Glasgow Times* had reached the Scottish city instead of being sent to the Kentucky one.

In Glasgow Village, St Louis, they had also heard of Glasgow, Scotland, and had even adopted the coat-of-arms of the Scottish city. In actual fact, Glasgow Village, St Louis, is named after a man called Glasgow who had a vineyard on the site of the modem development. But the Glasgow Villagers prefer to think of their area as Scottish in background and the streets are given such names as Brigadoon Circle, Campbell, Macrae and McLellan Streets, and the most prominent feature, an eminence of more than two hundred feet, is known as Ben Nevis.

In the other American cities of Glasgow which I visited, Glasgow, Scotland, was practically unknown. I was asked to speak to the children in one or two schools, and you have to be very brave indeed to speak to American schoolchildren. When I explained to a group of kids in a schoolroom in Glasgow, Virginia, that Glasgow, Scotland, had a population of just under one million I could see that they regarded me as a city-booster who didn't worry much about the truth.

This irked me a little, and I proceeded to explain that Glasgow had one of the biggest football stadiums in the world in Hampden Park, that Glasgow had the second largest cinema in Europe (Green's Playhouse, holding nearly five thousand), possessed more than sixty major parks, owned a school older than Eton (Glasgow High School), had the biggest single building devoted to education in the world (then the Royal College of Science and Technology, now part of the University of Strathclyde) and had a climate so useful that it was produced artificially in India.

Then I played my trump card and revealed that during World War II the Clyde shipyards built and repaired more vessels than all the shipyards of the USA put together. That was true, but a mistake. I could tell that these children disbelieved me utterly. When it came to question time a fat boy with large glasses rose and said, 'Sir, is it true that boys who go to school in your Glasgow wear skirts?'

This got a big laugh. I tried to explain what a grand garment the kilt is, but my audience refused to believe it. Some day they'll grow up and maybe one or two of them may even visit Glasgow, Scotland. If they remember what I said to them in Glasgow, Virginia, they'll be most disappointed at the number of kilts they'll see in my Glasgow.

Yes, it's a sad thing to say, but however important Glaswegians consider Glasgow, it's either practically unknown to the rest of the world or known for all the wrong things.

There was a time, around the beginning of this century, when Glasgow was known as the Second City of the Empire. Indeed, a Russian grand duke, carried away by the success of a launching on the River Clyde, once called it 'the centre of intelligence of Europe'. Today, though, Glasgow is not even the Second City of Britain. Birmingham, by extending her boundaries, claimed that honour a few years ago. The last time I looked up Glasgow's position among the world's most populous cities, I discovered that it came 164th. I haven't had the heart to look it up since.

It may be 164th to the rest of the world, but it is first to me. I have been in love with the City of Glasgow, Scotland, for more than seventy years. For me, Glasgow was the greatest town in the world from the moment I realised I was seeing it. And now, after seeing London, Paris, Berlin, Moscow, Mexico City, Brussels, Helsinki, Copenhagen, Stockholm, New York, Bangkok, Toronto, Milan, Zurich, Prague, Cologne, Leningrad, Singapore, Amsterdam, Tbilisi, Rotterdam, Chicago, Dublin, Montreal, Edinburgh, Hamburg, Washington – to name, as they say, but a few – I'd rather live in Glasgow.

If this marks me out as an eccentric I should point out that there are about a million of us, all as mad as coots, all daft about Glasgow. And it's surprising how many Sassenachs and foreigners come to Glasgow, much against their will and purely for business reasons, and decide to settle here for good. You will doubtless be astonished to know that, judged on a population basis, there is a bigger percentage of English people living in Scotland than there are Scots living in England. A great many of them are now acclimatised and have no intention of returning to the Deep South.

It's difficult to explain the hold that Glasgow gets on its natives and its visitors. There is plenty of beauty in Glasgow, but you have to search for it. Glasgow must be seen through the eyes of love. Edinburgh, the capital of Scotland, is a mere forty-five miles away and yet completely different, in any way you like to mention, from Glasgow.

Edinburgh is obviously beautiful (you will get Edinburghers who run the place down, but they're trying to make a name for themselves!). Indeed, every time I emerge from Waverley Station, and see that wonderful skyline of Edinburgh Castle and the Princes Street Gardens flowing in front of me, I feel that Edinburgh is presented to the visitor on a plate.

A great deal is made, of course, of the feud between Glasgow and Edinburgh. I belong myself to a sodality known as the All Saints, composed of an equal number of Glasgow and Edinburgh members and devoted to keeping the feud alive. I'm all for a feud between cities, and I think it's wonderful that in a country as small as Scotland you should find two such completely divergent towns less than fifty miles apart.

One night I arrived in Paris and was intrigued to see posters around the Champs Elysees advertising an 'illustrated lecture' at the Salle Pleyel on 'Scotland, Land of Monsters and Legends'. Fortunately this lecture was to be delivered on the following evening, so, first thing in the morning, I went along to the Salle Pleyel and booked a seat. It was a good thing I did, for the enormous auditorium was packed with Parisians who had come to hear and see all about Scotland.

My French is vestigial, but the lecturer told so many stories and made so many quips, which I already knew, that I was able to follow him without the slightest difficulty. He drew all the usual contrasts between Glasgow, the industrial town, and Edinburgh, the cultured city. He made that prize joke, beloved of Glasgow provosts since ever there was a provost in Glasgow, 'Edinburgh is the Capital, but Glasgow has the capital!' He said that Glaswegians, if asked what was the finest thing out of Edinburgh, would reply, 'The Glasgow train from Waverley Station.'

Just to redress the balance, he told the famous story of the competition run in Edinburgh where the first prize was one week's holiday in Glasgow. The second prize was two weeks' holiday in Glasgow!

The Parisians loved it. All around about me I could hear them chortling. True, the part of the lecture which enthralled them most was the bit about the Loch Ness Monster, and they were undoubtedly thrilled by a colour film of the Military Tattoo at the Edinburgh Festival. But at the interval, when they have the civilised French habit of opening the bars even at a lecture, I heard the names of Glasgow and Edinburgh mentioned time after time.

I'm not at all sure what effect the lecturer had on his audience. It might be that they would decide to see

Edinburgh if they ever visited Scotland, and would give Glasgow the go-by. This is the sort of thing which happens in quite a number of countries outside the United Kingdom. I have met American tourists who were booked for one night in Glasgow because they had to arrive there, and then went straight to Edinburgh. What worried them was that they'd rather liked the look of Glasgow and after flying visits to Glasgow Cathedral and the Kelvingrove Art Galleries they felt they wanted to see more of the city. Other people, particularly Russians, had one look at Sauchiehall Street and wanted to spend their whole holiday there.

To say that Glasgow is industrial and Edinburgh is beautiful and cultural is just plain nonsense. Edinburgh has a great deal of industry within its boundaries, particularly such very fine industries as printing and brewing. To my mind, Glasgow has much more genuine, native culture than Edinburgh. I got into trouble with a Lord Provost of Edinburgh some years ago when, during an Edinburgh International Festival edition of the BBC programme *Tonight*, I said, 'The difference between Glasgow and Edinburgh is that Edinburgh has culture for three weeks in the year, while Glasgow has culture for fifty-two weeks in the year.'

I don't mean to be anti-Edinburgh. I just like to stick up for Glasgow. And what saddens me is that while the vast majority of Glaswegians go to visit Edinburgh, very few Edinburghers think of visiting Glasgow. I was asked one night to give a talk about the two cities to an audience in a pretty well-off kirk in Edinburgh. At one point I asked everyone in the hall who had visited Glasgow to put up his or her hand. Out of an audience of more than two hundred, only a score of hands were raised. And afterwards I discovered that nearly a dozen of those who raised their hands were Glaswegians whose work had taken them to settle down in Edinburgh.

All the same, there is the perfectly true story of the BBC radio unit which visited the great swimming pool in the Edinburgh suburb of Portobello to make some recordings. It was a lovely day and the place was packed with Edinburgh children. They were asked to sing anything they liked, so that it could be recorded with the swish of the artificial waves behind the song.

What did these Edinburgh weans do? With one voice they broke into *I Belong to Glasgow*!

The first time I visited Russia – with a Scottish Cultural Delegation, of all things – I taught Russians in Leningrad and Georgians in Gagra to sing *I Belong to Glasgow*, and Ina, one of our interpreters, translated the city's anthem into Russian. So it may very well be sung there to this day.

When the words were translated to a group of women factory workers in Leningrad, they said they understood and appreciated the meaning of the song very well. Just in case you don't know, the chorus goes:

> *I belong to Glasgow, dear old Glasgow town,*
> *But there's something the matter with Glasgow, for it's going roun' and roun'.*
> *I'm only a common old working man, as anyone here can see,*
> *But when I get a couple of drinks on a Saturday, Glasgow belongs to me.*

I have also sung *I Belong to Glasgow* in the language spoken in the Garden of Eden, the Gaelic. When I appeared on a Scottish Television programme called *Highland Air*, the fear-an-tighe (or compere), the late Lord Bannerman, and the singer, Alasdair Gillies, translated the song into Gaelic and I learned it off by heart.

This is only right, since Glasgow is the greatest Highland town in the world. There are more Highlanders in this city than there are in any other place in Britain (including all those policemen in London), and even Canadian towns cannot compete with Glasgow in their Gael force.

After this paean in praise of our song it's maybe an anticlimax to tell you that the words were written by a man from Dundee, the great comedian, Will Fyffe; an Aberdonian has claimed that he wrote the tune; and I discovered that in Wagner's 'Siegried', Wotan has an aria the first line of which is identical to *I Belong to Glasgow*. This has been homologated by none other than the famous Scottish conductor, Sir Alexander Gibson. This just shows how Glasgow affects even foreigners!

Do I protest too much when I praise my city? Well, I think of the people who have visited Glasgow with the general idea of dark, satanic mills and dirt and drunkenness, and have remained to praise a vital, lively city with all sorts of unexpected beauties. I think of the people whose thoughts of Glasgow, if they think of it all, are based on reading *No Mean City*, or seeing the play *The Gorbals Story*, or watching the ballet *Miracle of the Gorbals*.

I remember, too, the intelligent girl cutter in our Army Kinematograph Service studios at Wembley during the war who asked quite seriously, 'Are there any gardens in Glasgow?' She'd heard about the razor-slashers, though.

Most people who run down Glasgow have never been in the city. I like to recall that Gilbert Harding, a man much readier for blame than praise, found Glasgow 'real' compared with Edinburgh.

I took Sir John Betjeman round Glasgow and he went into raptures. He described it as 'the greatest Victorian city in the world'. Once that would have been regarded as denigration, but not now. He said he felt it was all wrong that London should be the headquarters of the Victorian Society, for London couldn't compare with Glasgow in the matter of fine Victorian buildings. I have taken many people round Glasgow but never one as enthusiastic as Sir John Betjeman.

There is, however, a very big fly in the amber. Glasgow has been undergoing a sea change, anything but rich and rare. Good old buildings are disappearing and multi-storey office blocks are taking their place. The Glasgow I have known and loved for more than seventy years seems to be losing its shape. Only a matter of a few years from now the centre of Glasgow may well be unrecognisable to the older generation. We are not fortunate in our City Council in Glasgow and too often buildings of character in the city have been sacrificed for a matter of expedience.

One of Glasgow's greatest characters was a man named David Dale, born in 1739. He was the typical Glaswegian, although he was actually born in Stewarton – small, stout, strong, pawky, kind and enterprising. It's said that Sir Walter Scott, when he wrote *Rob Roy*, modelled the character of the great Bailie Nicol Jarvie on David Dale. Dale was a weaver when weavers were important people in Glasgow, and went out on a Sunday in their braws, carrying a cane with a golden knob on the top of it.

Eventually he gave up weaving for the linen-yarn business and opened a shop near Glasgow Cross. From linen he went to cotton with great success, and then he met George Macintosh, from the Highlands, who had invented 'cudbear', a dyeing system which was perfect for cotton goods. David Dale and George Macintosh formed a partnership, out of which the first Turkey Red works in Britain were started. Macintosh was so keen to keep his methods a secret that he built his cudbear works out at Dunchattan Street (which no longer exists) and engaged only Highlanders as workers. At that time the Highlanders spoke only the Gaelic tongue, and so no Lowlanders could ferret the secrets from them. It was the Macintosh family who invented the rainproof coat named after them.

Banking in Glasgow in those days was on a very small scale compared with banking in Edinburgh, which was then twice the size of Glasgow and considered a greater industrial centre! David Dale decided that there should be a Glasgow branch of one of the biggest Edinburgh banks, the Royal. He knew that he could get the other half of the shop he owned at Glasgow Cross for £2 10s a year, and he proposed to turn this into the Glasgow branch of the Royal Bank with, naturally, himself as agent.

David Dale had a fine house, built in the Robert Adam style in Charlotte Street, between Glasgow Cross and Glasgow Green. He invited some of the directors of the Royal Bank to come by coach from Edinburgh and dine with him at his home. On the day of this visit there was torrential rain. Two famous burns, the Molendinar and the Camlachie, which ran down into the Clyde about this point, overflowed and the river rose too. The water swept over Glasgow Green and the houses at the lower end of Charlotte Street were soon flooded.

The cook rushed up from the kitchen in the basement to tell David Dale that the dinner was ruined. The water kept rising and the wine cellar as well as the kitchen was awash.

What a situation for a Glasgow man to be in! His kitchen and his wine cellar under water, and a coach full of important Edinburgh bankers rapidly approaching from the east. David Dale didn't hesitate. He ran up Charlotte Street to his neighbours who were not affected by the flooding. He explained the position to them, the importance of securing a branch of the Royal Bank for Glasgow. Being true Glaswegians, they responded at once. In three different houses a new dinner was cooked, to be taken to David Dale's house when the Edinburgh gentlemen arrived.

As for the wine, David Dale's daughter climbed on to the back of a six-foot porter. They went down into the flooded cellar and Miss Dale knew so well where each bottle of claret or burgundy or brandy or usquebaugh was, that she could direct the porter just where to dive and bring up the requisite number.

The Edinburgh bankers arrived. They found the situation, with floods extending from the river right up to Charlotte Street, exciting. They were delighted with their dinner and with their wine. Glasgow (and David Dale) got a branch of the Royal Bank.

Some two hundred years later the Royal Bank of Scotland celebrated what David Dale had done for them by putting his portrait on their bank notes. His native Stewarton, by the way, keep his memory green by way of the David Dale Restaurant built alongside the ruins of the house in which he was born.

David Dale's daughter, who did this notable rescue work on the porter's back, went on to marry Robert Owen, a socialist who is internationally known today, when his father-in-law, from whom he took many of his best ideas, is quite forgotten. Dale, with Richard Arkwright, opened the great cotton mill at New Lanark, and Owen carried it on. It became one of the showpieces of Scotland, and most of the illustrious visitors imagined that it was all because of Owen.

I have in front of me at this moment one of David Dale's 'monitors', which he introduced at New Lanark. It's a small, four-sided piece of wood, with a little wire loop at the top so that it can be hung on to a piece of machinery. The four sides are painted white, yellow, blue and black. This 'monitor' was hung beside each cotton operative, and the colour showing outwards revealed the supervisor's opinion of the operative's work. If the 'monitor' showed white, the work was excellent; if it showed yellow, the work was good; blue meant that the work was passable, but could be improved; and if black, well, it was a black outlook all round.

David Dale had the sort of conscience that he hoped his workers would have. He was forever interested in good works. He fed the poor, he found homes for orphans, he provided work for the unemployed, he built houses and encouraged schools. One might have said that he was the epitome of a good Glasgow bailie ('alderman' is the word in the South).

Altogether, David Dale was a Glaswegian worth remembering. His home in Charlotte Street should have been worth remembering too, not only because of David Dale himself but of Robert Adam who inspired it. However, the Education Committee of the Corporation of the City of Glasgow decided in their wisdom that an extra playground was needed for an adjoining school, so they proposed to ding doon David Dale's house and make the new playground there.

There was, to the credit of Glasgow, an immediate objection. But any objection was overruled because the City Council had discovered that this house had no damp-courses. That meant, according to the City Council, the distillation of the wisdom of the city, that the building must come down. It was pointed out that in Denmark and Sweden similar houses of historical interest had been preserved – without damp-courses!

Protests were of no avail. David Dale's house was razed. The playground was eventually built, but the general effect is dispiriting in the extreme. And nowadays, when Glasgow school children are so intensely interested in Old Glasgow – think how much David Dale's house would mean to them.

What makes this David Dale episode all the more discouraging is that other towns in Scotland have done so much better in this matter of preserving good historical buildings. Edinburgh City Council must be commended for the restoration of the Royal Mile. Stirling City Council have done yeoman work in restoring their ancient buildings up the hill towards the castle. Aberdeen City Council have several fine restorations to their credit. Little Inverary, on Loch Fyne, has made a wonderful job of remaking a row of old 'lands'.

Glasgow City Council have had quite a record in getting rid of their history in stone, though things were improved here and there. The frontage of the city's oldest club, The Western, was preserved, although the club itself went round the corner into Royal Exchange Place. And fornenst the club the Glasgow Stock Exchange frontage was preserved. But, on the other hand, there was a proposal that the 17th-century Tolbooth Steeple should be removed because it was said to be in the way of traffic moving round Glasgow Cross. There is certainly congestion round Glasgow Cross and most of it is the City Council's doing. One of the clever things they did was to place a gentlemen's lavatory just behind the Tolbooth Steeple. I suggested that if they wanted to improve the traffic, all they had to do was to remove the lavatory and then they would secure a better motion. They did and the better motion was secured.

One foolish suggestion from the City Council was that the Tolbooth is dangerous. They said it was built on an insecure foundation – in fact, it is a house built on sand. It may be news to the authorities, but most of the buildings on the immediate north of the River Clyde are built on sand. Several enormous buildings along Argyle Street are built on piles and have sand below them. I have not heard that they are considered dangerous.

In actual fact, the Tolbooth Steeple has a bed of a kind of primitive concrete six feet deep below it. Experts I have met say that it is one of the safest buildings in Glasgow. I can't help comparing it with the City Chambers in George Square, where Glasgow District Council meet. The City Chambers are built on sand too, and the general level of the bed of concrete below them is a mere four feet. I can only say that on a stormy night I'd feel a lot safer in the Tolbooth Steeple than I would in the City Chambers!

But, after all, our modern District Councils are merely following in the well-trodden path of their predecessors. In

1723 Daniel Defoe, author of *Robinson Crusoe* and *A Journey through Scotland*, wrote in the latter work of Glasgow: 'The beautifullest little city I have seen in Britain.'

A century, or near enough, before, Defoe, a demobilised soldier of Oliver Cromwell's Ironsides, wrote: 'What to think, or what to say of this eminent Glasgow, I know not, except to fancy a smell of my native country. The very prospect of this flourishing city reminds me of the beautiful fabricks and the florid fields of England. However, I'll superscribe it to the nonsuch of Scotland, where an English florist may pick up a posie.'

Between the ex-Ironside and Defoe another Englishman had a word about Glasgow. He was the Reverend Thomas Morer, and he wrote, in part: 'Glasgow is a place of great extent and good situation; and has the reputation of the finest town in Scotland, not excepting Edinburgh, tho' the royal city.'

If Glasgow was so wonderful in times past how did it come to be the place described by William Bolitho in 1924 as 'The Cancer of the Empire'? Well, Glasgow was a city which grew too fast. As the Industrial Revolution grew, so did Glasgow. It turned from a university town and country market into a great workplace. From all over Scotland, from Ireland and even from England, people flocked to Glasgow to find work. They had to be housed and there were builders prepared to house them at the cheapest possible rate. They flung up tenements everywhere. If there was enough space they'd build a second tenement in the backyard of the first. And these are the slums of yesterday, and even today.

Certainly these men were what we call jerry-builders, but the material in which they built was so strong that the outsides still stand today. Under a more enlightened administration the interiors have been completely remodelled and the exteriors cleaned up in many cases, though much has still to be done.

Few Glaswegians in these pre-Victorian and Early Victorian days worried about buildings of historical or architectural merit. If they were in the way of some new scheme they went just as rapidly as David Dale's House and the Peel of Drumry that went in later years. The Victorians, in particular, were as great vandals as any Glasgow City Council we had in the 20th century. They swept away the fine buildings round the old Glasgow Cross. They mutilated the front of the great Glasgow Cathedral. They allowed ancient and important buildings to be turned into pubs, barbers' shops and Jenny-a'-things.

Everything they did was in the name of progress. The Glasgow Victorians thought a great day had dawned when in 1866 they got a City Improvement Act through the Houses of Parliament. The intention of this Act was to get rid of the slums. Well, they got rid of some slums, only to replace them with new ones. (The parallel today is the building of such barracks as Drumchapel, Castlemilk and Easterhouse, destined to become the slums of the future.) But the Victorians also got rid of much of the history of Glasgow. The railway companies assisted them. A great deal of old Glasgow was demolished by the building of St Enoch and Glasgow Central stations, and the lines into them.

Glasgow has been described, by no less a person than a former Provost of Paisley, as 'the oldest town in Scotland'. And if a Paisley buddy says that about Glasgow it must be true! But what is there left of the oldest town in Scotland? I am glad to say that there is still something to be seen, although it takes almost detective work to ferret it out at times. In the following pages I am going to do my best to show what remains of Glasgow as our forbears saw it.

As I have already said, Glasgow should be looked on through the eyes of love. That is the way that I look at my adopted city. Yes, I must admit that I am not really a Glaswegian. I was born in the village of Tollcross in 1906, and Tollcross did not become part of Glasgow until 1912. Still, my parents did the best they could for me by flitting from Tollcross to Glasgow when I was three years of age.

This means that I am really an 'incomer'. But over the years I have found Glasgow a genuinely romantic city, an exciting place to live in, a town full of vitality. I cannot imagine myself living anywhere else.

You will note, I hope, that I find many things wrong with certain aspects of Glasgow. But the good outweighs the bad.

13

Walking down Renfield Street on a wet day is to me a more rewarding experience than promenading Fifth Avenue on a fine day, and I have done both.

As you can see, I take a romantic view of Glasgow. That means, in the following pages, that I will have no hesitation in embellishing a legend, telling a doubtful tale (I mean 'doubtful' in the nicest sense!), or even pulling the long-bow. It is my experience, after many years of research, that the original stories are regarded as fairy tales, rejected, discarded, blown upon, and then, all of a sudden, they come back to full, fair life. It's found that they are true, after all.

That's the line that I pursue. If there is a good story I'm going to tell it, whether there's an iota of factual evidence or not. There have been many Glasgow story-tellers in the past, and if they have told a good, stirring story, far be it from me to cry them down. On the contrary, it is my intention to cry them up.

At the same time I shall still regard facts as sacred and give them due honour. I hope, too, that the picture of Glasgow which I present will be a true one. Sure enough, it will be through the eyes of love, but surely that is the best possible view of anybody, anything, or anywhere.

2

THE BEGINNING OF GLASGOW

The famous bromide says: 'Glasgow made the Clyde, and the Clyde made Glasgow.' Like most bromides, this is true enough, but some people have taken it to mean that Glasgow started on the River Clyde. There was, it is true, a small village of salmon-fishers about the foot of where Stockwell Street is now, and there were various little settlements around the many hills on which today's city is built.

These hills are remains of the Great Ice Age and, then, this part of the world had an Arctic temperature. Some people say it still has, but the fact is that although, as the *Third Statistical Account of Glasgow* picturesquely puts it, 'George Square and the City Chambers lie closer to the Arctic Circle than Red Square and the Kremlin', Glasgow's summer temperature is, on an average, only seven degrees Fahrenheit colder than Moscow's, while our winter temperature is warmer than Moscow's by an average of twenty-five degrees Fahrenheit. Berlin lies two hundred and fifty miles to the south of Glasgow, and yet the mean annual temperature is the same. Glasgow, in fact, is a very temperate place – as far as the weather is concerned.

I don't think anybody has counted the number of hills within the boundaries of Glasgow. One difficulty is the definition of a hill. But when, some years ago, a Glasgow City Council committee were concerned in the renaming of streets, they found there were sixteen Hill Streets in the city. Like other big cities, Glasgow has kept extending over the years and each time it took in another place it seems to have taken in a Hill Street as well.

Dug-out canoes have been found as far from the present River Clyde as the Drygate, and that shows that prehistoric men who lived in this vicinity looked out on to a wide estuary where the narrow river runs now. It is believed that the river started up about Rutherglen and widened rapidly down to what is the Firth of Clyde today.

The Romans would know the Clyde, but it's almost certain that they did not know of any Glasgow or any settlement big enough to be dignified by a name. They built their wall across Scotland from Dumbarton, by Hillfoot, to Falkirk and the east coast of Scotland.

So, apart from that tiny salmon-fishing village, there was no Glasgow until it was founded by St Mungo in the 6th century. And he did not found Glasgow on the River Clyde, but by a little burn named the Molendinar. Strange to say, he founded the place on where a minor Roman road came down a glen and across a ford, so the Romans had something to do with the foundation of Glasgow, after all.

There are some spoil-sports who say that St Mungo (Kentigern is his other name) never existed. They even doubt the existence of his mother, St Thenew, whose name has been corrupted and carried into our present day by St Enoch Square. At one time, just across St Enoch Square to the south-west, there was a St Thenew's Chapel. It disappeared many, many years ago and there's no telling how the name was transformed from St Thenew to St Enoch.

I don't care whether he existed or not. St Mungo is the patron saint of Glasgow. He is shown on our coat-of-arms, which also depicts his miracles. That is good enough for me. When I was a small boy we used to have a riddle in Dennistoun which went:

> Where's the tree that never grew,
> Where's the bird that never flew,
> Where's the fish that never swam,
> Where's the bell that never rang?

The answer to all these questions was the same – 'On Glasgow's coat-of-arms.' I've been told since then that we asked this riddle because we were Protestants and we were really supposed to be making fun of Roman Catholic beliefs. But we certainly didn't know that at the time, or even think of it. Perhaps my calf country, the Glasgow suburb of Dennistoun, was a sheltered spot, but I knew so little about these things that I didn't even know what to say when some belligerent boy seized me by my sailor collar and said, 'Billy or a Dan?' However, I found out in time.

In any case, if I seemed to insult the memory of St Mungo then, let me make up for it now. He is a real fine figure to me and I revere him as the first Glasgow Man. What a title!

St Mungo's mother, Thenew, was the Christian daughter of King Loth of Lothian, who wasn't quite sure whether to be a Christian or not. He was like a lot of other kings at that time. Thenew was young and innocent, besides being beautiful – so innocent, indeed, that when a neighbour, Prince Ewen, dressed himself as a girl and asked to share the bed with her she trustingly welcomed him to her arms.

Princess Thenew had vowed to be a virgin, and there was a terrible scene when her royal father discovered that she was going to have a baby, especially as she said that she didn't know how it had happened. Prince Ewen had disappeared from the scene and was not on hand to admit paternity. King Loth ordered that his daughter should be taken to the Bass Rock in the Firth of Forth and be thrown over the highest cliff there.

His men obeyed orders. But when the Princess hurtled from the top of the cliff a flight of white birds suddenly appeared. They flew below and round her, and carried her to the North Berwick shore. On the beach was lying a coracle and Thenew was guided into it. The boat pushed itself out and sailed across the Firth of Forth to the opposite shore. It beached itself at the holy place of Culross, where there was a monastery and school run by St Serf.

Thenew's baby was born as soon as she went ashore at Culross. It was a boy and St Serf not only looked after Thenew but decided to bring up the child. He named the boy Kentigern, meaning 'noble lord' in the Highland tongue, and Mungo, meaning 'dear one' in the Lowland language. Kentigern is regarded as official, but Mungo is popular, and you'll get very few Glaswegians referring to their patron saint as Kentigern.

St Serf dearly loved Mungo, and the boy became his favourite pupil. Accordingly, most of the other boys at the Culross school disliked him and called him 'teacher's pet'. They tried to get him into trouble too. It was a rule of the monastery that one of the boys had to sit by the fire all night to make sure it would not go out. One night it was St Mungo's turn. By some trick the bad boys of the school managed to get Mungo sound asleep. When he awoke the fire he was supposed to tend was black out. But this did not worry St Mungo one whit.

Although it was a winter's night and the ground was frostbound, out he went and plucked a bough from a bare tree. He brought this in, put it in the fireplace and commanded it to burst into flame. So he rekindled the fire and discomfited his would-be tormentors.

This just encouraged them to further evil-doing. St Serf had a pet robin and one day some of the boys caught it and twisted its neck. They proposed to throw the blame on St Mungo. Mungo was equal to this occasion too. He took the robin in his palm, commanded it to return to life and immediately it sat up and sang.

This is why the bird and the tree are on Glasgow's coat-of-arms. The bell and the fish were still to come.

Eventually his unpopularity became too much for St Mungo and, like a wise man of the east, he decided to go west. He bade farewell to St Serf and set out towards the setting sun and Glasgow's destiny. He knew of a lodging along the way where a holy man named Fergus would take him in for the night. But when Mungo crossed the Forth, and reached Carnock (near what is now Stirling), he found Fergus on his deathbed. Fergus's dying wish to St Mungo was that his body should be placed on a cart drawn by two untamed bulls. Mungo was to follow the bulls and where they stopped Fergus was to be buried.

There was a cart there, but no bulls. The old man died and the next morning two wild bulls appeared at the place. St Mungo harnessed them to the wagon and placed Fergus's body on it. The moment this happened, the bulls started for the west, with St Mungo following them. They tramped

The tree, the bird, the fish and the bell: Glasgow's Coat of Arms.

Glasgow Cathedral, from an engraving of 1760, showing the ruins of the Bishop's Castle to the right and the hill that would become the Necropolis behind.

Rottenrow in 1872.

The Bell O' The Brae. The crossing at the Drygate and Rottenrow, around 1860.

The Bridge of Sighs leads across the Molendinar to the Necropolis, 1834.

Provand's Lordship, the oldest house in Glasgow, built in the fifteenth century.

Buchanan Street in 1828, with St George's Church on the right and St Enoch's Church on the left.

Glasgow's Valhalla. The statues of Sir Walter Scott, Robert Burns, the Cenotaph and the City Chambers on George Square.

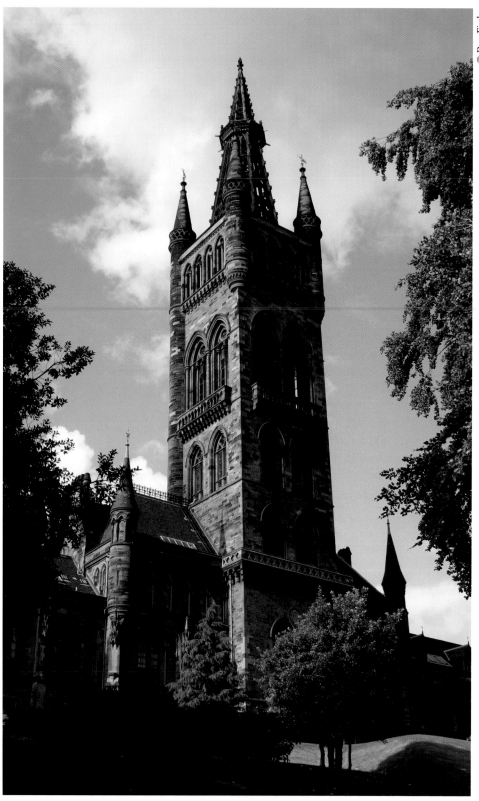

Glasgow University today.

some thirty miles before stopping in a charming glen, with a great grey rock on one side of it, and a beautiful burn beneath. There was also, handily enough, an early Christian burial place so that Fergus could be interred without difficulty.

St Mungo liked the look of this place so much that he decided to build his cell here. According to Robert Alison, who published his *Anecdotage of Glasgow* in 1892, St Mungo had as a couch a stone in the form of a coffin. His food 'consisted chiefly of bread, and his drink of milk; and of even these he partook but sparingly'.

Alison goes on: 'He would rise from his not too luxurious couch in the middle of the night, and rush, in all weathers, into the Molendinar, where he would remain until he had chanted or sung the whole of the one hundred and fifty Psalms of David. When he had finished, he would lay himself down on a stone on the hillside to dry.'

The Molendinar, of course, was the beautiful burn at the foot of the glen. The grey rock was later called the Fir Park. I may say that Robert Alison's account of an ascetic saint does not match with our ideas of St Mungo today. He is always depicted as a buirdly chiel, stout and jolly and red of face, with a beaming smile.

Sandy Rodger, the Glasgow poet who now lies in the Necropolis which was built on the Fir Park over the Molendinar, wrote this:

> St Mungo was a famous saint,
> And a canty carle was he.
> He drank o' the Molendinar burn
> When better he couldna pree.

> But when he could get stronger cheer,
> He never was water dry,
> But drank o' the stream o' the wimpling worm
> And let the burn run by.

> St Mungo was a merry saint,
> And merrily he sang;
> Whenever he liltit up his spring
> The very Fir Park rang.

But though he well could lilt and sing
And make sweet melody,
He chantit aye the boldest strains
When primed wi' barley-bree.

St Mungo was a godly saint,
Far famed for godly deeds,
And great delight he daily took
In counting o'er his beads.

But I, St Mungo's youngest son,
Can count as well as he.
But the beads which I like best to count
Are the beads o' barley-bree.

For the benefit of the uninitiated, perhaps I should explain that 'the wimpling worm' is a whisky still and the 'barley-bree' is the resultant nectar.

Whichever view we take of St Mungo – and there is something to be said for Sandy Rodger's because Glasgow's first industry was brewing and distilling by the monks on the banks of the Molendinar – we are told that he set up a monastery on the very ground where Glasgow Cathedral now stands. The date generally given for the foundation of Glasgow is 543 AD. And the name Glasgow? Now we come to some real trouble.

It is said that St Mungo called the place Glaschu because of his monastery. According to some people, that means 'dear community'. But others, and especially experts in Gaelic (who, it often appears to me, make a virtue of disagreement), have a long list of very different explanations. I have just started to learn Gaelic, so I have no right to speak. But it seems to me, as a naive neophyte, that 'glas' and 'chu' are the Gaelic for 'grey dog'. I am encouraged in this because one group of authorities makes it quite clear that Glasgow means 'greyhound', and that was an affectionate nickname for St Mungo.

Other experts say that the words which make up the name of the city come from 'Glas' and 'ghu', and aver that these words mean, respectively, 'green' and 'dear'. So to them Glasgow is the 'dear green place'. Mungo, of course, meant 'dear one', so it would seem appropriate to name St Mungo's habitation a 'dear place'. Incidentally, at one time in the very early days Glasgow was spelt 'Glesco', and you can hardly get nearer the native wood-notes wild than that pronunciation.

However, other interpretations of the city's name include 'a grey smith', 'dear stream' (presumably the Molendinar), 'dark glen' (again the burn of Glasgow's birth), 'green hollows' and 'the place of the grey rock' (otherwise Fir Park). I must not omit this last derivation because once when I was talking about Old Glasgow I was asked by an elderly gentleman what the derivation of the city's name was. I said it was virtually unknown, and gave a good selection of the guesses I have written above. The elderly gentleman arose in wrath. 'I have been wasting my time,' he said. 'Anyone who knows anything at all about Glasgow knows that the name means the place of the grey rock.' Then he swept out, and I felt I had lost my hold on my audience after that.

And when I was appearing in *Highland Air*, the Scottish Television programme I have already mentioned, I suggested to Johnny Bannerman that we should discuss the Gaelic derivation of Glasgow. 'Oh, gosh, no!' he cried. 'Anything but that! We'd never be done arguing.'

In the event, I wonder if it wouldn't be better to return to the great joke of my childhood about the name of Glasgow. When we were wee, we were told by bigger boys that Glasgow got its name because a chap was driving a horse-drawn lorry, bearing a load of glass, up the steep High Street. The horse started to falter and then came to a dead stop. The driver was lashing away at the poor beast when a bystander shouted, 'Stop that and let the glass go!' Accordingly the town was named Glassgo, later corrupted to Glasgow.

Yes, that's a piece of nonsense, but when I study the experts I feel it's as valid a theory as the next one.

Let me return to St Mungo, who now appears not such a legendary figure, after all. Historians are as notoriously credulous as are hagiographers; language experts are even worse. So I write of St Mungo with renewed faith. Nobody,

21

so far, has suggested that he was King Arthur or William Shakespeare, or even Robin Hood, and that is always something.

St Mungo established his monastery on the green hill overlooking the Molendinar Burn. He had, what every religioso of his time had, a bell to summon the faithful to worship. That is the bell in the Glasgow coat-of-arms. Whatever else is doubtful in our St Mungo legend, it is at least true that the man who founded the religious centre where the Cathedral now stands must have had a bell.

A Christian community grew up around St Mungo. The monks' cells became a settlement. St Mungo was the blessed teacher and outstanding leader, and whatever local king was reigning over that little bit of Scotland at that time asked him to become the Bishop of Glasgow. This lasted as long as the local king had power. According to Robert Alison, Clydeside was eventually ruled by King Morken of Cumbria. He was a despot and brought nothing but hardship to the land. St Mungo and his disciples faced starvation on the banks of the Molendinar, so the Bishop appealed to King Morken for corn.

The king replied, 'Cast thy care upon the Lord, and He will sustain thee, since nothing is lacking to them that fear God, as thou hast been accustomed to teach others.' King Morken felt so pleased with this reply that he did as so many of us do – went on to say too much. He added, 'If, trusting in thy God, and without human assistance, thou shalt be able to transfer to thine own mansion all the corn which thou seest contained in the barns, I willingly consent.'

Morken's barns, which were full of corn, lay along the banks of the River Clyde. St Mungo prayed and prayed, 'and lo, in the same hour, the River Clyde, rushing from below, began to swell and overflow its banks, and carried along with it the entire barns of the king, with the corn in them, up to the very place, Molendinar by name, where the saint was accustomed to reside'.

When Morken saw this happen he was so infuriated that he attacked St Mungo. He knocked the saint down with a kick. But at that very moment he was attacked by gout in the foot which had touched the saint. Shortly afterwards he died from that disease. His courtiers accused the saint of sorcery, and Mungo found it expedient to visit Wales for a spell.

His journey south shows why you will find the name of St Mungo attached to various churches in England and in Wales. He returned to Glasgow only when a new king, who was a Christian and his friend, took over the district. This was King Rydderch, who loved St Mungo so much that he insisted on his deathbed that he should be buried beside his already-dead bishop in the holy ground beside Glasgow Cathedral.

But, as the good old Victorian authors used to say, I am anticipating. Rydderch and Mungo had many fruitful years before them when the saint returned to the Molendinar. If you have been following me closely you will realise that I have not yet dealt with the fourth figure in Glasgow's coat-of-arms, the fish. Look at it closely and you will see that it has a ring in its mouth.

King Rydderch of Strathclyde had a beautiful, and susceptible, wife named Languoreth. She should have been happy with the king, but she fell deeply in love with one of his courtiers. After dallying with this handsome young man, Queen Languoreth was injudicious enough to pull a ring off her finger and present it to her lover. Probably she didn't realise it at the time, but this ring had been a gift from her husband the king.

Now Rydderch was a wise king, and he had suspected his queen's relationship with the young courtier from the start. He arranged a royal hunt and, when the hunters were resting on the banks of the River Clyde, the king contrived to take the ring from the finger of the sleeping courtier. He then threw it into the river.

When he returned to his castle he met Queen Languoreth and demanded that she should show him the ring. She made a pretence of going to look for it, but actually went to see her bishop, St Mungo. She confessed everything to him, explained that this dalliance had been a passing fancy and asked that he should help her to be reunited to her husband. Meanwhile her courtier lover, realising the danger he was in, had fled south.

St Mungo was stern, but he relented. He saw that she had truly repented, so he told her to send a trusty man down to the River Clyde and cast a line into the clear, sweet water. The trusty man must have been an angler as well, for, as soon as he cast, he picked up a fine salmon and, as he removed the hook from the salmon's mouth, there was King Rydderch's ring. The trusty man took the ring back to his mistress. The Queen showed the ring to Rydderch and, without actually saying so, the king forgave her.

And so the fish with the ring in its mouth was added to the city's coat-of-arms, and the pious motto appeared below, though many years after the time of Rydderch and Languoreth: 'Lord, let Glasgow flourish by the preaching of the Word and praising Thy Name.' The Victorians, finding this unwieldy, shortened it to 'Let Glasgow Flourish', which is the official motto of the city today. The only time the original motto has appeared in well over a hundred years was in electric lights on the front of the Kelvin Hall during the Billy Graham campaign of the 1950s.

The first Glasgow did flourish under St Mungo. It had started as a religious settlement, was gradually taken under the wing of the ruling authorities and became so important in the Christian world that St Columba came to visit St Mungo. They strolled by the banks of the Molendinar and it is said that they liked each other so much that they exchanged pastoral staves 'in token of the esteem they bore for each other'.

St Mungo died, it is thought, in the year 603. If you visit Glasgow Cathedral you will see his grave, over which a lamp is always burning. This is not a shrine. It is a simple, satisfying place. You look through the ancient arches at that little lamp and think of the first Glasgow Man. You may also think of the saint, but to envisage the first Glasgow Man is a much more solemn thought. There are many saints. But just look at Glasgow men today and consider that once there was an original!

In the centuries after St Mungo the town round the upper reaches of the Molendinar moved slowly south, along the line of the burn and roughly corresponding to Castle Street and High Street today. Eventually it linked up with the salmon-fishing village on the Clyde.

And then gradually the emphasis changed, as far as the future of Glasgow was concerned. This was not a town with a centre from which roads radiated and along which buildings were erected. Glasgow began to have two centres, a religious and a lay one. The shape of Glasgow was a long line, running from the Cathedral down to the Clyde. Round the Cathedral were the oldest thoroughfares of Glasgow – the Drygait, Rottenrow and the High Street.

But down by Glasgow Cross there was another complex. The High Street joined the original Glasgow with the new one, and the oldest thoroughfare continued the road down the Saltmarket, across by the Briggait, to Stockwell Street and the first bridge across the River Clyde. This was the direct link between St Mungo's Glasgow and the salmon-fishing village.

From Glasgow Cross there were two other streets, one going east and one west. To the west there was the short Trongate. To the east there was the long Gallowgate. Perhaps I should make it plain at this point that the word 'gate' does not signify an entrance into a walled town – Glasgow was never walled.

The word is, properly, 'gait', as I have given it in Drygait and Briggait. It is an old Scottish word meaning 'the way to'. So Briggait is the way to the bridge – that is the original bridge over the Clyde – and Trongate is the way to the tron, or town weighing machine, which was a very important part of any commercial town in Scotland. Gallowgate is the way to the gallows. (Or is it? I'll go into Gallowgate's derivation later.) When the Trongate was extended the new street was known as the Westergait before it became Argyle Street. It was, of course, the way to the west.

Percipient readers will be asking now, 'And what about the Drygait?' I just don't know. The Drygait was the original Roman road and is, therefore, the oldest street in Glasgow. In swampy days it may have been the only comparatively dry street. Or it may have been the way to the drying greens on the banks of the Molendinar.

It could be a corruption of 'Righ', the Gaelic for king, and mean the way to the king's castle. Rottenrow, for example, is supposed to have no connection whatever with Rotten Row in Hyde Park, London. It is derived from the Gaelic, 'Rat-an-righ', meaning the road of the king.

Hundreds of years, of course, passed between the Glasgow of St Mungo's time and the Glasgow of the eight original streets. But today there is nothing to show for them. If St Mungo returned tomorrow he would not recognise a single feature of his Glasgow. On his dear, green place there are buildings everywhere. Over on the grey rock there is the remarkable Cemetery of the Merchants House of Glasgow.

As for the Molendinar, in which he was wont to plunge when tormented by the desires of the flesh, he couldn't see it at all. This source of Glasgow's greatness was turned by our thoughtful Victorian ancestors into a sewer.

I have followed the Molendinar from its source at Hogganfield Loch to the point, by the weir above the Albert Bridge over the Clyde, where it trickles drably from a projecting pipe. At first it runs under the road to Stirling and by a Scottish Milk Marketing Board depot on one side and a field of rhubarb on the other. Then it makes its modest way to the suburb of Blackhill, which is regarded even by Glasgow City Council as one of its worst efforts.

Here a pathetic attempt has been made to show off the Molendinar. It is brought down between carefully planted rocks to a little park, which was in a derelict state when last I saw it. Its colour becomes steadily more gruesome. It runs under the finished Monkland Canal and is seen for a moment in the hinterland of Dennistoun. It is now indescribably filthy and, mercifully, it dives underground to become an official sewer.

Where St Mungo built his cell the Molendinar is completely covered over by Wishart Street – the name is in honour of Archbishop Wishart! It comes to the surface again beside Glasgow's oldest thoroughfare, the Drygait. You can hardly believe it, but it looks even worse than when you saw it last. It runs by a building where they used to dip sheepskins. When I last visited this building the owners told me proudly that they had an ancient charter giving them fishing rights in the Molendinar Burn.

The burn goes underground again and crosses under Duke Street, emerging for the last time as a narrow channel, much frequented by rats, between a school and a working men's hotel. And then you don't see it again until, as I have reported, it comes out of the sewer pipe and joins the River Clyde.

When I was demobilised after World War II I started a campaign to have the Molendinar cleaned up and returned to something of its former beauty.

Ah, well, we were all full of wonderful ideas in those days, weren't we? All that ever happened out of that campaign was the said waterfall in Blackhill.

So I cannot show you anything in Glasgow today which St Mungo saw. But I can show you something of what Daniel Defoe saw, a matter of twelve hundred years later. Despite the vandals, official and unofficial, there are still fine little pieces of Old Glasgow to be seen. It is my purpose to take you around the heart of Glasgow and show you the sights and tell you the stories which accompany them.

I have wanted to write this book for years. Now I realise I must do it while there is yet time to see the remnants of a beautiful city. True, there are plans of a sort to make a new Glasgow, but if I must be truthful I feel little confidence in them. What has happened since the last war does not inspire me with confidence.

This is not meant, though, to be a guide to Glasgow's past. It is meant to show what a great city Glasgow has been and can still be. And if I appear to hate at certain times it's because I love so much.

3

DANIEL DEFOE'S DELIGHT

D aniel Defoe is only one of many Englishmen who have been captivated by Glasgow over the years. He was not the first, by any means. In 1650 an English invader wrote: 'The town of Glascow [sic], though not so big, nor so rich, yet to all seems a much sweeter and more delightful place than Edinburgh and would make a gallant headquarters were the Carlisle forces come up.'

Some eight years later the author of *The Perfect Politician* wrote: 'In Glasgow the streets and houses are more neat and clean than those of Edinburgh; it being also one of the chiefest universities in Scotland.'

Then there was Franck, a satirist who wrote his *Northern Memoirs* in 1658 and suddenly became serious when he wrote about Glasgow. 'Now,' he said, 'let us descend to describe the splendor and gaity [sic] of this city of Glasgow, which surpasseth most, if not all the corporations in Scotland. Here it is you may observe four large streets, modell'd, as it were, into a spacious quadrant; in the centre whereof their marketplace is fix'd; near unto which stands a stately tolbooth, a very sumptuous regulated, uniform fabrick, large and lofty, most industriously and artificially carved from the very foundation to the superstructure, to the great admiration of strangers and travellers. But this statehouse, or tolbooth, is their western prodigy, infinitely excelling the model and usual built of townhalls.'

It would not surprise me if one day Mr Franck's opinion of the Tolbooth at Glasgow Cross is quoted to the myopic members of Glasgow City Council.

Moving steadily over the years towards Defoe, we turn to a Master Ray from England, who wrote: '1661. From Stirling we went, Aug the 22nd, to Glascow [sic], which is the second city in Scotland, fair, large, and well built, cross-wise, somewhat like unto Oxford, the streets very broad and pleasant.'

The anonymous author of *The Present State of Scotland*, published in 1715, said of Lanarkshire: 'The chief city of this county is Glasgow, the best emporium of the west of Scotland; it is a large, stately, and well built city, and for its commerce and riches is the second in the kingdom; it is pleasantly situated upon the east bank of the river Clyde.... The city is joyn'd to the suburbs on the west bank of the Clyde by a noble and beautiful bridge of eight arches built with square hewen stone.

'Most of the city stands upon a plain, and lies in a manner foursquare; in the middle of the city stands the tolbooth, a magnificent structure of hewen stone, with a very lofty tower, and melodious chimes, which ring pleasantly at the end of every hour. The four principal streets that divide the city into four parts centre at the tolbooth a magnificent structure, and all of them are adorned with several publick buildings.'

And so we arrive at Daniel Defoe, who came to Scotland to write about the country and spy for the Government in London. He is not the first, nor the latest author to combine the two jobs. He had obviously done his homework before he produced the first edition of *Defoe's Tour*. Some authorities give the date as 1723, others as 1727, but you know what authorities are. I quote extracts from the fifth edition, published in 1753, and don't blame me if you recognise some of the phrases from previous works on the subject of Glasgow.

'Glasgow', wrote Defoe, coining a phrase, 'is the emporium of the west of Scotland, the second in this northern part of Great Britain. It is a large, stately, and well-built city, standing on a plain, in a manner four square; and the four principal streets are the fairest for breadth, and the finest built that I have ever seen in one city together. The houses are all of stone, and generally uniform in height, as well as in front. The lower stories, for the most part, stand on vast square Doric columns, with arches, which open into the shops, adding to the strength, as well as beauty, of the building. In a word, 'tis one of the cleanliest, most beautiful, and best built cities in Britain.

'Where the four principal streets meet, the crossing makes a very spacious marketplace, as may be easily imagined, since the streets are so large. As we come down the hill from the north-gate to this place, the Tolbooth and guild-hall make the north-west angle, or right-hand corner of the street, which is new rebuilt in a very magnificent manner. Here the town council sit, and the magistrates try such causes as come within their cognisance, and do all their other public business; so that, as will be easily conceived, the Tolbooth stands in the very centre of the city. It is a noble structure of hewn stone, with a very lofty tower, and melodious hourly chimes. All these four principal streets are adorned with several public buildings.'

I don't think there's any doubt that Daniel Defoe had read the winged words of his Sassenach predecessors in Glasgow. But the point I think I have made is that the centre of Glasgow had changed, by the 17th century, from St Mungo's Cathedral on the Molendinar to Glasgow Cross near the River Clyde. So much so that these English visitors recognised only four streets in the city when there were actually eight.

Standing below this much-praised Tolbooth Steeple they saw the ancient High Street to the north, the Gallowgate to the east, the Saltmarket to the south and the Trongate to the west. But there were older thoroughfares up the hill of the High Street (or High Kirk Street, as it was called by some people, since it led to the High Kirk, which was what Presbyterians preferred to call the Cathedral).

Off the High Street were two roads which together made the Old Roman road across the Molendinar. They were the Drygait and the Rottenrow. That brings our total to six streets. The remaining two showed the way from the Cross to the great bridge of eight arches, which took daring travellers across the River Clyde. To get to the bridge you went down the Saltmarket, bore westwards along the Briggait and turned into Stockwell Street for the bridge in front of you.

One wonders if these 17th and 18th-century visitors to Glasgow ever got outside the ambience of the Tolbooth and Glasgow Cross. At any rate, all these panegyrics gives us our cue. If we are to see Glasgow we should not start at Glasgow

Cathedral, even though it represents the origins of the city, but at Glasgow Cross. It is the first place I take visitors. When they see the Tolbooth Steeple they are suitably impressed. I wish I could affect Glasgow city councillors in the same way.

Even today, if you stand at Glasgow Cross, you get the strong, exciting feeling of the city. And this is in spite of the 'improvements' which have been made over the years. The Cross in Daniel Defoe's day was more spacious than it appears now. It has been cluttered up with a railway station. It has six off-shoots instead of 'the four principal streets'. There has been a half-hearted attempt to turn the area into a composite whole. You can see that an architectural effort has been made to make a sort of circus in the London style. But there are only two bits of arcs and the rest of the Cross remains uncompromisingly square.

The Tolbooth Steeple stands entirely on its own. It lives up to the descriptions of the visiting Sassenachs. Yet it looks as if something is missing. That is true, because it was originally part of a building which had an imposing frontage to the Cross. The Tolbooth, built in 1626, was the tower attached to the jail and the court-houses. Much later, in 1740, the Town Council of Glasgow built their chambers alongside the jail, presumably for convenience. Then there was the Tontine Coffee Room, where the elite of Glasgow, the merchants, gathered to drink their 'meridian' – claret or whisky at noon – and read the newspapers from Edinburgh and London, which had been brought by stagecoach.

Glasgow has always been an intensely democratic town, and a measure of this is shown in the fact that the waiter who looked after the coffee room collected the newspapers in his arms, marched into the room and threw them all in the air, so that the distinguished citizens had to fight for their news.

According to Sir Walter Scott in *Rob Roy*, that eminent freebooter was actually in the Tolbooth at one time. This, I regret to say, is untrue, but I never say so to visiting foreigners. It is my experience that people from the Continent and America and Russia are much better informed about the works of Sir Walter Scott than anybody in Scotland. When I show an American the Tolbooth I say, 'And that is where Rob Roy was incarcerated.' Even that isn't true, since, according to Scott, he was just inside the jail to meet a friend. But you should see the awed look on the American's face.

And I remember, too, a visit to the Institute of Fine Arts in Leningrad. At one point I was detached from the rest of my party and was being conducted through the building by a pleasant young Russian who, so it seemed, knew no English. He took me up a winding stone staircase and, all of a sudden, he rapped his knuckles against the rough stone of the wall and said, with a beaming smile, 'Rob Roy!'

I was impressed because, as a matter of fact, that winding stone staircase was very like the way you climb up the Tolbooth Steeple. I have been to the top twice, which is 200 per cent more than a million Glaswegians can claim. From the outside appearance you'd imagine that the twisting staircase was very narrow, but actually there's plenty of room and it's better lit than most twisting stairways I have climbed.

You come to a landing where you can see the works of the clock, and then you go up to the little room from which the carillon is played. The bells of Glasgow were once a great feature of the city. They were played several times a day. Now you hear them, on an average, twice a year – if that. The same City Council that is quite happy to provide a jazz band in George Square seems to worry about the money for somebody to play the traditional Tolbooth chimes. The one night on which they melt is Hogmanay – New Year's Eve. Just in case anybody is gathering round Glasgow Cross to see the New Year in, the authorities engage Miss Jessie Herbert to ring the bells. I doubt if Miss Herbert needs the fee. Indeed, I know that she does it to maintain a family tradition. Her family members have been the Tolbooth bellringers since the year 1830.

In 1830 the bellringer was a Bayne, but the job passed to the Herberts on the distaff side. The first time I went to the top of the Tolbooth was with William Herbert, father of the present bell-ringer. It was a cold, windy night and I felt as if the high tower was swaying slightly. I mentioned this to Mr Herbert.

He just laughed. 'The first time I felt the sway, I worried too,' he said. 'In fact, I went up to see the City Engineer and told him about it. Do you know what he said to me? He said: "That's all right. The first time you're up the Tolbooth on a windy night and it *doesn't* sway, get the hell out of it!"'

In the little turret room there was a keyboard, with a double bank of handles sticking out like baseball bats. Mr Herbert put on a pair of small boxing gloves (at least that's what they looked like to me) and with a cardboard sheet of hieroglyphics in front of him began to pound out 'The Rowan Tree'.

Then he asked me if I would like a try. I have never been one to say no, so I put on the boxing gloves and tried my 'prentice hands on 'Crimond'. I made mistake after mistake and how glad I was when Mr Herbert took me aloft to the belfry and I looked out on the cold, wet night and realised there wasn't a soul about to hear my execution.

The second time I went up to the top of the Tolbooth was with William Herbert's daughter Jessie. She was very proud to be carrying on the family tradition of bellringing after more than one hundred and thirty years. But while her father had a regular daily engagement to ring the chimes, Miss Herbert found it remarkable if she was asked to play them on any other date than Hogmanay.

She had, however, rung the Tolbooth bells on at least one notable occasion. In December 1745, on their way back from Derby, Bonnie Prince Charlie's Highland Army blockaded Glasgow. They were in an ugly mood and they knew that the Glaswegians didn't like them. They were all for putting Glasgow to the fire and sword. In any case, they had nothing to lose. The Prince was swayed by the argument of Cameron of Lochiel, who said that Glasgow should be treated in kindly fashion and asked to provide food and clothing for an army which needed these two things badly.

Cameron of Lochiel won the day. Glasgow was mulcted to the tune of £10,000, but that was a great deal cheaper than having the city burned out. The magistrates were most grateful to Cameron of Lochiel and they said that in time to come, if he or any of his descendants came to Glasgow, the bells of the Tolbooth would be rung in honour of Lochiel.

This promise was taken so seriously that a few years ago the present Cameron of Lochiel went to Glasgow Cross and Miss Herbert put on a special carillon programme in his honour.

As I've said, the only regular date for the Tolbooth chimes is Hogmanay. At one time a huge crowd of Glaswegians gathered at the Cross to hear the chimes and see (if that is the right word) the New Year in. The custom is more honoured in the breach than the observance now, although some twenty thousand folk turned out on a New Year's Eve when it was announced that the proceedings were going to be on television.

In the old days the statue of King William of Orange, better known to the natives as 'King Billy', stood near the Tolbooth. It was a gift to Glasgow from a Glaswegian who had become Governor of Madras. King Billy was carved in the form of a Roman emperor, wearing a toga and astride a vigorous horse. To this day newspapers in Glasgow receive letters from credulous people who say, 'I have seen the statue of King William of Orange, but surely this is really Julius Caesar or some other Roman Emperor.'

To explain that there was a fashion for portraying eminent men as Roman emperors does not really convince the letter-writers. The fact is that King Billy has been a sort of religious totem ever since he was put up at Glasgow Cross, and you can't expect clear thinking on the subject from either the Protestants or the Roman Catholics.

This controversial statue stood, at first, fornenst the Tolbooth. Then, when Glasgow Cross was remade, King Billy was taken back along the Trongate towards Argyle Street. He was still much revered by Orangemen, who expressed their reverence as the Tolbooth rang in the New Year by smashing their empty bottles against the plinth of the statue.

And now stories diverge. One is simply that King Billy's statue was in the way of the traffic and was eventually moved to a monumental sculptor's yard until its fate could be decided.

The other story is much better and, naturally, it is the one which I believe. One Hogmanay, when the crowds around Glasgow Cross were toasting the New Year and preparing to go on their first-footing expeditions, a fellow who had had a few found himself looking up at a peculiar-looking chap astride a horse. This peculiar-looking chap seemed to be arrayed in just a blanket, and his complexion was very grey indeed.

The happy wanderer below decided that he must bring in the New Year with this cauldrife man on the horse, so he got out a bottle from his hip pocket and started to climb up the plinth and the horse towards King Billy. Whether it was the Glasgow weather which had eroded the statue, or whether it was the strength of the happy wanderer, nobody knows. All we do know is that when he grasped the horse's tail it came off in his hands.

This was too much for the reveller, who dropped the tail and made off. Fortunately, some civic-minded character retrieved the tail of King Billy's horse and returned it to the Corporation of the City of Glasgow. It was soon after that that the statue, with the tail in a separate parcel, was moved to Mossman's, the monumental sculptors. And there they both remained until the City Council, in their wisdom, decided that the statue of King William of Orange should be re-erected in Cathedral Square.

It could not be put up, however, without its tail. The ingenious renovators fixed the tail on to the hind quarters of the horse by means of a ball-and-socket arrangement. The result is that when strong winds blow through Glasgow you can see the tail of King Billy's horse swaying in the breeze. If you are showing visitors around Glasgow, and you've all had a very good lunch, it's better to warn them in advance that they must not be surprised if they see the horse's tail moving.

As far as I can find out, Glasgow is the only city in Europe with a statue which has a moveable part. I have to be cautious about this, and confine myself to Europe. The moment this claim becomes known I'm pretty certain that both America and Russia will enter claims for statues in their countries with moveable parts. We must wait and see.

I return rapidly to Glasgow Cross. If the spirit of Daniel Defoe came back today he would certainly recognise the Tolbooth, although he'd think it looked rather naked. But would he see anything else that reminded him of the Glasgow Cross he admired so much? He knew it as a big open space with piazzas all round it. The citizens could then do their shopping without fear of the weather. It has always surprised me that Glasgow has been so badly off for arcades. Perhaps the piazzas were considered old-fashioned when the day came to make a new Glasgow. But standing at the Tolbooth Steeple, even today, you can get one little glimpse of what the Cross looked like to Defoe.

You must look west, along the Trongate, and there you will see the tower of Tron St Mary's Church. It is squarely built on a stout archway, and that archway is the last remnant of the piazza system at Glasgow Cross. I'll have a great deal more to say about Tron St Mary's later. At the moment, I merely direct your attention to the kind of architecture, which Daniel Defoe admired.

Just across from the Tolbooth Steeple is Glasgow Cross itself – a solid, round, stone building with the arms of Scotland and of Glasgow represented and a pillar rising from it. This is not the original Glasgow Cross. It is a replica, put up in 1929. Strange to say, Glaswegians have never treated it seriously. The Tolbooth is real to them, but the Cross is not. Nor do Glaswegians seem to notice the various rather naive architectural attempts to persuade them that the Cross is still surrounded by 18th-century Scottish buildings. An imitation façade has never impressed the natives. But often it impresses the visitors and when I introduce the Cross of Glasgow to an impressible tourist I never say a word about its dating back only to 1929 – unless he asks me questions, of course.

Many dramatic things occurred at Glasgow Cross. Men and women were hanged in front of the Tolbooth. Witches and malefactors were scourged there. The Provost and magistrates of the City Council paraded around the Cross. Great gatherings mustered there. The coaches from Edinburgh, and even from London, arrived there. But eventually the City Council moved to pastures new – if you can call Wilson Street pastures new. The centre of Glasgow moved west, and was established in George Square – a place where game was shot and snared when Glasgow Cross was the city centre. Daniel Defoe would have thought he was in the wilds if he had ever got as far as George Square.

A few Glaswegians, and a great many visitors, go to Glasgow Cross today to admire the Tolbooth Steeple and the tower of Tron St Mary's kirk. But they don't seem to know that in this very place one of Glasgow's greatest gifts to the world was born. If you stand with your back to the Tolbooth and look south-south-east you will see the corner of London Road and the Saltmarket. In Defoe's day, of course, London Road did not exist. The Saltmarket came up to join the Gallowgate.

But just about that spot there was an inn, one of the very many in Glasgow in the old days. There are more than a thousand inns in Glasgow today, but, judging by per head of population, Glasgow of the 19th century was much better off – or much worse off, if you happened to be a Prohibitionist.

In the late days of the 18th and the opening days of the 19th centuries drinking in Glasgow was divided by classes. If you were a well-to-do merchant or shopkeeper or university professor you went to certain hostelries where you drank claret and punch and whisky. Claret, of course, was the great drink, and horse-drawn vehicles paraded around Glasgow selling claret by the jug or bowl to housewives who wanted to keep their husbands happy.

Claret kept its popularity by reason of the 'Auld Alliance' between Scotland and France. Punch was popular because so many Glasgow merchants had an interest in America and the West Indies, so they imported their own rum and their own limes. Bailie Nicol Jarvie attributed the success of his own particular punch to the fact that the limes were grown on his plantation. And whisky was popular because it was cheap, being home-made, and very, very strong.

These things were for the well-off people, and Glasgow then was sharply divided between the rich and the poor. If you were poor and went into an inn you had to count your pennies. The usual thing was for a group of three or four men to go in together and buy a bowl of ale. They would sit round a table and pass the bowl of ale from one to another, much as a loving cup is passed round at a university dinner today.

If they had a little money they might buy a bottle of whisky and share it in the same way. This was a chancy business, though, because bottles varied so much in size.

The inn at the corner of the Saltmarket was kept by an Irishman. It was patronised mainly by the poorer people and the Irishman's soft heart was disturbed by the sight of a group of men sharing a bowl of ale or a bottle of whisky. All of a sudden the answer came to him: Why should he not serve the mercies in smaller measures?

And so he contrived to get small containers for the ale, and even smaller containers for the whisky. Each man now could order for himself a small measure of whisky and a somewhat larger measure of beer. And so Glasgow gave its inestimable gift to the world – 'hauf an' the hauf-pint'. That is to say, the half-measure of whisky, followed and washed down by the half-pint of beer. For many years it was regarded locally as the quickest way in the world to get drunk. Such are the benefits of science that some Glaswegians know quicker ways now.

In some parts of Glasgow, whisky was thought to be far too expensive, and it was also rejected because it had become swanky. It was found that you get pretty much the same effect (and the devotees drink for effect, and not for taste) by drinking a glass of cheap red wine and following it with a 'chaser' of beer. Pubs which sell this combination are known in Glasgow as 'wine shops'. They are not notable for their amenities, but their quick service could hardly be quicker.

One morning I went into a wine shop near the centre of the city. The opening hour was eleven, and I was, maybe, some ten minutes late. I entered a small outer room which was the public bar. On the gantry were enamel trays in great profusion, and each enamel tray was laden with glasses of cheap wine, already poured out. The staff stood ready at the beer machines to provide the accompaniment.

Already, in a number of back parlours, the addicts were at it. Any moment now they were going to reach the singing stage. I could only conclude that, since it was shortly after official opening time, they had been drinking all night.

This sounds dreadful, but I must point out that there are very few wine shops in the city. Some psychologists think they serve a useful need. One chargehand of a wine shop told me that on Friday and Saturday nights women with fur coats and 'Kelvinside' accents arrived at opening time and left, in taxis, at closing time. 'Did you see that picture *The Snake Pit?*' he asked me. 'It's not in it with this place on a Saturday night!'

In Daniel Defoe's day they drank heavily in Glasgow, but they didn't know of later refinements. Some two hundred years after Defoe, in the days of the depression, the early thirties, there were two drinks known as Jake and Red Biddy. These were mixtures of methylated spirit and cheap red wine. The effect on the addict was frightening. I have seen Red Biddy drinkers brought into the Central Police Station in Glasgow and slid, literally rigid, from the Black Maria into the cell.

In those days in Glasgow, the chief object of the down-and-out was to achieve oblivion. One way was to attach a tube to the gas bracket on the stair landing of a tenement and send a whiff of gas into a glass of milk. Mind you, while this was certainly done, it was not general. It achieved fame because of newspaper reports that I might describe as picturesque.

Scent-drinking was fairly popular, though very much an acquired taste. Any cheap scent would do, but at one time there was an Eau de Cologne, or so it said on the label on the bottle, which sold at sixpence and was a great favourite.

Experts on oblivion told me that between the wars it was possible to be drunk for a fortnight on less than a shilling. In those days an oblivious addict could buy sixpence-worth of spirit of salts from any chemist. That is forbidden now. He also bought a large bottle of lemonade, which cost about fivepence. Into the bottom of a glass he put a very little spirit of salts, and filled it up with lemonade. When he swallowed this mixture he became unconscious almost immediately.

As soon as he came back to his detested life – and that might take some time, depending on the strength of the original mixture – he took a glass of water. The effect of the water on his interior made him drunk again. Next time he recovered he took another drink of water and left the world. He just kept on drinking water until it no longer had any effect. Then he made a new mixture of spirit of salts and lemonade and started all over again. And by ringing the liquid changes in this way he could remain drunk for two weeks.

This kind of dreadful drinking hardly exists in Glasgow now. The much-criticised younger generation go in for vodka and Bacardi rum, chased down by Scandinavian beers. But the real Glasgow man sticks to his hauf an' hauf-pint. In a way, of course, a vodka and a Carlsberg Special is just another version of the hauf an' the hauf-pint. From my own studies in Scandinavia and Russia I should think that this kind of drinking is an escape medium for the north of Europe. However, I'm not claiming that it was invented in Glasgow for the benefit of the north of Europe. The hauf an' the hauf-pint were for Glasgow and ever since that Irishman in the Saltmarket introduced the idea Glaswegians have swallowed it.

There is still a pub on the site of the Irishman's inn at the top of the Saltmarket, so we can enter and have what is called, in the best Glasgow circles, 'a refreshment'. The word 'drink' is taboo in genteel society. And over our refreshment we can consider how next we shall probe the heart of Glasgow. Where would Daniel Defoe have gone? I should say that he'd have walked towards the sun, down the Saltmarket. We'll take the same road.

4
A' THE COMFORTS

G lasgow has as many old sayings as any other historical place, and one of them is 'A' the comforts o' the Sautmarket'. It's difficult to say just how old this old saying is, because Sir Walter Scott used it in *Rob Roy*. His Glasgow magistrate, Bailie Nicol Jarvie, was wont to describe his affluent life in terms of where he lived. And, since he lived in that fashionable thoroughfare known as the Saltmarket, he talked about his creature comforts there with great nostalgia when he was compelled to leave the town for any time.

But, of course, Sir Walter may very well have taken this phrase from life. Even though he had aristocratic longings, he was much more au fait with the ordinary people of Scotland than he was with the aristocracy. Not that the bailie would have considered himself an ordinary person. Glasgow bailies, even today, do not consider themselves ordinary. But some of them would have to talk about 'a' the comforts o' a cooncil hoose'.

The Saltmarket did, in its time, house some very special people. Oliver Cromwell had his lodging here when he occupied Glasgow. Provost Bell had a house in the Saltmarket, and King James VII, when Duke of York, lived in Provost Bell's house.

The name of the street, surprisingly enough, comes from the fact that this was the site of the market which sold salt for the curing of salmon. When Glasgow was solidly established as a town, the salmon were cured at a station where the Molendinar joined the Clyde. On the west side of the Saltmarket, buildings proliferated. Between the Saltmarket and Stockwell Street became the most densely packed area of the town. As you look down the street from Glasgow Cross you see that the view is obliterated by a railway bridge. It brings the line in to St Enoch Station. And, though it may look like a blot on the landscape to you, the coming of the railway was hailed by respectable Glaswegians because it enabled them to cut a swathe through one of the worst parts of the city.

When Daniel Defoe walked down the Saltmarket it was a fine street in pleasant surroundings. Some one hundred and fifty years later the whole area round Glasgow Cross – the Saltmarket, Princes Street, Goosedubs, Bridgegate, King Street, Trongate, High Street and Gallowgate – was described as 'a citadel of vice'. In an area of less than one-sixteenth of a square mile there were a hundred and fifty shebeens and two hundred brothels.

The coming of the railway swept many of these away, but it also swept away some fine old buildings. There is not a historical building left in the Saltmarket, unless you count late Victorian, with Gothic curlicues, as historical. I've always liked the wee shops of the Saltmarket myself, and I was especially attracted to Moffat, the clog maker, on the left of the street near the top. Moffat was not only famous for making stout clogs for the male and female workers of the town who wore clogs to the factory or workshop, he also made special clogs for champion clog-dancers.

When I was a young reporter you could still see clog-wallopers on the stage, but they were a dying race. Even before that Dan Leno had found it worth while to give up clog-dancing in favour of comicking. In Moffat's shop window there were photographs of the world's champion clog-dancer, and the clogs he had worn were displayed below. I wrote in my newspaper about this, and then the heavens fell. It turned out that the West of Scotland was full of world champion clog-dancers. The real question was – what *is* a world championship? It's asked today about world champion beauty contests.

A controversy like this would be regarded by a newspaper nowadays as something rather good and interesting. Then, in 1928, I was told off for starting a row. Later the assistant chief reporter took me aside and said: 'Listen, Jack, I'm going to give you a tip worth its weight in gold. Never discover anything!'

42

You must go under the railway bridge in the Saltmarket before you discover anything old around the street, and even it wasn't there when Daniel Defoe paid us a visit. It has been my experience to take a Londoner this way, and when we have reached the corner of the Saltmarket and St Andrew Street, he looks to the east and a glow of something approaching recognition comes into his eyes. He is looking at St Andrew's Parish Church, the kirk of Glasgow City Council, thought of in 1734 but not opened as a church until 1756.

Why should that glow of recognition gleam in a Londoner's eyes? Well, when the City Council decided to have their own kirk they had a competition for architects. This competition was won by a Glasgow architect, Allan Dreghorn. It's not known whether any of the judges on the City Council had ever visited London. If so, they might have recognised in Master Dreghorn's work a copy of St Martin in the Fields in Trafalgar Square. The only difference is that the Glasgow architect has given the church a spire, which is not considered a very successful one.

When the City Council decided to build their own kirk most of the ground behind the Saltmarket was open. The Molendinar Burn ran down between the Saltmarket and a piece of ground called Bell's Yard. It was in 1734 that the City Council decided to buy Bell's Yard and put up their church.

But it was five years before they arranged to transport stone from the Crackling House Quarry to Bell's Yard. The Crackling House Quarry is now Queen Street Station, so beloved of Sir John Betjeman. I remember his eyes sparkling as he stood on the south side of George Square and looked at all the glass and ironwork on the front of the station. 'Oh, how lovely!' he said.

Some six years after the stone was transported from the quarry the walls were not completed. And in that year, 1745, Bonnie Prince Charlie brought his Highland Army into Glasgow. You will note, and you will note again, that, for a man who visited the city only once, Charles Edward Stewart made a great impression. His troops encamped in and around the walls of the unfinished kirk. It's said that the men slept outside the kirk, but the horses, being considered more important, were stabled inside it.

St Andrew's might have been the oldest church still standing in Glasgow today (not counting the Cathedral, of course), but the City Council were beaten in building by the Episcopalians. Just down the road to Glasgow Green, a matter of about fifty yards, they started building their chapel, St Andrew's by the Green, in 1751. They also finished building it in 1751, and opened it in the same year. St Andrew's Parish did not open until 1756, so St Andrew's by the Green is the oldest church in Glasgow. There were, of course, seven or eight churches before that, but they have all disappeared.

As a building, the Episcopal Church is small and has been allowed to fall into a state which is no credit to the Scottish Episcopal Church (or is it the Episcopal Church in Scotland? – I can never remember). It can be said for the parish kirk that it is a fine building, both outside and in. Indeed, the interior is much fancier than you will find in most parish kirks in Scotland.

It was made by a great Glasgow man, Mungo Naismyth, the master-mason. He had built the Town Hall attached to the Tolbooth and is supposed to have carved the famous 'Tontine Faces', which can now be seen in different parts of Glasgow. The same year that he finished work on St Andrew's, the spire of Glasgow Cathedral was struck by lightning. The authorities condemned it, but Mungo Naismyth stepped in and saved it by his reconstruction.

In the case of St Andrew's, Mungo Naismyth left an architectural conundrum which has not been solved to this day. There are six fine Corinthian columns in the portico and you are invited to look at the lintels over them. The joints of the stones are perpendicular, and give no appearance of being keyed. Some people call them 'flat arches'.

Mungo's workmen, apparently, did not like this idea at all, and others joined them in their fear that when the props supporting the lintels were removed there would be a disaster. Naismyth heard of this and on the night before the props were to be removed he went along to the church, climbed up to the lintels and slackened the wedges below one

44

of the unsupported arches. Then he had a bed made up for him just below the arch and slept there all night.

When the workmen came along in the morning there was the master-mason, still (apparently) sound asleep under one of the 'dangerous' arches. After that there were no more criticisms and, so far, the lintels have stayed safe for more than two hundred years.

St Andrew's Square, once a most fashionable place, was not built until much later, and in 1784 the famous balloonist, Lunardi, made two flights from the back of the church. These were great occasions, when crowds estimated at a hundred thousand turned up to see the balloon take off. Considering the entire population of Glasgow at that time numbered about seventy thousand, there must have been a lot of people in from the country.

Lunardi was a handsome young man, who wore a brilliant uniform and was very gallant to the ladies. His balloon was brilliant too. It was attached by a rope to the back of the church. While it was being slowly inflated, the band of the 27th Regiment played. Then, when Lunardi gave the signal, the band played a stirring march, the church bells of all the kirks in Glasgow rang and up went the balloon. Some ladies fainted, others wept, but most of the crowd cheered and waved.

'The daring navigator', says one author, 'managed his aerial ship with splendid skill, and, carried along by a fresh gale, landed in two and a half hours in the Valley of the Ale in Selkirkshire, to the great astonishment of the scattered shepherd population, who escorted him and his strange machine into Hawick, where he was publicly feasted and presented with the freedom of the burgh.'

Lunardi didn't stay long in Hawick, however. He knew a great welcome was waiting for him in Glasgow and got back to his laurels as soon as possible. A week or two later he made a second ascent from the back of St Andrew's Kirk, but this time flew no further than the foot of the Campsie Hills, a few miles to the north.

St Andrew's by the Green, as an Episcopal chapel, installed an organ a few years after it was opened in 1751, and hence it was known to witty Glaswegians as the 'Whistlin' Kirk'. The Presbyterians would not tolerate the idea of artificially made music in a church. The precentor conducted the choir and the congregation. He would sing a line of a psalm and then the rest would repeat it, right through all the verses.

But in 1805 a new minister was appointed to St Andrew's Parish Church, a Dr William Ritchie, a 'man of the world' type of clergyman who had travelled on the Continent and had up-to-date ideas. He found, in one of the outer rooms of the church, a small chamber organ which had been made by a former member of the congregation named James Watt. At that time James Watt had been working for Glasgow University, but one day, during a walk across Glasgow Green, he was suddenly struck with a new idea for the condensation of steam. This brought him such fame that he moved from Glasgow to Birmingham, where his ideas were taken up in a big way. Mr Watt left his organ, which looks more like a liarmonium than an organ, to the kirk.

Dr Ritchie liked the idea of music in his church and he allowed the organ to be played during choir practice. Though they were all strict Presbyterians, most of the congregation actually liked the sound of the music, and, since St Andrew's Square had now been built round the kirk, and the Molendinar buried beneath the ground, a large number of well-to-do Glaswegians were members of St Andrew's.

In 1806 they took the daring step of presenting a petition to Glasgow City Council, asking that they should be allowed to remove certain seats in the church so that they could use the organ in public worship. This petition was accompanied by a letter from Dr Ritchie and it said, in part, if the request was granted 'our Heritors, Magistrates of one of the first commercial cities of Europe, will thus give new evidence to mankind that the genius of commerce is not the contracted spirit of hostility to the liberal arts, but the enlivening sun of science, dispelling, in its progress, the gloomy fogs of prejudice that have too long benumbed the energies and untuned the feelings of our country.

'Glasgow has the honour of having first made the public proposal of introducing into one of its churches the most perfect of musical instruments, and of employing it for the generous purpose of tuning the public voice for the exercise of praise. And the present Lord Provost, and magistrates and Council, will, we doubt not, eagerly embrace the opportunity of accomplishing a measure which will give additional lustre to their names, and render the period of their administration the opening of a new era in the annals of our national advancement.'

But the Lord Provost, magistrates and Council wished no part in opening a new era. They said no. All the same, the organ was moved into the church, but kept under a green baize covering. Then one summer's day in 1807 these anarchic members of St Andrew's decided to defy the City Council. At the afternoon service on 23 August the congregation were excited to see that the green baize covering had been removed. There was the organ, all ready for playing, but no organist was to be seen.

The psalms and paraphrases were sung in the usual unaccompanied fashion, until Dr Ritchie announced the final psalm. Then who should appear but the elderly organist of the 'Whistlin' Kirk', John Fergus. He sat down at the organ and played the music while the congregation sang.

The next day this outrageous act was the talk of Glasgow and soon it was the talk of Scotland. There was bitter controversy all over the country, and finally the Presbytery announced that organ music was 'contrary to the law of the land, and to the law and constitution of the Established Church, and prohibited it in all churches and chapels within their bounds'.

So the organ which James Watt had built was removed from St Andrew's. It was sold to a Glasgow music shop where the owner 'improved' it by building up gilt pipes along the front. Then the famous Bailie McLellan, who gave Glasgow the McLellan Galleries and the collection of paintings which formed the nucleus of the Art Galleries, bought the organ. After that it went from house to house, and now, I am glad to say, it is on view in the People's Palace on Glasgow Green. And the ghost of James Watt, to say nothing of the spirit of Dr Ritchie, will be glad to know that it can still be played.

The organ was not the only piece of furniture in St Andrew's kirk to be cast into outer darkness. With it went a fine-carved eagle reading desk. Apparently this lectern was considered too 'fancy', so it too had to go. However, it was quickly snapped up by a man who was just opening a new hotel in the city. He put the bird above his door and called his place the Eagle Hotel. This Eagle Hotel was swept away by the railway, and the eagle itself eventually landed above the door of an ice-cream shop. From there it was at last rescued by representatives of the kirk and put back in its place on the top of a lectern in St Andrew's Parish Church.

Back in the Saltmarket, in the year before the 'Whistlin' Kirk' was built, Glasgow's first bank was founded. In 1750 all the existing banks had their headquarters in Edinburgh. The Glasgow and Ship Bank (better known just as the Ship Bank) was opened at the corner of the Saltmarket and the Bridgegate, where the Ship Bank Tavern stands today.

If you examine the panels in the walls of the Ship Bank Tavern you will see a representation of what that corner looked like when the Ship Bank stood there. It remained there for twenty-six years and then flitted to the Trongate. Later came the Thistle Bank in the Bridgegate, and later still the Ship and the Thistle amalgamated to become the Union Bank of Scotland. Now the Union Bank has been swallowed up by the oldest bank in the country, the Bank of Scotland itself. But it's a remarkable thing that, whether it was the Ship Bank or the Union or the Bank of Scotland, the insignia of the ship has been retained, and you will see it on the back of any Bank of Scotland note you are fortunate enough to have in your pocket.

We shall be looking more closely into the Briggait later, so now we walk on down the Saltmarket (originally known as the Walker-gait, by the way) and, where the road widens, Jocelyn Square is in front of us. In my young days it was known as Jail Square, but the City Fathers thought that name inappropriate and changed it to Jocelyn to commemorate the Glasgow bishop who gave the town its famed 'Glasgow Fair'.

Bishop Jocelyn was the founder of the present Glasgow Cathedral. There was a church by the Molendinar, of course, ever since St Mungo decided to stay there. But the building of our cathedral was started by Jocelyn in the 12th century. Bishop Jocelyn was also the man who got King William the Lion to make Glasgow a burgh – not a Royal Burgh, but one 'held of the Bishop'. A second charter was granted by William in 1189 for an annual fair in Glasgow, and that is the origin of our present Glasgow Fair holiday.

It was Jail Square before it was Jocelyn Square, because the South Prison stood where the Justiciary Buildings stand now. But we end this chapter at the end of the Saltmarket.

5
YOU'LL DIE FACING
THE MONUMENT

I started my last chapter with an old Glasgow saying – 'A' the comforts o' the Sautmarket'. I start this with another – 'You'll die facing the Monument'.

They couldn't be more different. The first refers to comfort and well-being. The second is an insult. 'You'll die facing the Monument' means, to elderly Glaswegians, that you're going to be hanged.

When, in the 19th century, the South Jail stood in Jail (now Jocelyn) Square, any malefactor who was to be hanged was, as they say, 'turned off' between the two pillars of the entrance to the jail. Hangings were in public then and the scaffold was built outside the entrance. It faced straight across to Glasgow Green and Nelson's Monument, so that the last thing the poor wretch saw was the Monument.

The last person to be hanged in public in Glasgow was Dr Edward William Pritchard, an English practitioner who had settled down in Glasgow and poisoned his wife and his mother-in-law in his house on Sauchiehall Street. Dr Pritchard was a card. As a doctor he was not much more than a quack, but he shone as a lecturer, a Freemason and a ladies' man. Indeed, he had to leave Filey, where he had a very good practice, because so many incensed husbands of his female patients were after him.

He was tall, slightly bald and had a fine beard. He was always the glass of fashion and when he promenaded Sauchiehall Street he carried a packet of picture postcards with him. Each of these postcards was one of Dr Edward William Pritchard himself and if he liked the look of someone approaching him, the doctor would make a courtly bow and present him, or more usually her, with a postcard.

He killed his mother-in-law swiftly because she was suspicious about her daughter's lingering illness. Mrs

Pritchard was originally an Edinburgh girl and her parents still lived there. While she was in Glasgow she was always unwell. But when she left her ever-loving husband and went through to Edinburgh to stay with her parents, she immediately started to recover. Parents and daughter attributed this to the fact that the air of Edinburgh was so much purer than the air of Glasgow. It was only when the doctor's mother-in-law came to Glasgow to nurse her daughter that she suspected the doctor might have something to do with this strange illness.

While Dr Pritchard was killing his wife by slow torture, he was making love to their young Highland maidservant. If this situation seems familiar to you I should point out that the Glasgow dramatist James Bridie used the story of Pritchard as the basis for his play *Dr Angelus*. The two deaths were traced to Dr Pritchard, who insisted on his innocence until just before he was due to be hanged, when he confessed. Since, just before the funeral of his wife, and before he was suspected, he had had the coffin lid opened so that he could kiss his victim on the lips, he was known in Glasgow as 'The Human Crocodile'.

He was hanged facing the Monument in 1865, and thirty thousand people gathered to see justice done. I have met men whose fathers saw the hanging, and they told how preachers harangued the crowds for hours, how pickpockets had a good day and how bakers and piemen did a roaring trade. Dr Pritchard dressed for the occasion. His beard was freshly combed. He had on his newest suit. And he wore a pair of new patent-leather boots. He was duly hanged.

Now, when you leave the Saltmarket and enter Jocelyn Square, you will see a red brick building on your right and the High Court Buildings beyond it. This is the city mortuary – the morgue to American visitors.

Before the mortuary was built the ground had to be prepared for the foundations and the pipes. This ground was within the boundaries of the Justiciary Buildings and it was the place where people who had been hanged in public were buried. Workmen digging in the ground came across the skeleton of Dr Edward William Pritchard, and the story goes that his patent-leather boots were still in a perfect state of preservation. These boots were promptly sold, so that, for some time, somebody was going around Glasgow in Dr Pritchard's boots. The workmen discovered, too, that there was some financial value in Dr Pritchard's skull. It is alleged that there are no fewer than three of Dr Pritchard's skulls in existence. But if you happen to know of anybody who possesses one, don't say a word to him about this. After all, for all we know, his might be the real one!

Most Glasgow murder trials, and other 'big' cases, are heard in the Justiciary Buildings. There is not much pageantry in Glasgow, although Glaswegians dearly love a show and crowds gather to see each High Court start, with bewigged judges, trumpeters and attendants. Crowds gather at the end of a big trial to hear the result and to see the leading figures in the case – including the accused, if he has been freed.

When I was a young reporter (you might as well get used to that phrase now!) they gathered on the other side of the square, in front of the entrance to Glasgow Green. The police had some trouble with them there. They didn't like the idea of a large group, supporting a Glasgow gangster who had just been sentenced, collecting in a body when some witnesses, belonging to rival gangs, were about to leave the court-house.

This was solved in a remarkably simple and effective way. The Parks Department of Glasgow Corporation merely put down a few flowerbeds there, thus breaking up the open space. Glaswegians, even gangsters, are very law-abiding. They wouldn't think of tramping down a flowerbed. Even if chased by the police a Glasgow 'ned' would run round the flowerbed, and the policeman chasing him would do the same.

You see the same kind of thing in operation in George Square, now the centre of the city. Protest meetings and all sorts of assemblies are held in George Square, but nobody thinks of walking on the grass plots. The last man who picked some daffodils in George Square was fined £5 so there is a good reason for keeping to the by-laws.

In a way I am sorry to see the flowerbeds in front of the entrance to Glasgow Green. This was once Glasgow's Hyde Park Corner. Famous orators stood here and vied with one another. They were very much admired and attracted big crowds. One of them was that much-loved anarchist Guy Aldred, who also knew the inside of the building across the way. Guy Aldred was the nicest anarchist who never threw a bomb. His bombs were all verbal ones.

After the flowerbeds got in the way the forum was transferred to the foot of the Nelson Monument in Glasgow Green. But it was never the same again.

Long before it was a forum, however, this part of Jocelyn Square was, appropriately, the place where the Glasgow Fair was held. That's to say, the Glasgow Fair when it ceased to be an annual market place and became a centre for a one day's round of the delights of the fleshpots. From the foot of the Saltmarket down to the River Clyde there were circuses, booths, merry-go-rounds, freak shows, pie shops, wrestlers, theatres, oyster stalls, geggies, beer tents, performing bears, waxwork shows, cock-fights, whisky vendors, performances done by mirrors and all the other wonderful things our forefathers enjoyed. Some of them I still saw in my youth, and oh, how I envy my forefathers!

For many years the Fair was held on Glasgow Green, on a great open space which provides football pitches in the winter. There was a circus – Pinder's Royal Number One – where you could find a freak show and a boxing booth and a tent with 'magic' mirrors, and there were merry-go-rounds and all sorts of rides like the Moon Rocket and the Whip, but the booths were given over to bingo and other games of chance, such as rifle-shooting and Aunt Sally. And if you think these last two are not games of chance you're more innocent than I thought you were.

Jocelyn Square became a popular place for theatres at one time. In 1835 a Mr Mumford built a wooden theatre near the foot of the Saltmarket. He charged only a penny per performance, and this fee included one or two plays, several songs, a dancing performance and quite often a lecture by Mr Mumford himself on the evils of drink. When he was sober Mr Mumford was an expert with the Italian marionettes, but he'd go off on a 'blind' for weeks at a time and his wife had to carry on the show.

When Mr Mumford, who seems to have been a real
Bohemian, returned to his theatre he would insist on giving a
moral lecture to the audience as they gathered outside the
booth. Immorality was his theme, and he would explain how
his mother had told him that he must not follow the usual
showman's practice of putting on an entertainment by day
and stealing by night.

If he was drunk, however, Mr Mumford gave his audience
a lecture on the teetotal theme. A typical example is given by
the actor Walter Baynham in his book *The Glasgow Stage*.

I quote Mr Baynham on Mr Mumford: "'If you knew," he
hiccuped one day, while supporting himself by one of the
posts supporting his exhibition, "if you knew the advantages
to be derived from abstaining from intoxicating drinks you
would shun whisky – hic – as you would the very devil."

"You're drunk yourself!" cried one of the crowd. "I know
it," continued Mumford, "but what did I get drunk for? Not
for my own gratification, but – hic – for your profit, that you
might see what a beast a man is when he puts an enemy to his
lips. I got drunk – hic – for your good.'"

Mumford was really a harmless soul, but John Henry
Alexander, the manager of the Theatre Royal in Dunlop
Street, not so very far away, didn't see him in that light. Mr
Mumford presented plays, and Alexander had a royal patent
that gave him the sole right, as he saw it, of presenting plays
in Glasgow. John Henry was not only a man of the theatre, he
was a man of the law, and he engaged in constant litigation
while he was in Glasgow. He brought an action against Mr
Mumford, who was forced to give up the drama and stick to
the marionettes and lectures on immorality and strong drink.

The odd thing is that Mumford's name long outlasted John
Henry Alexander's. In later years, when the Theatre Royal,
Dunlop Street, had disappeared, there was still a Mumford's
Penny Geggy on Glasgow Green. Mrs Mumford carried it
on, and became famous for presenting a drama, a comedy and
a farce or pantomime for one penny. There are people in
Glasgow who still remember Mumford's Penny Geggy, and
some of its imitators.

The geggies were rude wooden frameworks with canvas
coverings and rudimentary seating arrangements. The price

of admission was always one penny for adults and a halfpenny for juveniles – although they might also be admitted for an empty jam jar, which in those days had a monetary value. In latter days the performances grew shorter and the idea was to get through as many as possible in a single evening, so that there might be five or six different audiences with their pennies.

Will Fyffe, the great Scotch comic who wrote 'I Belong to Glasgow', was brought up in a penny geggy. His father, Jack Fyffe, was the leading man and was renowned for his performance as Rob Roy. In the years when his son Will was famous for the brilliance of his character acting, in such a part as 'Daft Sandy', he owed it to the training he had had as a boy actor in a geggy.

The transpontine drama was the greatest attraction in the penny geggies. *Rob Roy* came first, because it was a patriotic piece as well as high drama. In some geggies the performance could be affected by the booth's proximity to a pub, of which there were plenty around Glasgow Green in those days. It is told of one production of *Rob Roy* that Rob himself thundered on to the shaky stage, rather late and with his red beard festooning his cheek instead of his chin.

Somebody in the audience shouted – it seems to have been the favourite cry of theatrical audiences in Victorian Glasgow – 'You're drunk!' Rob Roy stopped in his rodomontade and turned to the audience. 'Me drunk?' he cried. 'You wait till you see Bailie Nicol Jarvie!'

One of the hits of Glasgow Green drama was a thriller of *The Stranglers of Paris* and *The Face at the Window* type. The penultimate scene showed a mountainside, made of orange boxes over which canvas was draped, up which the villain had to climb, pursued by the arms of the Law. As he almost reached the top a shot rang out and he was apparently hit. Then he fell dramatically down the whole mountainside, landing in a heap at the foot.

This was known to the faithful patrons as 'The Deid Man's Drop', and if it was well done they applauded until the villain arose from the dead, bowed and did it all over again.

Four years after Mr Mumford built his geggy on the Green another rival to John Henry Alexander of the Theatre Royal appeared. He was David Prince Miller, a penniless showman who came to Glasgow Fair and managed to get into the wooden theatre where the Wizard of the North, the Great JH Anderson, was showing the Glasgow public the conjuring tricks with which he had baffled the Crowned Heads of Europe. (Just to make the matter clear, we have had three Wizards of the North in Scotland. The first was Michael Scott, a medieval magician; the second was Sir Walter Scott, who made magic with words; and the third was the Great JH Anderson.)

Anderson's most famous piece of magic was the 'Great Gun Trick'. It has often been done since – indeed it killed the Aberdonian Chinese Conjurer, Chung Ling Soo – but the Great JH Anderson claimed to have invented it. It consisted of having a volunteer from the audience fire a loaded rifle at the conjurer's head. When the audience recovered from the flash and the bang they saw that the conjurer was holding the bullet – marked, and therefore the one which was fired – between his teeth.

Miller watched Anderson's performance several times and gradually worked out how the trick was done. He tried it in private and succeeded. So he built a booth just opposite the Wizard of the North's pavilion and charged the public one penny to see the same trick that was being done across the way at a charge of sixpence. He cleaned up to the tune of £70.

With this money he decided to build a theatre on Glasgow Green. It was a wooden building, like most of the others in the Saltmarket area. But Miller's plays had been running for only two or three nights when the Royal Patentee, Mr Alexander, charged him with infringement of the Theatre Royal's rights. Miller fought back with spirit and put on a pantomime entitled *The Licensed Murdered*. But the legal proceedings went inexorably through and Miller finished by spending thirteen weeks in the adjacent jail.

When he was released David Prince Miller reopened his theatre. But he took care not to present any plays. Catching bullets in his mouth was safer. But the stranglehold of Alexander was broken when a Bill was passed in Parliament enabling local courts to grant licences. Miller applied for a licence successfully and opened a new theatre in Jail Square. He called it the Adelphi and opened with a performance of *As You Like It*. He brought the great actor Phelps to Glasgow in *Hamlet* and he produced a pantomime, *Baron Munchausen*, which conquered Alexander.

But Miller was to be sorry that he had ever learned the 'Great Gun Trick' from the Wizard of the North. In 1845 JH Anderson, the Wizard himself, came back to Glasgow and announced that he was going to build a new great theatre on Glasgow Green, just beside the Adelphi. Miller decided to follow a policy of appeasement. After private talks between them it was agreed that Anderson should pay £1,000 to Miller and become a partner. This arrangement fell through, and the Wizard of the North built the City Theatre on the Green. It was the biggest and finest theatre that Glasgow had ever seen.

At first the entertainment consisted mainly of magic and dancing, but then Anderson applied for a dramatic licence and, when he got it, started a season of opera with Sims Reeves as the star. In *The Bohemian Girl* Reeves was the darling of Glasgow.

The success of the City Theatre worried both the Adelphi and the Theatre Royal. But they did not have to worry long. On 18 November 1845, the City Theatre caught fire and everything, including scenery, costumes and the night's receipts, went up in flames. The Wizard of the North tried to enter the burning building to save the money, but he was held back. The Adelphi, next door, was only saved because the firemen, realising the City Theatre was beyond hope, concentrated on throwing water against the walls of the Adelphi.

The Adelphi was saved, but only for another three years. The great actor Macready, who had not been seen in Glasgow for fourteen years, appeared at the Adelphi, but Glasgow opinion was crystallised by the critic who wrote: 'To see Macready once was to see him always'. Still, the Adelphi was doing well, until the unfortunate afternoon in November 1848 when the company were rehearsing a drama called *The Ocean Monarch, or Ship on Fire*.

The actor who was playing the part of the ship's captain was just addressing his passengers on the dangers of smoking aboard ship when his eye caught a sudden glare in the gallery. He stopped short in his speech, but, even before he could shout a warning, a sheet of flame shot right along the gallery. By the time the fire brigade arrived the Adelphi was well alight, and this time the firemen had to concentrate on saving the Episcopal church of St Andrew's by the Green. Although the roof had caught fire the church was saved, which was more than the firemen could do for a horse which happened to be passing as the flames burst out of the theatre. The heat was so intense that the hair was burned off the horse's back.

This ended the era of big theatres in Glasgow Green, although the booths and the geggies were to continue for many years to come. They were followed by the forum, and the forum was followed by the flowers, and now we are ready to go into Glasgow Green, which is considered to be the oldest public park in Britain. Mark that word 'public'. Many public parks today started as royal or private parks. But Glasgow Green was town property in the 15th century and, although part of it was sold during the 16th century (owing to bad management on the part of Glasgow Town Council), it was bought back again in the 17th.

Its greatest danger was when a later City Council was told that there were five seams of coal below the Green. The Council, in their search to make Glasgow ever more beautiful, were quite prepared to turn the Green into a series of coal mines. Fortunately, tests proved that the 'experts' were wrong. A city surrounding a coal mine is an awesome thought.

Nowadays we walk into a pleasant park, with the River Clyde curving to the south. Down near the Clyde at this point there was the famous Arns Well, where most of the inhabitants of the tenements to the north of the Green drew their water. When more than a hundred years ago a proper water supply was piped into Glasgow from Loch Katrine, some of the older people refused to touch it and still took their pitchers to Arns Well. One old lady from Monteith Row was asked why she didn't use the water from the tap. 'I've tried it,' she replied, 'and it has neither taste nor smell!'

If you take the path by the river you come across the boathouses of the various rowing clubs, including Glasgow University and the Glasgow Printers, who race regularly on the Clyde. There's also a jetty where you can hire a rowing boat, and behind the jetty is a rescue station, occupied by a family named Parsonage who have been pulling people out of the Clyde for years.

But going straight ahead into the park the first thing you see is the yellow, glazed Doulton Fountain, the only memento of the first of the famous Glasgow Exhibitions. Most people in the city would tell you proudly of the exhibitions of 1901 and 1911. Some looked back nostalgically on the Empire Exhibition of 1938. But the first was held in Kelvingrove in 1888, and this fountain was made by the firm of Boulton to honour Queen Victoria. Though very much smaller, it has an affinity with the Albert Memorial in London. The Queen sits in front, glowering a little, and is surrounded by representatives of the Empire on which the sun never set in those days.

It is an odd example of Victoriana, and I'm sorry now that I did not show it to Sir John Betjeman on his visits to Glasgow. But I did show it to a Tovarich Agapov, from the *Literary Review* of Moscow. He was entranced by the Doulton Fountain and insisted on taking shots of it from all angles. I don't know if they all came out, but I counted thirty-four photographs before he was finished. Perhaps I should make it clear to those who have not visited Russia that there is a very strong Victorian streak in housing, decoration and general surroundings there. I think Mr Agapov felt at home, though he was to feel even more at home later in the Green.

Mr Agapov was not quite so interested in the Nelson Monument, even though I told him the story of 'You'll die facing the Monument'. Glasgow, by the way, was the first place in the whole of Britain to erect a monument to Nelson. I have to be careful of my words here, because the first *memorial* to Nelson's victory at Trafalgar was made by some English workmen who heard the news while they were engaged in iron work at the village of Taynuilt, on Loch Etive in the Highlands. They got hold of a fair-sized boulder and rolled it into the village, and inscribed a patriotic message on it. The boulder can still be seen behind the church in the middle of Taynuilt.

But Glasgow put up an official monument in honour of Nelson long before any town or city in his native country did. Subscriptions were started in 1805 and a column in the style of Cleopatra's Needle was erected by 1807. The Glasgow magistrates were considering the inscription for the monument when a noted wise man, Sir John Carr, was in the city. They asked his advice and Sir John recommended something simple. He thought it should just be, 'Glasgow to Nelson'.

It's a pity to have to explain a joke before it's made, but I must tell the non-Scottish reader that the town of Neilston, near Glasgow, is pronounced very like 'Nelson' by some people. So, when Sir John Carr said 'Glasgow to Nelson', one of the bailies replied: 'Aye, just so. An' as the toon o' Nelson's close at hand, might we no' just say "Glasgow to Nelson, six miles", an' mak' it a milestone as weel as a monument!'

I hope this story is not apocryphal, because I have always bracketed it along with the one about the great Glasgow Exhibition of 1901. When the City Council were discussing the exhibition someone suggested that as an attraction on the River Kelvin, which ran through the Exhibition, they should get six gondolas from Italy. One bright bailie immediately said: 'Six? Why no' just buy two gondolas an' let them breed!'

The part of Glasgow Green around Nelson's monument was the first golf course in the town, and it's also where James Watt was walking one Sunday in 1764 when he got the idea of a separate condenser for the steam engine. By rights James Watt should not have been walking across the Green at all on the Sabbath, and if he had been caught by zealous Presbyterians he might have been fined or even imprisoned.

This, unfortunately, kills that romantic story about James seeing the steam coming from the kettle on the hob in the kitchen, and getting his great idea then. On the other hand, I sometimes wonder what would have happened if he had been caught walking in Glasgow Green. Might his arrest not have wiped for evermore the idea of the separate condenser out of his mind? Even so, no doubt somebody else would have discovered it. It's just that at times I feel how much better off we'd have been without the steam engine.

A few meetings in the old style of Jail Square are still held at the foot of the Nelson monument. Just fornenst it is, or rather was, another source of entertainment, the park bandstand. In the days of my youth Glasgow park bandstands were popular places. Not now. The glamour of the Black Dyke and Foden's and the Argyll and Sutherland Highlanders under the conductorship of Captain FJ Rickets has gone. I'm glad that when I was a boy I was still able to experience it. Some of the happiest hours of my life were spent on summer's nights standing outside the railings at Alexandra Park, listening to the band.

To the north of the Nelson monument, is the McLennan Arch. I mention it only because visitors to Glasgow seem to think it is of some special significance. It is part of the façade of the Assembly Rooms, built on Ingram Street by Robert Adam at the beginning of the 19th century. Later it became the entrance to the Glasgow Athenaeum. A Bailie McLennan, in the goodness of his heart, had the archway pulled down and rebuilt on Glasgow Green.

From the McLennan Arch you can see Monteith Row, once the most fashionable terrace in Glasgow. It has sunk far down in the world, but still has an air about it. There was a great Chartist riot in Glasgow in 1848. It started with speeches on the Green, and some of the rioters looking for weapons tore the iron railings from the front of Monteith Row.

Across from Monteith Row is the People's Palace, which houses the Old Glasgow Museum and has a Winter Garden, where – since I have mentioned bands – I recall hearing the great Kneller Hall Band play one Sunday evening, among the palms and tropical plants. Kneller Hall houses the Army School of Music, and the cadets' band remains in my memory as the finest military-cum-brass-cum-jazz band I have ever heard.

The relics of Old Glasgow in the People's Palace include what I call the 'scalps' of the city. There is a series of enormous maps on which the growth of Glasgow is shown. Below these maps are the chains and insignia of the various burghs which Glasgow, in the nicest sense, took in. One chain belonged to the Provost of Partick who, on the day that Partick became merely a district of Glasgow, threw his robe, his three-cornered hat and his chain on a table in Partick Burgh Hall and cried, 'There they lie – the abandoned habits of the Provost of Partick!'

There is an interesting old orrery in the People's Palace, and it actually works, showing miniature planets revolving round miniature sun. Among the paintings is one purporting to show the old Glasgow Fair on Glasgow Green. Included among 19th-century characters is a figure, which can only be Charlie Chaplin. Nobody knows how he got into the picture, which includes characters famous in Glasgow a century or so before him.

Some of the many yachting trophies presented to Sir Thomas Lipton, Glasgow's (and Britain's) greatest grocer, are now on show. He sailed one Shamrock after another against the Americans for the America's Cup, and they called him 'the world's greatest loser'. It's appropriate that his yachting trophies should be shown in the People's Palace because Tommy Lipton, when a boy in 1861, founded a yacht club, confined to those who built their own boats, on the River Clyde at Glasgow Green.

I have called him Glasgow's and Britain's greatest grocer, but in some respects he was the world's greatest grocer. Lipton's Tea, I believe, is known everywhere except in China, where they seem to have a preference for their own brand. He was the son of Irish parents who came to Glasgow during the Hungry Forties. His father had a butter-and-egg shop and when Tommy was twenty-one he started a grocer's shop of his own in Stobcross Street. He worked hard all day and slept under the counter at night. He had a wonderful advertising sense, and it is to him that we owe the habit of constant tea-drinking that obtains today.

From the People's Palace you go across the park by the drying greens where Glasgow women once washed their clothes as well as dried them. Glasgow has always been famous for beautiful girls, and still is. To English visitors in the 18th and early 19th centuries one of the sights was the girls, with their skirts kilted to near the waist, tramping out the washing in their 'bynes' (or tubs) with their bare feet.

At the end of the 18th century Glasgow Green was the principal promenade in the town, and a local poet, John Mayne, wrote proudly:

> Whae'er has daundered oot at e'en,
> And seen the sights that I hae seen,
> For strappin' lasses, tight and clean,
> May proudly tell
> That, search the country, Glasgow Green
> Will bear the bell.

There was a washing house (or 'steamie', as it was called hereabouts) and a swimming pond, but they have disappeared. In my young days I still saw the washing hanging out on the clotheslines on Glasgow Green but, alas, there were no girls with their skirts kilted up.

I have mentioned Mr Agapov, of the *Literary Review* of Moscow. I took him right across the Green to this point for a special purpose. You see in front of you a remarkable building – Templeton's carpet factory, the biggest carpet factory in Britain and one of the biggest in the world. In this factory two golden carpets have been made for Coronations and special carpets have been made for Glasgow Cathedral, for maharajahs in India and for Atlantic liners.

On my first day in Moscow I saw the Kremlin. At first, with its battlements, spires, turrets, cupolas and what not, it reminded me of an old-fashioned pantomime set in the days when the Theatre Royal in Hope Street was at its best. But when I had a closer look I felt even more at home. I saw then how much the Kremlin resembled Templeton's carpet factory on Glasgow Green.

There is, of course, a good reason for this. Templeton's carpet factory was built in the style of the Doge's Palace in Venice. Part of the Kremlin, particularly the outer walls, was built by an Italian architect of the same period. So you see the same architectural features on the Kremlin – the Italian fish tail battlements, for example – that you see on Templeton's carpet factory. As I say, I felt at home in Moscow and I may add that when I took Mr Agapov as far through Glasgow Green as Templeton's carpet factory, he felt at home too.

Glasgow Green comes to a thoroughfare and a bridge now, and on the other side is the Fleshers' Haugh, where the ground is given over mainly to football pitches, except during July when something approaching the old time Glasgow Fair is held. There are no theatres or penny geggies, but there are still rides and stalls and entertainments of all kinds. Perhaps it's significant that today the booths where there are the biggest queues are the fortune tellers.

On the Fleshers' Haugh Bonnie Prince Charlie reviewed his Highland Army in December 1745. By this time some of the ladies of Glasgow, notably Clementina Walkinshaw, had given in to the Prince's gallantry – in the pleasantest way, I hasten to add – and a fair number of townspeople turned out to watch the parade. It was noted that, with the clothes and shoes and other accoutrements provided from Glasgow's common purse, the Highlanders looked much better dressed than when they had arrived in town. Well, so they should. According to one historian, Glasgow provided them with 12,000 shirts, 6,000 cloth coats, 6,000 pairs of shoes, 6,000 pairs of stockings, 6,000 waistcoats and 6,000 bonnets. By which token, I'd say the Highland Army numbered about six thousand, wouldn't you?

Despite the gallant show, Prince Charles was unhappy. One Glaswegian said afterwards: 'He had a princely aspect, and its interest was much heightened by the dejection which appeared in his pale, fair countenance and downcast eye. He evidently wanted confidence in his cause, and seemed to have a melancholy foreboding of that disaster which soon ruined the hopes of his family forever.'

And it was after Culloden that a Glasgow poet, of all people – William Glen – wrote that sad Jacobite ditty, 'Oh, wae's me for Prince Charlie'.

The Fleshers' Haugh was always a favourite place for parades, and various corps of volunteers marched and drilled over it. Samuel Hunter, the eighteen-stone editor and proprietor of the *Glasgow Herald*, was one of the notable figures on the Fleshers' Haugh. He was Colonel of the Glasgow Highland Volunteers and then of the Glasgow Corps of Gentlemen Sharpshooters. Once, when he was putting the Gentlemen Sharpshooters through their paces on the Green, he fell from his horse. A sympathetic crowd gathered round him, but Samuel just said: 'Oh, never mind. I was coming off anyway.'

Nowadays you don't see so many parades on Glasgow Green, but occasionally you may catch the Glasgow Mounted Police at exercise here. They may not come up in magnificence to the Royal Horse Guards, but they have a glamour of their own when seen through an early-morning mist.

We have walked right across the Green, but you can also take the road by the side of the River Clyde. This could be made into as fine a promenade as you'll see in any city, but so far there are proposals but no action. Across the river you see the skyscrapers of the new Gorbals, where Glasgow's new Left Bank may yet gain something of the fame of the Left Bank in Paris.

Most people imagine that the parkland on the other side of the river is still Glasgow Green, but it is actually Richmond Park.

Behind it is Polmadie, and there used to be a saying in Glasgow – 'Oot o' the world and into Polmadie'. A sad waterway, reminding you of the old Molendinar, runs through it and on the Left Bank at Richmond Park you can see it join the Clyde. It is Mall's Myre, or Jenny's Burn.

Polmadie is pronounced 'Polmadee', with the accent on the first syllable. They'll tell you there that the reason for the name is that when Mary Queen of Scots was fleeing from defeat at the Battle of Langside she was riding her favourite horse Poll. But in trying to get across Mall's Myre Poll fell and had to be destroyed. Still, it was obvious that the Queen had escaped and, as she gazed upon her dying steed, she said sadly, 'Poll may dee that I may live.'

Those present were so impressed that they gave the place the name of 'Poll-may-dee', which became Polmadie in the course of time. This is a good story (and we shall come across some more Mary Queen of Scots tales of equal verity), and

I'd be glad to believe it were it not for the fact that maps of the district drawn before Mary Queen of Scots was born show the name of Polmadie or Polmaddy. It is a corruption of a Gaelic name meaning 'pool of the wolves' and within living memory there was a lonely pool on the way to Hampden Park. As for the wolves, they have always been with us.

Glasgow Green and Richmond Park, though regarded by Glaswegians as in the middle of the town, are actually on the periphery. The boundary between the city and the Royal Burgh of Rutherglen runs close to them. Just across the road from Richmond Park is Shawfield Stadium. The boundary line runs across the football pitch, only some twenty yards from the western goal. So it is possible for a player to kick the ball in Rutherglen and score a goal in Glasgow.

Rutherglen became a Royal Burgh before Glasgow did and has always claimed seniority. And every time Glasgow has attempted to take Rutherglen over, the opposition has been so strong that the proposal has never had the slightest chance. To this day the atmosphere of Rutherglen is quite different from the Glasgow ambience, and even Glaswegians who go to live in Rutherglen are so affected that they change sides.

If you walk back across Glasgow Green on a fine winter's afternoon, when a frosty sun is setting, you get glimpses which remind you irresistibly of the paintings and drawings of the Green made two or three hundred years ago. There are even the same spires to be seen as in an 18th-century print of the scene. Daniel Defoe wouldn't feel altogether lost even today.

6

PADDY'S MARKET

Halfway down the Saltmarket, on the eastern side, is the Bridgegate, or Briggait – otherwise, the way to the first Glasgow bridge over the River Clyde. It doesn't look much of a street. There are drab tenements and shops which specialise in second-hand goods of all sorts. A railway bridge crosses over it. Even in sunlight it has a sad air. And yet this was once the most fashionable street in Glasgow. In the 17th century the rich merchants of the city built their dwelling-houses in the Briggait, and towards the brig itself Sir William Bruce built the Merchants' House with a picturesque steeple in the Dutch style.

In the Merchants' House the great assemblies and balls were held, and so on the appropriate evenings the Briggait would be full of sedan chairs, borne by Highlanders taking the ladies of fashion to the gay occasion. For some hundred years the height of Glasgow fashion paraded in the Briggait and then the merchants and their families started to move out. The merchants gave up their Merchants' House too, and it was sold. The Briggait went steadily down in the world.

The Merchants' House was sold in 1817 and the new owners demolished it, leaving only the fine old steeple, built in 1659. Just thirty years after the sale came the great Potato Famine in Ireland and the Hungry Forties, when the Highlands of Scotland were nearly as badly affected as Ireland. The Irish began to emigrate in great numbers. If an Irish family had any money they went to America. If they had only a little money they went to Liverpool. And if they had no money at all they came to Glasgow.

The cost of transport from Belfast to the Broomielaw was four-pence per skull – and skull was often the operative word. In order to make the voyage pay, the ship-owners crammed their human cargo as tight as it would go. Irish men, women and children spent the whole voyage across the Irish Sea and up the Firth of Clyde standing upright, jammed so tightly together that when a passenger died he was held in position by the other bodies and his death was only discovered when the ship berthed.

And at the same time as these ships full of Irish people were sailing up the Clyde into Glasgow, other ships were sailing past them, full of Scots, particularly Highlanders, seeking their fortune across the Atlantic. And yet in those days the Government and the Establishment and the people at the top thought that all things were working together for good. Perhaps in London they didn't even realise that ships of Irish were coming into Scotland while ships of Scots were sailing out.

The arrival of the destitute Irish created a great problem in Glasgow. There were already Irish people in the city, and they did their best for the incomers. A great many liberal-minded Glaswegians got together and provided soup kitchens and depots for clothing. Peter Mackenzie, whose *Reminiscences* are at once the most individual, erratic and best account of Glasgow at any particular period, has described the harrowing scenes in the centre of Glasgow, where poor Irish women would hold up their ill, and sometimes dying, children to the gaze of the passers-by, and an Irishman would stand in the gutter in the Briggait, attempting to sell the shirt he had just taken off his back.

I mention the Briggait advisedly. By the 1840s the street had come down so far in the world that a number of the old mansions belonging to the 17th-century merchants were still standing, but were empty. Many Irish people moved into these empty rooms and became, as it were, our first 'squatters'. Soon the street, which had once been the most fashionable thoroughfare in Glasgow and homed the first city banks, became an Irish quarter.

To the incoming Irish the first problem was the simple one of existence, and the men were prepared to take any kind of job. If starvation had affected their strength, determination to make a living for their families more than made up for it. Glasgow was already a great industrial city. In 1801 the population was 77,000. Fifty years later it was 329,000. And in another fifty years it had reached 762,000. These figures are impressive, but perhaps the best comparison is that between 1801 and 1871 the population of the whole of Scotland doubled. In that same time the population of Glasgow increased over six times.

Nowadays it is said that one-third of the population of Glasgow is Irish or descended from the Irish, which does not mean, of course, that one-third of the population is Roman Catholic. But most of the Irish who flooded into the Briggait and nearby streets in the Hungry Forties were Roman Catholics. St Andrew's Roman Catholic Cathedral on Clyde Street, built in 1816, had a bigger congregation than ever.

The Irish were poor, hard-working and well behaved, but they had their characters, and Peter Mackenzie tells how it was a common sight on a Saturday night to see a big, drunk Irishman literally trailing his coat down the Briggait in the hope that somebody would step on it and so provoke a fight. At this time the Briggait was surrounded by shebeens and it was very easy indeed to get fighting drunk.

Today the Briggait, though drab, is much more respectable than it was in the Hungry Forties. The extraordinary thing about it is that there are still two strong remnants of those days.

First there is the Ship Bank Tavern, which I mentioned already as the site of Glasgow's first bank. For many years this pub was the unofficial headquarters of the Irish in Glasgow. It was the address given to young men who were leaving their native isle to seek a fortune in the big city. If you came from Donegal all you had to do was go along to the Ship Bank Tavern in the Briggait and tell anybody behind the bar where you came from. Right away you'd be put in touch with other people from Donegal. You could be among friends within an hour or so of arriving, a poor, lost soul, at the Broomielaw.

The parallel with this is the Highlanders' Umbrella over Argyle Street. Between Union Street and Hope Street the bridge of the railway from Central Station makes a fair-sized shelter, with many shops below it. Some people today imagine that this is called the Highlanders' Umbrella because of the thriftiness of the Highlanders. The idea is that when it rains the Highlanders rush to get under this cover and so save themselves the cost of buying an umbrella. As a matter of fact there are several shops selling umbrellas under the Highlanders' Umbrella!

But the reason for the name has nothing to do with the thriftiness of the Highlanders. Indeed, the Highlanders have always been known for being very free and easy with their money, when they had any. It was the Lowland Scots who were the thrifty ones and, of all the Lowlanders, the Aberdonians worked hardest to get the 'near' reputation. (The line between the Highlands and Lowlands in Scotland runs diagonally from the Clyde to about Inverness, and Aberdeen, though farther north than many places in the Highlands, is actually a Lowland city.)

No, the reason for the name of the Highlanders' Umbrella was that in the days when many young men and women from the Highlands were coming to Glasgow to find work and opportunity, this was the place where they met on their one free day, the Sabbath. If you were a girl from Tiree you'd be told before you left your island that all you had to do on a Sunday afternoon or evening was to go to the front of a certain shop under the Highlanders' Umbrella, and there you would meet other exiles from Tiree.

The shops were all closed, of course, but in front of almost every one you would see a little gathering of people from Mull or Inveraray or Mallaig. Nowadays there's a fine big Highlanders' Institute up near Sauchiehall Street, but underneath the Central Station bridge is still known as the Highlanders' Umbrella.

So the Highlanders met, in their day, under a railway bridge on Argyle Street, and the Irish met in a pub in the Briggait. Historically, the Irish had more reason on their side. And the Ship Bank Tavern is not the only historical connection.

If you go along the Briggait towards the railway-bridge you'll find a narrow opening on the south side with the legend, 'Shipbank Lane'. Go down it and you will find yourself in the midst of Paddy's Market. There is a little courtyard with a restaurant of sorts and a few second-hand shops. Down the lane from the Briggait to Clyde Street there are more second-hand emporia made out of the archways under the railway line. One of them, indeed, is called 'Paddy's Market'.

But right down the whole length of the lane there are individual sellers of all sorts of second-hand goods. A small boy stands holding out a knife. A shifty-eyed gentleman has a camera for sale. Several 'rag-women', having scoured the suburbs, now display a variety of clothes, tablecloths, bed linen and even hats. The only person missing, I am glad to say, is an Irishman trying to sell the shirt off his back. Nevertheless, the tradition of Paddy's Market has come straight from him.

Devotees of Paddy's Market say that you get far better bargains there than you do at the more sophisticated Barrowland in the Gallowgate. I am not really in a position to judge. But I do like, every now and then, to pay a visit to Shipbank Lane and see what they have to sell underneath the arches. I am not so keen on the vendors who stand along the lane. It is said that you should not visit Paddy's Market with a tall man wearing a soft hat, a raincoat and big boots. Strange to say, at his appearance most of the vendors will disappear like snaw aff a dyke. This may be because they are not licensed hawkers. Or there may be another reason.

I can tell you this, though. Not long ago I was concerned in the making of a film about Glasgow. Edward McConnell, who was making the picture along with Laurence Henson, asked me to go with the camera unit to Paddy's Market because I was known there. The idea was that I should jolly the vendors and the customers along and that we should get some good pictures of the real, unvarnished Glasgow.

All went well at first. I was soon surrounded by a group of people who either wanted to say hello or else complain to me about too much police activity in the neighbourhood.

At one time I had a crowd like an execution around me. Then people noticed the camera being set up. This takes some time especially when, as on that afternoon, the sun is dodgy. Gradually people started to move away. I noticed that those who were left, still talking to me, kept their backs to the camera.

Then even the old die-hards left me. When the camera was ready there wasn't a soul in the lane for a score of yards on either side. I couldn't coax anybody back either. They had their own good reasons, no doubt, why they should not have their pictures taken.

Back to the Briggait, you walk under the railway bridge and there is the Glasgow Fish Market to your left and the Goosedubs to your right. The Fish Market, as I have said, takes the place of the old Merchants' House, and you can see the 17th-century tower rising above it. The Victorian decorations of the Fish Market are not too out of keeping with the tower, and most visitors imagine the building and the tower are all of one piece. I find the Fish Market an entrancing place, but it's seldom that I am there early enough to see it at its best.

I find the fish we get in Glasgow much fresher than in any city I have visited in England. Perhaps it's not quite as fresh as the fish in Aberdeen, but it will do. It has always surprised me that there aren't more restaurants in Glasgow specialising in fish dishes. I am not counting our fish-and-chip shops. I am thinking of restaurants proper. At one time, for instance, we had a profusion of oyster bars in Glasgow. Now you have to look for them.

Part of the Fish Market was once a church, and it was noted for its outdoor pulpit. Every now and then the minister would hold an outdoor service in the Briggait and address whatever congregation had collected in the street from his vantage point.

The old steeple, along with the Merchants' House, was built by Sir David Bruce, who was a favourite architect of King Charles II in 1659. It is possible, but not advisable, to climb the steeple. You can see the old clock and a bell that is never rung. On the bell is the inscription: 'John G Wilson, Founder, Glasgow. AD 1861. Lord, let Glasgow flourish by the preaching of the Word.'

Rather rickety ladders lead from one balcony to the next. From the topmost of the three balconies, about 170 feet high, there is a fine view down the Clyde, and in the days when this was part of the Merchants' House those merchants who had ships were supposed to climb to this vantage point to see if their argosies, richly lade, were coming up the Clyde to the Broomielaw.

These Glasgow merchants were very go-ahead. In this Merchants' House, as far back as 1783, they founded the first Chamber of Commerce in the British Isles. It was called the Chamber of Commerce and Manufactures, and it was the second in the world. The first Chamber of Commerce had already been established in New York.

All visitors to Glasgow are intrigued by the name Goosedubs. To most Scots who know their own tongue the meaning is quite plain. A 'dub' is a puddle or a small pond. One of the Glasgow bailies had his house fronting Stockwell Street and his gardens stretching back to the Briggait. He kept a flock of geese and these geese enjoyed themselves in the dubs or wee ponds that he had made for them. When a lane was made, connecting Stockwell Street with the Briggait, it was naturally called Goosedubs. There were houses here, too, and in one of them was born Mrs Grant of Laggan, an authoress and song-writer who composed *Oh, where, tell me where is your Highland laddie gone?* some thirty or forty years after the principal Highland laddie, Bonnie Prince Charlie, had left Glasgow for good. In early Victorian days there was quite a rage for writing Jacobite songs, particularly as Queen Victoria approved of them.

Mrs Grant of Laggan was so highly thought of in Glasgow that when first *Waverley* and then *Rob Roy* came out, a great many Glaswegians thought she had written these novels. Sir Walter Scott, of course, was still remaining anonymous. And, naturally, the more Mrs Grant disclaimed authorship, the more the knowing ones became quite certain that she was the mysterious 'Author of *Waverley*'.

Oddly enough, when Sir Walter Scott visited Glasgow he came to this same Briggait district. In King Street, which runs between the Briggait and the Trongate, stood the Institution Tavern, a howff popular with university professors and students, and with Radicals who planned risings and rebellions. The Institution was Scott's favourite tavern in Glasgow and he often tied his horse to the ring at the door.

This howff had a low roof, the floors were sanded and all the drink was served in silver tankards. It had also a Wishing Stone, and if you were superstitious you sat below this stone while you drank and your wish would come true.

How wonderful it would be if one could visit the Institution today, sit under the Wishing Stone and ask that the Briggait should return, just for an hour or so, to its former grandeur. As it is, when you walk along the street you must send your imagination constantly back into the past, for the present is not pretty.

7

BEYOND THE PLAINSTANES

When I was a boy my father took the *Strand Magazine* regularly, and though in the Dennistoun suburb of Glasgow we were more than four hundred miles away, I felt when I looked at the cover that I was looking at the heart of London. It was always the same piece of the Strand that was shown, and the only difference was at Christmas time, when all the well-known buildings were suddenly transformed by a fall of snow. It struck me that London was fortunate in always getting snow at the right moment.

Just about the same time, and for a wheen of years before, the equivalent Glasgow picture was a view of the Trongate, taken from about King Street and showing Tron Saint Mary's Steeple, the Tolbooth and Glasgow Cross in the distance. There was no equivalent of the *Strand Magazine*, but any time a general view of Glasgow was to be presented this was the scene which was chosen.

Well, the *Strand* has gone, more's the pity. And few people today would choose the Strand as the typical street scene of London. It's just the same with the Trongate. Although it was one of the eight original streets of Glasgow, it has almost lost its identity. Most of the people who walk along Argyle Street on a Saturday afternoon don't even realise that they are in a different street when they reach the Trongate.

And yet Argyle Street is a mere whippersnapper of a thoroughfare compared with the Trongate. For hundreds of years after the Trongate was already known and respected there was no street at all past the West Port, a gateway which stood where Glassford Street joins the Trongate now. There was merely a track to the West and as it developed it became known as the Westergait ('the way to the West'). Then, when it had been considerably built on, and the funeral cortége of the 4th Duke of Argyll had proceeded along the way, it was renamed Argyle Street. (They didn't bother much about spelling in those days, as I'll remind you later.)

But the Trongate was a change in name too. It was known originally as St Thenew's Gait, and that meant the way to St Thenew's Chapel, which stood near to where St Enoch Square is today. Need I remind you that St Thenew was the mother of St Mungo? Yes, if you skipped my opening chapter.

In 1491 the Bishop of Glasgow negotiated a royal charter which gave him the right to have a free tron, or weighing machine, in the city. At this tron goods coming into Glasgow were weighed and customs were exacted. The money went to the bishop and, through grants given by him, some of it went to Glasgow University, which was now forty years old. The place for a tron was, naturally, at the mercat cross of Glasgow. So, because people coming into Glasgow to sell their merchandise had to go to the tron, the name gradually changed from St Thenew's Gait to the Trongate.

Although, as I have said, the Briggait became the most fashionable street in Glasgow, the Trongate was the most important. The rich city merchants maybe had their houses in the Briggait, but they did their business in the Trongate. Many of them lived in the Trongate too, and the only reason that the Briggait had the edge over the Trongate was the fact that the Merchants' House, where the assemblies and balls were held, was in the Briggait.

It's odd that the two most fashionable streets of Glasgow in the 18th century were the two smallest. The Trongate is only a little longer than the Briggait. But the Trongate was considered so important that it was the first street in the city to have a pavement. Flagstones were laid along the front of the Tolbooth, the City Chambers and the Tontine Coffee House, and these were known to Glaswegians as the Plainstanes.

At this time there was a group of self-made men in Glasgow who were called the Tobacco Lords. They had cornered the tobacco trade between America and Europe. They owned estates on the other side of the Atlantic and they paid for the tobacco by sending over locally-produced goods, as well as slaves transported from Africa. The Glasgow Tobacco Lords were among the biggest slave-traders in Britain. This is a side of their business life which has been conveniently ignored by most Glasgow historians, who will tell you how various factories were built to provide America with hats, bottles, cotton goods and all sorts of other goods, with never a word about human beings.

The Tobacco Lords were not accepted by Glasgow society of the time. There were few aristocrats in Glasgow, but the merchants had formed themselves into an aristocracy of their own and they did not recognise the Tobacco Lords as belonging to it. And yet the Tobacco Lords were making far more money than were the merchants. They reacted in a way which Freud and his friends would certainly have regarded as completely normal. They made themselves into a superior society of their own.

First of all, they dressed up. A Tobacco Lord wore a scarlet gown over his coat and breeches. He wore a silvered wig with a three-cornered hat on the top of it. And he carried an ebony cane with a silver top to it. Just to show how completely powerful they were, the Tobacco Lords decided that they, and they alone, had the right to walk on the Plainstanes in the Trongate. So when they took their leisure they paraded up and down the Plainstanes and if any ordinary Glasgow citizen dared to tread on the sacred ground, the nearest Tobacco Lord would take a swipe at him with his ebony cane.

They made their pile, they bought their estates, but most of them came to a bad end, from the business point of view. The American War of Independence finished them off. Their plantations and their tobacco businesses were taken over by the revolutionaries. The only man who made money out of this was William Cuninghame of Lainshaw. In the 1780s, when his colleagues were depressed by the news from the American colonies, he said he would take over their stocks of tobacco, worth threepence a pound, at sixpence a pound. The colleagues knew a sucker when they saw one, and sold gladly. William Cuninghame hung on to the tobacco until it reached a price of three shillings and sixpence a pound. Then he sold out and made an immense killing. And, although some of the other Tobacco Lords are still remembered by street names or in obscure histories, Cuninghame is the one who has a building in the city associated with his name. I shall come to it later.

Fornenst the Plainstanes was the statue of King William of Orange, the King Billy monument whose story I have already told. I should just add that it was given to Glasgow by James MacRae, a Glaswegian of humble birth who became Governor of Madras. In nine years he made an immense fortune, and he presented the statue to Glasgow in 1743. By this time he had returned to Scotland, and he looked for surviving relatives. He found that his mother had latterly lived and eventually died in the house of a travelling fiddler named Hugh McGuire, who had married James MacRae's cousin Bell.

The fiddler and his wife had four daughters and Governor MacRae treated them as his family. He showered money, education and clothes on the girls, brought them out in society and saw them well married. Leezie, the eldest, became the wife of the Earl of Glencairn, and on her wedding day she received from her fond uncle land and jewellery to the value of £70,000. The second daughter got an estate and became Lady Alva. The third daughter married Governor MacRae's 'nephew' (otherwise, his illegitimate son) and was given an estate in Dumfriesshire. And the fourth daughter owned Orangefield in Ayrshire and married very nicely.

Robert Burns, who wrote A Man's a Man for A' That, was delighted with the patronage of Leezie's second son, the 14th Earl of Glencairn, and he also found the Dalrymples of Orangefield among the kindest of Ayrshire society people. As far as I can discover, Burns never knew that they were descended from an itinerant fiddler and a poor girl whose cousin had had an eye to the main chance in Madras.

If you are in the Trongate today, and stand where the Plainstanes were laid, you may have some difficulty in recapturing the 18th-century scene. Our Victorian ancestors removed Paton's Land, an old tenement which stood opposite the Plainstanes, so that they could improve the scene by putting a railway station there. Paton's Land belonged to a famous Glasgow worthy called Captain Paton, immortalised by Sir Walter Scott's son-in-law, John Gibson Lockhart, in his

Lament for Captain Paton. I give a verse or two of the Lament here because it shows what life was like in the Trongate at the beginning of the 19th century.

> Touch once more a sober measure,
> And let punch and tears be shed,
> For a prince of good old fellows,
> That, alack-a-day, is dead;
> For a prince of worthy fellows,
> And a pretty man also,
> That has left the Saltmarket,
> In sorrow, grief and wo'!
> Oh! we ne'er shall see the like of Captain Paton no mo'!
>
> His waistcoat and breeches
> Were all cut off the same web,
> Of a beautiful snuff-colour,
> Or a modest gentle drab;
> The blue stripe in his stocking,
> Round his neat slim leg did go,
> And his ruffles of the cambric fine,
> They were whiter than the snow.
> Oh! we ne'er shall see the like of Captain Paton no mo'!
>
> And whenever we foregathered,
> He took off his wee three-cockit,
> And he proffered you his snuff-box,
> Which he drew from his side pocket;
> And on Burdett or Bonaparte
> He would make a remark or so,
> And then along the plainstanes
> Like a provost he would go.
> Oh! we ne'er shall see the like of Captain Paton no mo'!

I have already mentioned the West Port. There was a public well there which was the gathering place of the maidservants of Glasgow. Lockhart brings it into his Lament and he also gives the American background of a Glasgow gentleman of the time.

Or if a bowl was mentioned,
The Captain he would ring,
And bid Nelly to the West Port,
And a stoup of water bring;
Then would he mix the genuine stuff,
As they made it long ago,
With limes that on his property
In Trinidad did grow.
Oh! we ne'er shall taste the like of Captain Paton's punch
no mo'!

As you can see, if you look around you at this part of the Trongate, Victorian architects have made a vague attempt to capture the spirit of the old buildings. But the only old building, once you have left the shadow of the Tolbooth, is the steeple of Tron St Mary's Kirk, set on its archway. Today there is the steeple, then a small courtyard and behind that an ecclesiastical edifice (I use these words advisedly!) used as a store by Glasgow Corporation.

I can remember when it was still a church, and the Presbytery of Glasgow met there. But it was a comparatively modern church in the place of the 16th-century building attached to the present steeple, which was finished in 1636. The first church was burned down by the Hell-Fire Club in February 1793.

There were Hell-Fire Clubs in various parts of Britain in those days. Some of them were devotees of Thomas Paine. Others were just out for a lark. The Hell-Fire Club in Glasgow was composed of well-to-do young men who wanted to brighten their evenings.

At this time there was no proper police force in Glasgow (the first was started in the year 1800). There were elderly watchmen, usually Highlanders, who were called 'Charlies', for no known reason. And there was the city night-guard, a body of burgesses who took turns to go round the town in a patrol. The night-guard were, to put it politely, somewhat erratic. The burgesses who were to go on duty prepared for the night by taking something to keep them warm. They also took a flask or two with them so that they could continue to keep warm. It was a natural precaution.

There was no street lighting at that time, but the Charlies were provided with lanterns. Each Charlie had also a sentry-box, where he stayed for most of his watch, emerging now and then to walk his beat and perhaps give an occasional call of 'Four o'clock of a fine summer's morning, and all's well,' or something of the sort.

When the young men of the Hell-Fire Club decided to make their presence felt they would gather away out in the East End of the city, at the farthest environs of the Gallowgate. Each had a horse and when they had met they covered their horses with white sheets and muffled the horses' hooves in white cloth. Then the Hell-Fire boys put on white nightgowns and pulled white hoods over their heads. They must have looked very like the Ku Klux Klan.

Once they were all assembled and dressed they would ride into the city. With their horses' hooves muffled, they rode silently and you can imagine the effect on a superstitious Highland Charlie when he saw this ghostly cavalcade approaching him. Some Charlies fainted clean away. But, whether they fainted or not, the Hell-Fire Club saw that each Charlie they came across was laid on the ground and his sentry-box put on top of him. That meant he had to remain there all night, until some public-spirited citizens came along in the morning and lifted the sentry-box off him.

On St Valentine's Day, or rather night, the Hell-Fire Club had come into Glasgow. After their usual fun and games they were riding back to the Gallowgate when they came upon Tron St Mary's Kirk. This was where the city night-guard gathered before they went on their rounds. The Hell-Fire Club, which may very well have numbered some sons of the night-guard among them, knew that the burgesses left the session-house at three o'clock in the morning. They knew, too, that the burgesses always kept a good fire going.

They may also have known that the city night-guard were a trifle careless and didn't bother to lock the door of the session-house. In they went and gathered round the fire and, since they were merry, they boasted to each other about how much heat they could stand, which was important in view of the title of the club. So they kept adding to the fire anything in the session-house that would burn.

THE HEART OF GLASGOW

There is another story which says that the Hell-Fire Club were so lost to human shame that they had gone into the kirk to celebrate a Black Mass, but this may have been put about by opponents of Thomas Paine. At any rate, the fire grew too big, the session-house caught alight and the Hell-Fire Club fled. Strange to say, although the session-house and the church were gutted, and the north side of the Trongate was threatened by blazing embers, the steeple itself was not touched. It remains today exactly as it was in the 17th century.

Just across the way from the Tron steeple is the Candleriggs, and in Donald's Land, where shops and warehouses stand now (just before you reach the Candleriggs from the Tolbooth), one of Glasgow's great soldiers was born in 1761. He was Sir John Moore, the hero of Corunna and subject of a poem, *The Burial of Sir John Moore*, which every Glasgow schoolboy had to learn by heart in my young days. Indeed, it's one of the very few which I can make a stab at reciting today. There is a statue of Sir John Moore in Glasgow's Valhalla, George Square.

If you turn the corner from the Trongate into the Candleriggs you go past modern warehouses where there once stood small huts in which candles were made. There is a famous hostelry called Granny Black's on the western side and you pass it to reach the Glasgow Fruit Market, built on the site of an even more famous hostelry, the White Hart Inn. This is the city's equivalent of London's Covent Garden and it overflows into all the side streets around.

On one of these streets was a pub called the Hangman's Rest. It is alleged (and since we are now so near the Glasgow Sheriff Court I must pick my words) that in ancient days when the official hangman had done his job in front of the Tolbooth he would not be allowed into any of the inns nearby. He had to skulk away and take a devious route along country lanes behind the Trongate houses until he reached a little tavern on what is now Wilson Street.

There he could take his ease and spend his tainted money. An artist painted murals in the Hangman's Rest to give verisimilitude to what might otherwise be a bald and unconvincing narrative – if I may quote from the tale of another executioner.

82

In the Candleriggs, beside the Fruit Market, is the City Hall, which once was second only to St Andrew's Hall in the affection of the citizens who flocked to the 'Bursts', the Abstainers' Union concerts, the Saturday-afternoon concerts run by Glasgow Corporation, the soirees and the political meetings. Public halls were an important part of Glasgow life then (and I mean in my own lifetime). Most of them are neglected now.

Such great men as Harry Lauder, WF Frame and Charlie Kemble appeared at the 'Bursts', which got their name because every member of the audience received a poke containing cakes, cookies, biscuits and fruit. This was to accompany the tea, or sometimes milk, which was served during the evening. After the audience had consumed the contents of the poke they would blow up the paper bag and explode it. Hence the 'Bursts'. It is regrettable but true that the audience, if they did not like a turn on the stage, would soak a cookie in their tea or milk and throw it at the performer. Glasgow audiences are just not the same nowadays.

That's true, too, when we come back down the Candleriggs to the Trongate. On the south side there were various places of entertainment. The two outstanding were MacLeod's Waxworks and the Britannia Music Hall, both absorbed today in multiple premises. The Britannia was outstanding in the Victorian days when the music hall was the main entertainment in the city. It was in close competition with the oldest of Glasgow music halls, the Scotia, round the corner on Stockwell Street.

In the 'Brit' all the great stars of Victorian days appeared, and some of them, the Great Leybourne, Lion Comique, for example, so arranged their Glasgow visits that they performed in two or three theatres each evening. They moved from one music hall to another in a specially-hired cab and if they had to alter make-up or costume they changed in the cab. Glasgow audiences, as I have indicated, were always ready for rude fun and games. If they didn't like an act they made no secret of it. At the Britannia doors, men and women were selling ripe tomatoes, squashed oranges, rotten eggs and other forms of ammunition. It was quite the thing to buy a parcel as you went in and, since you were a Scot and didn't approve of waste, you were bound to use it at some occasion during the performance.

Both MacLeod's Waxworks and the Britannia were bought by one of Glasgow's 'characters', a Yorkshireman known as AE Pickard. Albert Ernest died in 1964, in his eighties. He brightened the Glasgow scene for some sixty years. He described himself as 'AE Pickard Unlimited' and stood for Parliament in the Maryhill Division as the 'Millionaire' candidate.

He told me that he got his start in show business by buying a weigh-yourself machine for a pound or two and finding, when he got it home, that the contents were still inside it and amounted to £30. I understand, however, that the usual weighing machine can't take as much money as that at a time and that even if it did its weight would be so great that it couldn't be moved without using a crane.

That, however, didn't worry AE Pickard. He would happily reel off story after story and he would produce his eight great volumes of newspaper cuttings and other paper trophies to 'prove' that what he said was true. On one page there was a eulogy of AE Pickard as he opened a new cinema in the suburbs of Glasgow. On another was a telegram from a music-hall artist who assured Mr Pickard that he and his wife would not appear at the Panopticon, even if they were reduced to sweeping the streets.

The Panopticon was the name which Mr Pickard gave to the Britannia after he took it over. MacLeod's Waxworks were changed to Pickard's Waxworks, and in the basement Mr Pickard ran a zoo of sorts and constantly challenged Bostock and Wombwell's Menagerie on New City Road. There was really little comparison, but Mr Pickard had the edge on advertising and got the crowds.

Mr Pickard showed films at the Panopticon, but he also had a variety bill of several acts, and he carried on the Britannia tradition by having an 'Amateur Hour' every Friday night. The tomato and orange vendors carried on the tradition also and many people, whose interest in the theatre was otherwise slight, went to the Panopticon on a Friday night for 'some fun'. The stage manager was equipped with a long pole which had a sort of shepherd's crook at the end, and if the amateur act was getting the bird, to say nothing of the fruit and the vegetables, the stage manager would place the crook round the act's neck and pull him off stage.

Despite this treatment many amateurs went along on a Friday night to try and beat the audience. One of them was the great Jack Buchanan, the immaculate musical-comedy star between the two world wars. He was a Helensburgh boy who went to Glasgow Academy (although his name was strangely omitted in a list of famous old boys issued some years ago) and knew the Glasgow scene well. After appearing at the Panopticon, Jack Buchanan tried himself out at a music hall in Edinburgh. There his act was greeted by stony silence, and he said afterwards that he'd rather have the Panopticon audience, oranges and all.

Pickard's Waxworks and the Panopticon did not survive the Depression of the early thirties. They were both victims of a change in public taste. In his first days Albert Ernest Pickard had had a great success at the Waxworks with a succession of fasting men and women. The fasting man who broke the world's record in the Trongate was a great swell who dressed in the height of fashion and carried a silver-topped cane. He was exhibited in a glass case and at the back was a curtained recess where he could retire when the needs overtook him.

Every day a doctor called at the Waxworks and examined the fasting man, and his medical bulletin was put up at the entrance.

There was a constant crowd marching up the stairs and past the glass case, although they came down to one or two after midnight. The fasting man duly broke the record. His system was simple. The silver-topped cane was hollow, and inside it he had enough nutrition pills to keep him going for days on end.

Mr Pickard showed the fattest boy in the world, the fattest girl in the world, a number of bearded ladies, dwarfs, giants and freaks of all kinds. A report appeared in the Press that a leprechaun had been seen in Ireland. Immediately Mr Pickard announced that the leprechaun was here, in Pickard's

Waxworks. Crowds rushed to see a gnarled Irish dwarf, sitting amid vaguely Irish scenery, scowling at the audiences and muttering imprecations in what was thought to be Erse.

My own last visit to Pickard's Waxworks was to see the Armless Wonder. He was a rather refined-looking gent, with a waxed moustache, a high collar and a plain tie. Round his shoulders he wore a cloak, which concealed the fact that he had no arms (or, for that matter, that he did have arms!). As we say in Glasgow, he 'wore' his bare feet and he proceeded to show us that anything we could do with our fingers he could do with his toes. He threaded a needle with his toes and he hammered a nail into a block of wood with his toes. Finally, he took up a pen in his toes and signed copies of his autobiography at sixpence a time. It was a most impressive performance. You felt it didn't really matter whether he had arms or not.

The narrow entrance to Brunswick Street on the north side of the Trongate shows what the street was like in Victorian days. There were various wynds and closes on either side of the Trongate and a number of public houses and inns were so built that they could be entered from either end. You could go up a wynd, enter a pub, have a drink and walk out the other side and down a street into the Trongate. This was the case in Argyle Street too, and these pubs were much used by Victorian husbands who were accompanying their wives on shopping expeditions.

This seems fairly innocent, but the Trongate and round about was anything but innocent in Victorian days. Over one hundred years ago local legislation was brought in to deal with brothels and shebeens (drinking dens) in the centre of the city. The authorities made pious sounds about how everything had been cleared up and the district around the Trongate, King Street, Goosedubs, Bridgegate and Saltmarket had now been purged of such places.

And then in 1871 along came the *Glasgow Daily Mail* with an investigation into 'The Dark Side of Glasgow'. The newspaper revealed that proprietors were not keeping their tenants in order, and pointed to Glasgow City Council who owned the Laigh Kirk Close at 59 Trongate. In this one close there were twenty brothels and three shebeens. This was nothing unusual in the area. In less than one-sixteenth of a square mile there were two hundred brothels and one hundred and fifty shebeens.

According to the Glasgow volume of the *Third Statistical Account of Scotland*: 'The larger, respectable shebeens, which made great profits, consisted of a large room holding thirty or forty, a smaller room for favoured customers, and overflow accommodation in the kitchen. There were also, in descending order of decency, the smaller shebeens in the wynds, and the "wee shebeens" on the stairheads (particularly difficult to pin down), and, lowest of all, those establishments which operated at one and the same time as shebeens, brothels and thieves' kitchens.'

The Trongate today is such a respectable place that it's difficult to imagine that it was once Glasgow's centre of vice. Indeed, when these things were happening in the Trongate the much-maligned Gorbals was a substantial, well-doing district across the Clyde. Yet even in this century there were queer places in and off the Trongate and I remember, as a young reporter, seeing model lodging-houses and backlands just behind the business and shopping frontages.

The narrow entrance of Brunswick Street suddenly widens and there is a view of the ornate front to the County Buildings where the Glasgow Sheriff Court and a number of other courts sit. There is a sheriff and nearly a score of sheriffs-substitute and Glasgow and the surrounding districts keep them very busy indeed. Parts of this building, and particularly the side facing Ingram Street, were used as the Glasgow City Chambers for some years, but, like their predecessors, they became too small, and it was from here that the flitting took place to George Square.

Next to Brunswick Street along the Trongate is Hutcheson Street, and at the top of it you see Hutchesons' Hospital, with the statues of the Hutcheson brothers in niches on the front. This street is named after the Hutchesons, of course. George, the elder, had a house in the Trongate. He was a very rich man and when he died he left his money to his younger brother Thomas, with an injunction to build a hospital for aged men nearby. The hospital was built where Hutcheson Street is now and its 17th-century steeple is one of the old monuments of Glasgow which has been swept away.

The present Hutchesons' Hospital is the second, and it is not a hospital. It was built by David Hamilton at the beginning of the 19th century, and he deliberately made it look older, so as to keep something of the 17th-century atmosphere of the original hospital. The present building houses the offices of the Hutchesons' Trust, which administers, among other things, two famous Glasgow schools: Hutchesons' School for Boys and Hutchesons' School for Girls.

The Hutcheson brothers bought land out at Lambhill to the north of Glasgow, and when I walked along the Forth and Clyde Canal I used to pass their 'Castle'. It had fallen sadly in the world when I first inspected it. The building had been let out into separate rooms and flats and had become a sort of tenement. Hutchesons' Trust did not seem to be interested in it, and eventually Glasgow Corporation swept it away and built Council houses on its site. The Corporation even took away the good old names which were still in use after the First World War. On the Hutchesons' side of the canal the place was known as Sodom and across the canal it was, naturally, Gomorrah.

However, we return to the Trongate. On the south side there was the grocer's shop where gas lighting was first introduced in 1817. It was confidently expected that when the jetees were lit the whole shop would explode. It was also said that the smell of gas would affect the food and drink for sale. In general, it was held to be a Great Mistake.

There was a large crowd to see the explosion, and they held well back. But when the jetees flared into brilliant light the crowd came gradually forward. Some people stayed in front of the window until the gas was extinguished for the night. The grocer had a *succès fou* and it was the done thing for the youth and beauty of Glasgow to parade up and down in front of the shop in the glowing light of the gas.

That gas might have saved some lives a few years earlier. Near the grocer's shop were two narrow passages, the Old

Wynd and the New Wynd. When the resurrectionist scare was at its height in Glasgow, early in the 19th century, it was said that the local sack-'em-up boys were following the practices of Burke and Hare in Edinburgh. These jovial navigators had found that what the anatomists in the colleges wanted was bodies, no matter where the bodies came from. So Burke and Hare, instead of going to all the trouble and danger of robbing graves, got hold of credulous people, usually women, made them drunk and then killed them.

I don't know of any resurrectionist murders in Glasgow, though some may well have taken place. There was plenty of grave-robbing, as I shall tell you later. But the stories went round Glasgow that lurking in the wynds off the Trongate were body-snatchers with pads soaked in chloroform. When some unsuspecting person came along a couple of body-snatchers would spring from the wynd. One would pinion the victim. The other would put the chloroform pad over his mouth. Then they would take the unconscious victim away for treatment.

This story was told particularly of the Old Wynd and I have met elderly Glaswegians who assured me that their parents had warned them never to pass the Old Wynd by night without putting a hand over their mouths. This was to prevent the chloroform taking effect. I am assured that in this very century there were Glaswegians who always followed this practice as they passed the Old Wynd, though they had no idea why they did so.

If you keep to the north side of the Trongate you once came to an arched entrance with a legend painted above it – 'Spreull's Court'. This was an important part of old Glasgow, but it has been demolished. The Spreull family was one of the oldest in Glasgow. It is said that the name appears in Glasgow records as far back as the 13th century. The Spreulls had a land, or tenement, there for many years. The most famous of them was 'Bass John', a noted Covenanter who got his name because he was imprisoned on the Bass Rock in the Firth of Forth for his beliefs. But 'Bass John' Spreull came back to Glasgow and did well for himself.

Spreull's Court was built about 1784 and was a good example of an 18th-century land. It was only well-off

Glaswegians who could afford to live in this kind of tenement. Their flat, or house as it was called, consisted of a kitchen and several bedrooms. The kitchen was used as a general living-room, but when lady visitors called they were conducted into the principal bedroom.

There they would sit on the big bed, because there was often nowhere else for them to sit, and be served claret and cake. Tea was not served because it was considered a dangerous drug.

Most lands in the Trongate area of Glasgow were built in the form of a square. There was, of course, no indoor sanitation whatever, and what nice people call 'night soil' was taken from the house and piled up in the middle of the square. This might have gone on for months and if it was summertime the stench must have been dreadful. However, the pile remained there, always growing, until the proprietor arranged with farmers outside Glasgow to bring their horses and carts in and take it away – at a price, naturally, because manure was highly valued.

Spreull's Court was famous for its fine old hanging staircase. You stood in the lobby and looked up to the lovely oval spiral. If you climbed the stairs you would see how the doors were curved to suit the curve of the staircase and how the whole scene fitted the cupola at the top of the building. The flats and houses became offices and showrooms, but you could still see in some of them original fireplaces and ceilings.

Through the entrance to Spreull's Court there was another archway. On the last two or three occasions I visited the Court the second entrance was closed. On the other side was an elderly mansion, an odd thing to find behind a city building. This was at one time the office of Glasgow's oldest newspaper, the *Glasgow Herald*.

The Spreull family were also associated with Greenock and one of them, James, did so well in the herring line that it's said that he was responsible for the fish getting the name of 'Glasgow magistrates'. There seems to be no truth in the rumour that they were called Glasgow magistrates because they were red herrings.

Not far from where Spreull's Close once was (a modern office block went up in its place) was a branch of the Royal

Bank of Scotland at the corner of the Trongate and Glassford Street. It's now a shop, but on the corner is a plaque which states that this was the site of the Shawfield Mansion where Prince Charles Edward Stewart resided in 1745. To be very precise the bank was not quite the site. The Shawfield Mansion stood half on the bank site and half in what is now Glassford Street. In the 18th century the Trongate ran as far as Virginia Street. Glassford Street was opened in 1793, when the remnants of the Shawfield Mansion were swept away.

The Shawfield Mansion was considered the grandest house in the city in its day. It was built by Daniel Campbell of Shawfield, Member of Parliament for the Glasgow district of Burghs, early in the 18th century. He had already made himself unpopular with the Glaswegians because of his views on raising the tobacco tax, but what really inflamed them was when he voted in favour of the malt tax, which was threepence on every barrel of beer brewed.

The first day of the new tax was 23 June 1725, and when the excise officers tried to impose the tax there were crowds of citizens to oppose them. Mobs gathered here and there, shouting, 'No malt tax!' At the end of a day of excitement they were startled to see two companies of infantry marching into the town. They were making for the guardhouse at the corner of Candleriggs and the Trongate, but the crowd got there first. They attacked the town's officers, threw them out of the guardhouse, locked it and took away the keys.

Then the word got round that Campbell of Shawfield had ordered the troops into town. The crowds dispersed to find weapons, and then, with hatchets, axes, knives and scythes, they attacked the Shawfield Mansion, shouting: 'Down with Shawfield's House! No malt tax!'

Daniel Campbell had prudently removed himself and his family to his country residence several days before the malt tax was due to be imposed. The few servants he had left in the house were swept aside and the mob wrecked the mansion. The soldiers were occupied in trying to get into the guardhouse at this time, but later Captain Bushell, of Lord Deloraine's Regiment of Foot, decided to ask the Provost and magistrates if he should parade his men.

It was well after midnight before the Captain traced them to an inn off the Trongate. They were having a pleasant celebration there and had not even heard of the gutting of the Shawfield Mansion. It's doubtful how serious the Provost and his bailies thought the affair, but they told Captain Bushell not to parade the troops. By morning, however, they had more sober thoughts and decided to give the Captain the benefit of their advice.

But, as they advanced along the Trongate from the Tolbooth, they saw Captain Bushell form his men into a hollow square in the middle of the street. They were surrounded by a huge crowd who were throwing stones at the soldiers. Captain Bushell gave the order to fire and the troops aimed directly into the rioters. The crowd retreated, but to the town magazine, which they burst open and from which they armed themselves. Others ran to ring the fire-bell.

Provost Miller saw that the Glaswegians would annihilate the troops, so he recommended Captain Bushell to retreat. And this the gallant Captain did, with firing from both sides. By the time he had reached Dumbarton Castle the citizens of Glasgow had found that they had suffered nine dead and seventeen wounded. The Captain lost two soldiers, but one escaped from the mob and the other was rescued by some Glaswegians who thought things had gone far enough without a lynching.

The Government were vastly alarmed at this rioting and two weeks later General Wade marched on Glasgow with Deloraine's Regiment of Foot, six troops of the Royal Dragoons, one troop of the Earl of Stair's Dragoons, a company of Highlanders and one gun. This was enough to overawe even Glaswegians, and General Wade took over the town with no trouble. With him was the Lord Advocate from Edinburgh, Duncan Forbes of Culloden.

Duncan Forbes investigated the Shawfield Mansion riot and its results and ordered nineteen people to be apprehended. He also ordered that the Provost and magistrates should be incarcerated in their own Tolbooth.

From there they were taken under guard to Edinburgh Castle where they were again imprisoned. Next day they asked for bail. It was granted and they were at once released.

The Provost and bailies did not wait in Edinburgh one moment. As soon as they got their horses back they mounted and rode towards Glasgow. About six or seven miles from the town they were alarmed when they saw a great crowd of horsemen riding towards them. But then they heard the sound of cheering and realised that this was a Welcome Committee of two hundred of their fellow citizens who had ridden out to greet them. It must be one of the very few cases when any Glasgow magistrates saw a Welcome Committee.

The horsemen formed a guard of honour round the Provost and bailies and, as they entered Glasgow, the bells began to ring and the citizens turned out in their thousands to wave and to cheer their civic heroes. It was a triumphal procession.

No further proceedings were taken against the Provost and magistrates. The nineteen ordinary citizens were not so lucky. Two of them, a man and a woman, were sentenced to perpetual banishment, nine were whipped through the streets of Glasgow and eight received long sentences of imprisonment.

All this was bad enough, but the iron really entered into Glasgow's soul when Campbell asked the Government for compensation. Parliament granted him an indemnity of £6,080, an enormous sum in 1725, and Glasgow had to pay it. Together with other costs the riot cost the city nearly £10,000. But Daniel Campbell was all right, Jock. With his money he bought the islands of Islay and Jura, and became Campbell of Islay instead of Campbell of Shawfield.

Shawfield Mansion must have recovered from the beating it took at the hands of the rioters. Just over twenty years later, at the end of December 1745, Bonnie Prince Charlie marched his Highland Army into Glasgow. It did not take him long to decide that the finest house in the town was where he would reside.

According to one story, 'he ate twice a day in front of Shawfield House'. If this means what I think it does the weather that December must have been much better than it is now. But perhaps it means that he sat at a window in full view of passers-by in the Trongate. At any rate we are assured that he usually wore a coat of fine silk tartan with crimson velvet breeches, but sometimes changed this for an English court coat, with the ribbon star of the Order of the Garter.

Glasgow left the Prince severely alone. The ladies of the city did not flock round him as did the ladies of Edinburgh. Possibly that is why he so much admired Miss Clementina Walkinshaw, the youngest of the ten daughters of John Walkinshaw of Camlachie and Barrowfield, out Gallowgate way. At any rate, when he had eventually escaped to France, Charles Edward sent to Glasgow for Clementina and she lived with him for part of his unhappy life.

Shawfield Mansion had its greatest days after these stirring times. It was bought by John Glassford of Dougalston, one of the Tobacco Lords. He paid 1,700 guineas for it in 1760. And he could well afford that, for, according to Tobias Smollett in *Humphrey Clinker*, he owned twenty-five ships and his annual trade amounted to half a million pounds. John Glassford died in 1783 and nine years later his son, Henry Glassford, sold the mansion and grounds to a builder for £9,850.

When a street was made from the Trongate to the north it was named Glassford Street after the famous merchant. But before Glassford Street struck through the Shawfield Mansion this part of the Trongate was famous for banks and a hostelry known as the Black Bull. I shall leave them, however, until we come to Argyle Street, otherwise our geography might become rather mixed up.

And, ere we leave the Trongate, we'll walk up Glassford Street to Ingram Street. There are two important buildings on Glassford Street, but they are situated at the north end. The west side of the street has changed almost completely. Until the late 1960s, about halfway up the street, was the entrance to the City of Glasgow Bank, which failed so disastrously in 1878. It was started on Virginia Street, and so I shall leave its tragic history until we are going along Argyle Street.

Halfway up the east side, in a building which no longer exists, was Glasgow's General Post Office in 1840. The first Post Office, as far as anyone can determine, was in the Saltmarket around 1710. It moved gradually north and was in the Trongate for a while. The importance of its stay on

Glassford Street from 1840 to 1857 was that Glasgow postmen were provided for the first time with an official uniform.

The uniform came along in 1855 when there were more than seventy postmen in Glasgow. It included a scarlet, swallow-tailed coat, blue vest and tall black satin hat, with gold band and cockade. Unfortunately, after all this peacockery, the postmen had to supply their own trousers. Perhaps in those Victorian days nobody looked at a man below the waist.

Up at the top of Glassford Street on the west side are two buildings which deserve well of our city authorities. The first is the Trades House, built by Robert Adam in 1794. Apart from Glasgow Cathedral it is the oldest building in Glasgow still used for its original purpose. (That, by the way, is Glasgow's second most popular cliché. If you mention the Trades House to most Glaswegians they will reply, 'Ah, yes, the oldest building in Glasgow still used for its original purpose.' Just for the record, the most popular cliché is 'Glasgow built the Clyde and the Clyde built Glasgow.')

The Trades House is the meeting place of the fourteen Incorporated Trades of Glasgow. The origin of some of these trade guilds is very ancient but, since Glasgow was not a Royal Burgh, the guilds were not officially incorporated until 1605. For many years the Trades House and the Merchants' House shared the running of Glasgow City Council. Even today the Deacon Convener of the Trades House has an *ex-officio* position on Glasgow City Council, although attempts have been made to remove the position.

You must not make the mistake which the Duke of Edinburgh made about the Trades House of Glasgow. Many years ago he was to be sworn in as a Brother of one of the Incorporations. He assumed that this was some sort of trade union and prepared a speech accordingly. Then he marched in a stately procession from the City Chambers in George Square to the Trades House on Glassford Street and found himself in a magnificent hall, with fine murals and a beautiful Adam ceiling. He was facing a group of men, richly bedizened with chains and orders, obviously well-to-do, if not positively rich, exuding civic pride, benevolence and business acumen. The Duke realised at once that he had been misinformed and tore up his prepared speech.

Today the Trades House of Glasgow is mainly a benevolent society. The fourteen Incorporations include Hammermen, Bakers, Fleshers, Bonnet Makers, Wrights, Gardeners and the Weavers, and it is unfortunately the case that there are not many bakers among the Bakers, weavers among the Weavers or even hammermen among the Hammermen. The situation, perhaps, is not quite as bad as is the case with the only guild left in the Royal Burgh of Rutherglen. The last time I attended their annual dinner there was not one single tailor in the Incorporated Tailors of Rutherglen.

Apart from benevolence, the main function of the Trades House appears to be holding dinners. These are among the best in Glasgow, although they do not come up to the standard of when I was a young reporter and had to buy myself a dinner-jacket so that I could attend Trades House dinners as a representative of my newspaper. In those days evening newspapers, as well as the dailies, carried full reports of the speeches made at dinners. A reporter received no extra payment for this darg – except two shillings and sixpence for the laundering of his boiled shirt.

Trades House dinners in the late twenties could run to a dozen courses. There was a separate wine for each course and halfway through a sorbet (a kind of water ice) was served along with a half-sized cigarette. This was to afford a kind of interval before you attacked the second half of the repast. Dinners today are much more modest but speeches are just as long.

The original Incorporations of Glasgow were much interested in saving money, so it's perhaps appropriate that the other special building on Glassford Street, just a few yards north of the Trades House, is the headquarters of the Savings Bank of Glasgow. It's a first-class example of Late Victorian architecture. It was designed by Sir John J Burnet and built in the year 1900. It gives some dignity to a rather undistinguished corner.

The Savings Bank was founded in 1836 and out of it came the first Penny Savings Bank in Britain. The Bank itself is by far the largest Trustee Savings Bank in the country and it holds funds owed to depositors far in excess of £100,000,000.

Even John Glassford never knew money like that, but I'm sure he would approve highly of its being gathered in the street named after him.

8
NO MORE SALMON, PLEASE

There's a wonderful story which has been going round Glasgow ever since I knew the town, and that's not yesterday. It is that the Clyde and its attendant rivers and burns were so full of salmon that a clause was written into the indentures of all Glasgow apprentices that they must not be fed on salmon more than three times a week.

I couldn't tell you how many grave and reverend seigniors have assured me that this is the case. But the sad fact is that nobody has ever seen an indenture with this clause in it. It's true that some old firms and businesses in Glasgow can produce charters which allow them fishing rights in places where it is no longer possible to fish. There is a sheepskin-washing business on the banks of the Molendinar Burn, fornenst Duke Street. They can produce a charter to show that they have fishing rights in the Molendinar. But all they could catch today would be the odd used motor tyre or a bit of a pram or a piece of a bed.

True, also, the River Clyde was once famous for its salmon. But that was long ago, and the last salmon reported in the river at the Glasgow end was one which got as far as Govan in 1887 and then gave up. But still you'll hear the story of the apprentices who suffered from too much salmon.

As I have said, there was a salmon-fishing village about the foot of what is today Stockwell Street, and it was this village which eventually linked up with St Mungo's ecclesiastical centre and made the first Glasgow. So you will not be surprised to know that Stockwell Street was originally known as the Fishergait – or the way to the fishers.

When I looked down Stockwell Street from the Trongate it looked as drab and uninviting as the Saltmarket from Glasgow Cross. Each of these streets was then crossed by a railway bridge. When the Victorians brought the railway lines

98

into Glasgow they did not worry in the least about the buildings and the streets which were removed or changed. The Victorians knew that all that they did was for the good of mankind, and particularly the mankind of Glasgow. If they took away a building or truncated a street they knew that they were removing a part of the slums of the city.

Certainly they did not worry about the fact that Stockwell Street was one of the eight original thoroughfares of Glasgow. But, since it was the way to the first bridge over the Clyde, it was well known even in the days of Sir William Wallace, who started the fight for the independence of Scotland. There was a well in the road and the story goes that Wallace and his men fought and killed a number of Englishmen and threw their bodies into the well.

In order to encourage his henchmen, Wallace is supposed to have cried, 'Stock it well, lads, stock it well!' And from that slogan the name of Stockwell Street is supposed to have been born. To me this smacks of Mary Queen of Scots and Polmadie. Somebody, anxious to ensure that Wallace will be remembered, fathers this story on to our Scottish hero. All the same it was believed for many, many years. There was a well in Stockwell Street called the Ratton Well. It was notable for the unsavoury taste of its water, and it was said that this was due to the fact that Wallace and his men had thrust the dead Englishmen down it.

When you walked from the Trongate down Stockwell Street you didn't go far before you met a section of Glasgow's history. On the right-hand side there was an elderly building, No 24 Stockwell Street. This was once Garrick's Temperance Coffee House and Commercial Lodgings, later shortened to the Garrick Temperance Hotel.

It's a rather odd fact that the Garrick Temperance Hotel did not appear in the Glasgow Directory until 1845. Yet the building was known for more than a hundred years before that date. When Bonnie Prince Charlie brought his Highland Army into Glasgow in December 1745 it was here that Cameron of Lochiel lived. And as I have told you, it was Cameron of Lochiel who pleaded for Glasgow and prevented the city being given to the fire and the sword.

For a while His Majesty's Customs occupied this building, then it reverted to an hotel, and it was here that the Swedish Nightingale, Jenny Lind, stayed in 1847 when she gave several concerts and captivated the city.

You will look through the various histories of Glasgow in vain for any mention of the slave-trade. Nevertheless, it was an important part of Glasgow's life. The Tobacco Lords and many of their descendants dealt with all sorts of shipping commodities, including human beings. Since the slaves never came to Glasgow, the good Glaswegians were able to ignore the dreadful business. Even the upright Dr James Currie, who wrote the first biography of Robert Burns, was able to take part in a business administered from Glasgow which included slave-trading and not seem to be unduly worried.

About the middle of the 19th century, however, Glasgow awoke to the horrors of the slave-trade and the Glasgow Anti-Slavery Society was formed. Later it became the Glasgow Emancipation Society and under that name it held its meetings in the Garrick Hotel.

By the way, it is not known whether the name of the hotel had anything to do with the famous actor David Garrick or not. As far as we know David Garrick never visited Glasgow. He certainly never appeared in any of the city theatres, although there was a theatre poster in the Garrick Chop House opposite the Alhambra Theatre which had David Garrick's name in large type. When you examined it closely you found it gave the name of another actor in small type and announced that he would give his celebrated imitation of DAVID GARRICK!

On the last occasion I visited the Garrick Hotel it was being used as a sort of fun-fair, rather along the lines of Pickard's Waxworks. The main attraction, if that is the right word, was a gentleman who had been charged with a trunk murder at Brighton and got off. But what interested me most was the one and only flea circus I have ever seen. It was run by a Professor Smith and he had trained his fleas to take part in chariot races, fight a duel and juggle a silver ball on their feet.

Television hadn't started then, but I suggested to the BBC in Glasgow that they might consider broadcasting this flea circus. My idea was that the fleas might perform on a piece of parchment, so that listeners could hear the sounds of the chariot race and so on, and listen to the Professor's fascinating patter. But by the time the BBC agreed to the idea, the flea circus had left Scotland, so a world-shattering opportunity was missed.

As you go down Stockwell Street you come to the Goosedubs, which I have already mentioned. Directly across the way was once the frontage of the Metropole Theatre, but when last seen it was a dismal open space. This was the oldest music hall in Scotland, but it went on fire some years ago. Alex Frutin, who ran the theatre, transferred the name to the Falcon (formerly the Empress) Theatre at St George's Cross.

But the original Metropole was first of all the Scotia Music Hall, where Harry Lauder made his first professional appearance. The Scotia was founded in the second half of the 19th century and its greatest proprietor, out of a number, was a Mrs Baylis – no relation of Lilian Baylis of the Old Vic, as far as anybody knows. She engaged all the famous Victorian music-hall stars and regarded the Scotia as far ahead of the other Glasgow music halls. She also gave opportunities to growing talent in Scotland and after Lauder, still only a youth, had made his appearance at the Scotia, Mrs Baylis is supposed to have said, as she handed him his salary: 'Right, laddie. Awa' hame an' practise!'

This is a delightful and much-quoted story, but I knew Mrs Baylis's nephew, and he assured me that she spoke with a decided English accent. It may be that she uttered these words to the young Lauder and that, in repeating them in his own accent, he gave his listeners the impression that these were the actual phrases which she used. At any rate, many years later Sir Harry attended all the Metropole pantomime first nights and was very proud that it was this theatre which gave him his first professional chance.

In the days of this young Lauder, Irish and American, and to a lesser extent English, comedians ruled the roost. There had been the occasional Scotch comic (the word comic in Scotland takes the adjective Scotch, along with whisky, haggis, shortbread, broth and terriers), but the Scottish public

101

seemed to prefer incomers. As far as we know the first Scotch comic, who appeared naturally at the Scotia, was a tall, thin man named Harry Linn, whose big song was *The Fattest Man in the Forty-Twa*. He appeared at a command performance before Queen Victoria, and it is said that on this occasion the Queen *was* amused.

Harry Lauder, anxious for fame, felt he could not imitate American or English comedians, but anybody in the West of Scotland should be able to have a stab at the Irish accent. So, after he went home from the Scotia, what should he practise but an Irish comic song called *Callighan, Call Again*. With this song he made his first hit, and went on to become the greatest of all Scotch comics, though he preferred to be known as a 'character comedian'.

Sometimes the Scotia audience gave an act the bird. There was one famous Lion Comique from London who got the bird on his first night and went to Mrs Baylis in a great state. He said he would rather go back to London right away and take no money at all than be subjected to the insults of a Glasgow audience. Mrs Baylis replied that she had engaged him for the week and he would play for the week, and she would see that the audience behaved themselves. We don't know whether or not she did anything to the subsequent audiences, or whether it was merely that the Glaswegians felt that the Lion Comique was a brave man for staying on, but there was no more trouble and, indeed, he finished his Saturday-night show with a triumphant ovation.

One star of the Scotia was Charlie Coborn, famous for evermore for *Two Lovely Black Eyes* and *The Man Who Broke the Bank at Monte Carlo*. Charlie Coborn was a Highlander from Argyll, but he appeared as a London comedian and his Scottish audiences didn't worry about that a bit. In 1938, at the age of eighty-something, he came back to Glasgow for a radio programme about the Scotia Music Hall. He sang his two famous songs with the backing of the BBC Scottish Orchestra and a large chorus. When he finished, orchestra and chorus burst spontaneously into applause.

John Watt of the BBC was the compère and he paid very little attention to the script which I had written. As old

Charlie Coborn was bowing to the applause, John Watt said: 'Wonderful, Charlie, wonderful! If I couldn't do better than that I should be put up against a wall and shot!'

He meant exactly the opposite, of course, but it's so easy to get mixed up on the air. The people in the studio didn't notice the remark and, though those of us in the producer's box cringed, the show went on as if he had paid Charlie Coborn the greatest compliment in the world. But some of the listeners at home had heard what was actually said, and several of them phoned a Glasgow newspaper to complain about the 'insult' to Charlie Coborn.

Now this broadcast was a link-up between Broadcasting House in Glasgow and the Metropole Theatre, and when the newspaper got its reporters to work they apparently thought that the whole programme was coming from the theatre. So down they went to Stockwell Street to be faced by a bland representative of the BBC who explained that neither Charlie Coborn nor John Watt was appearing there. The reporters could see that for themselves. They went back and reported and the editorial powers apparently decided that their readers were imagining things. Not a word was ever printed about this incident. John Watt would not believe that he had said these words – until he heard a recording of the programme. Nothing has ever appeared in print about it until now.

Mrs Baylis died and the Scotia Music Hall was never quite the same again. New and more modern theatres opened up in the centre of the town. The music hall declined and was replaced by variety. But the Scotia was taken over and transformed from a music hall into a theatre, whose name was changed in time to the Metropole. The Metropole specialised in the transpontine drama. It was famous for *The Stranglers of Paris, The Face at the Window, Maria Martin, or The Murder in the Red Barn, The Silver King*, and *A Royal Divorce*.

This last was the story of Napoleon and Josephine, and, though I regret to say I never saw it, I recall the great coloured posters which showed Napoleon saying, 'Not tonight, Josephine!' and announcing that, for this week, the enormous company would be augmented by the brass band of the Highland Light Infantry.

The other Metropole poster which comes back vividly to my mind was one which showed a dastardly character with a villainous moustache entering the boudoir of a lady who was standing there in her nightie, ordering him out of the room. And right in the foreground was an armchair on which reposed a rolled-up pair of corsets! What a thrill! I can't recall the name of the play, but I remember the poster very clearly.

The manager at this time was a Mr Arthur Jefferson, a tall and dignified man in the old tradition. He had a young son named Stanley, and, out of school hours, Stanley was allowed to help in the theatre. As he grew up he became an assistant stage manager and was even permitted to appear in minor parts on occasion. But eventually the taste for the transpontine drama seemed to die and Mr Jefferson gave up the job.

What happened to young Stanley is not quite certain, but the next time he set foot on the stage of the Metropole he had a new name. He was Stan Laurel, the doleful half of that great pair of film clowns Laurel and Hardy. Many years after *The Royal Divorce*, and all the rest of them, Laurel and Hardy were making a personal appearance at the Empire Theatre in Glasgow. Glasgow has always gone daft over American film stars and they went daft in style over Laurel and Hardy. I think only Tom Mix's horse had had a bigger reception in the city.

But one day Stan Laurel succeeded in escaping the vigil of the fans who had camped outside the Central Hotel. By a devious route he made his way to Stockwell Street and got into the Metropole Theatre. There he met an attendant who didn't recognise him and explained that, as he had once worked there, could he just go in and stand on the stage for a little? The attendant said he could, and Stan Laurel went on to that stage, where Harry Lauder, Charlie Coborn, Marie Loftus, Gertie Gitana and his father had appeared. He just stood there for a while, looking round the empty stage and out into the auditorium, and then he thanked the attendant and left.

By this time the Metropole was in the hands of the Frutin family, who removed it from Stockwell Street to St George's Cross. The first Frutin was Bernard, a Russian Jew who had been the wig-maker for a theatrical company which travelled through Eastern Europe. Like many of his compatriots he came to Scotland. He found there was not much to do in the theatrical line, so he set up as a barber. After a time he made enough money to buy a cinema, and later he bought the Metropole. He was back in show business again.

The Metropole of the drama was renamed the New Metropole, but it reverted to a 20th-century equivalent of the Scotia. Variety and revue came back and practically every Scotch comic of the years between the Great Wars and since appeared on that stage – still the same one which Lauder and Laurel graced.

Of them all, the most indigenous was a man who could do no wrong in Glasgow but was quite unknown in London (except to the English comedians, who regarded him highly). His name was Tommy Morgan. He came from the East End of Glasgow – the district of Bridgeton. He had amazing powers of observation and his great appeal to his Glasgow audiences was that he was absolutely authentic. In this he was like an even greater Scotch comic, also unknown in the Deep South, named Tommy Lorne.

For years Tommy Morgan was principal comic of the Metropole Theatre pantomimes and it was while he was there that the theatre broke the world record for twice-nightly pantomimes. This was a run of twenty-six weeks. It has never been exceeded since. Glasgow, of course, is the real home of pantomime. The winter shows usually start early in November and go on at least until the end of March. Sometimes they continue into April, and one pantomime at the Royal Princess's Theatre (now the Citizens') only stopped at Easter because the management felt it was somehow wrong to keep a pantomime going after that date.

The Metropole stage was a fairly small one and there was nothing spectacular about the pantomime there, although it was here that James Currie's Dancing Fountains and Real Waterfall were first introduced. Now you see them all over Europe and America. But they were invented by a Glasgow man in the Metropole.

I remember one Metropole pantomime, *Robinson Crusoe*, in which the Scottish Nightingale, Ina Harris, appeared in the title role. At one point, for a reason which escapes me now, the scene turned to a forest of icicles. Robinson Crusoe entered in a very fetching white fur suit leading, or being led by, a couple of Borzois – a dog which was very fashionable at that time.

A moment earlier the Demon King had been uttering a particularly nasty spell. He disappeared as Crusoe brought the dogs on. Crusoe released the dogs, which bounded after the Demon King who was, after all, their owner. Then she uttered the immortal lines:

'Vice will be vanquished, virtue will prevail,
Even if I have to take the Oregon Trail.'

Crusoe then sang *The Oregon Trail*. I still regard it as one of the finest moments in a lifetime of pantomime-going.

Under Alec Frutin, a number of modern Scotch comics received their first big opportunity, including Jimmy Logan, who appeared there as a comic boy with the rest of the Logan family.

But before that, for a number of years, there was a remarkable reversal to the days of Mr Arthur Jefferson and his son Stanley. The transpontine drama came back. The wonderful posters were no longer there, but the plays were the same. They were presented by the Charles Denville Company, and Charles was the son of a Mr Alfred Denville who had been performing a similar social service in the North of England and the Midlands for quite a number of years.

The Silver King came back, and so did *The Face at the Window*. But the finest jewel in Mr Denville's crown was undoubtedly *The Horrible Crimes of Burke and Hare*. Of course, Glasgow audiences had seen *The Anatomist*, by the distinguished James Bridie. But they had never seen anything like *The Horrible Crimes of Burke and Hare*.

Perhaps if I tell you of a rehearsal for the play it may give you some idea of its power. The company were rehearsing the scene where Burke and Hare murder Daft Jamie. They have a tremendous struggle to kill him and keep breaking bottles over his head. Every time they think they have done for him he comes to life again and the fight is on once more. But at last they finish him off and Burke says, 'Who would have thought that the boy had so much blood in him?'

Now it is time for them to go off to church, so they carry the body over to a convenient cupboard and prop it up inside. They shut the cupboard door, turn the lights off and leave for the service. A green spotlight shines on the cupboard door and gradually the audience notices that a rivulet of some sort is coming from under the cupboard door. It spreads slowly down the stage and they draw in their breath with terror as they realise it is BLOOD!

At this moment the outer door opens and Mrs Hare enters. She is beginning to get suspicious about the number of dead bodies she finds lying around and, since she rather likes Daft Jamie, she has been worried about his safety when left alone with her husband and Mr Burke. So in the darkness she comes forward crying hoarsely: 'Jamie! Jamie! Are ye there, Jamie?' Then she sees the burn of blood. She follows it up to the cupboard, opens the door and out falls the body. Curtain!

Well, at this rehearsal an actress new to the part was trying out Mrs Hare. She was word perfect, but Charles Denville felt she was not giving the full performance that he liked. At last he went up on to the stage to do as producers have been doing ever since acting started – perform the part himself.

'You come in like this, see?' he said. 'You say your lines – "Jamie! Jamie! Are ye there?" Then you come forward. You see the blood on the floor. You get down on your knees beside it, look at it, put both your hands in it, lift them up – like this – and *let it drip!*'

Can you wonder that at the actual performance *The Horrible Crimes of Burke and Hare* was a *succès fou*? The Metropole was packed every night, and a large part of the audience were medical students from Glasgow University. They had already loaned a quantity of skulls and bones for the production. Every time the anatomist Dr Knox appeared he had a special horrid spotlight on him and the medicals booed and hissed. This was the one drama which had to be kept on for a second week.

I hope you don't think I am labouring too much over this particular Glasgow theatre. I am thinking of Sir Lewis Casson, who broadcast in an Arts Review programme in Scotland in 1947 on 'The Theatre in Scotland'. He said: 'Glasgow has one really native theatre – the Metropole. Their work may not be of high intellectual value, but it is vividly alive in its humour. I wish there were many such theatres, and others, too, that gave us emotional drama at the same unsophisticated level.'

For a number of years I am glad to say, the Metropole gave us unsophisticated, emotional drama. The man nearest Harry Lauder today is Andy Stewart. Through the medium of television he is already known to as many people throughout the world as Sir Harry was. On his way up, where should he appear but on that very same stage on Stockwell Street.

One night in the Metropole I went to see a transpontine drama, but in the 1950s and not the 1850s. It was a famous play entitled *The Black Sheep of the Family*. And who was the Black Sheep? None other than Andy Stewart, who, like Sir Harry Lauder, could ask to be called not so much a Scotch comic as a character comedian.

When I go down Stockwell Street I can't look at that empty space without a feeling of sadness. Alex Frutin had a plan to rebuild the Metropole, but, as I have said, all this part of Glasgow has a foundation of sand. The cost of putting in a new foundation was prohibitive, and he had to give up his idea of re-creating the Scotia Music Hall, let alone the home of plays for which audiences still cheered the hero and hissed the villain.

From the old Scotia down to the Clyde there isn't much to be seen. The buildings, by modern standards, are elderly but not beautiful. There is the entrance to the Briggait with an old tenement at the corner. Traffic lights guard the approach to the Victoria Bridge, which crosses the River Clyde just where Glasgow's first bridge spanned the shallow water.

Nobody can say just when the first bridge was built there. It is said that it was built of wood and it existed in the 13th century. Blind Harry, the Homer of Scotland and the poet of the wars of independence, described how Sir William Wallace and his men were concerned in a skirmish with my Lord

Percy's followers. They had seized Wallace's uncle's sumpter mule somewhere about Cathcart, well to the south of the bridge. Wallace, in his customary fashion, attacked and slew them. Then Wallace, his men and the mule had to escape. They reached the river and crossed the Clyde by a 'brig o' tree' and vanished into the dark north.

This wooden bridge was followed by the first real Glasgow bridge, one built about 1345 by Bishop Rae of Glasgow and Lady Lochow of what is now the Gorbals. It was twelve feet wide, which was considered quite broad enough in those days. The Regent Moray rode over Bishop Rae's bridge (it was always called Rae's bridge on the Glasgow side) when he was committing his forces to the Battle of Langside. The forces themselves had to ford the river somewhere higher up. But the officers and gentlemen used this bridge. It was considered unsafe for heavy traffic.

Bishop Rae's bridge was the only one over the Clyde in Glasgow for more than four hundred years. It is the bridge so much praised by Daniel Defoe and those earlier writers from whom he copied the paeans. Twice the old bridge was widened, but, apart from that, it remained essentially the same bridge for all those years.

The Broomielaw Bridge was built in 1768 and it was the city's second bridge. But the old Glasgow bridge was not replaced until long after that. The Duke of Atholl laid the foundation stone for the Victoria Bridge, to replace the ancient one, in 1851. It was opened in 1854 and still carries a great weight of traffic across into the Gorbals.

We are not going to cross the bridge. To the east there is Clyde Street, leading past the Fish Market and the High Court buildings to Albert Bridge and Glasgow Green. We turn to the west, still Clyde Street, a quayside where sand and gravel were once unloaded from vessels low enough in the water to come up under the down-river bridges. On the other side of the Clyde, however, there is Carlton Place, a fine piece of old Glasgow which has been charmingly renovated. The main feature is a terrace of houses, remarkably little spoiled by the Victorians. One of the houses in the centre is a showpiece and you can see how the original

Mr Laurie liked to live. In his day Carlton Place was so exclusive that there were gates at each end to keep *hoi polloi* out. Naturally, he called the district Laurieston.

On the north side of the Clyde the buildings don't appear to be so distinguished. As you walk along from Stockwell Street you come to a china warehouse which conceals the entrance to one of Glasgow's old houses. The warehouse has been built on to the original Dreghorn Mansion, put up by Allan Dreghorn in 1752. If you go in by the main entrance you will still see the pillars of the other entrance – the one to the Dreghorn Mansion.

When this house was built it was considered the finest in the city and all visitors to Glasgow were taken to see it. Allan Dreghorn was the first man in the town to use a four-wheeled carriage. All his ideas were on the same lines – he was thinking of status symbols long before they were invented. He had a plan with his brother Robert to found a great Glasgow family. It was all the rage in those days. But he had no children, and Robert had a son and a daughter. The brothers' ambitions centred on young Bob.

Young Robert Dreghorn inherited the estate of Ruchill from his father and the house on the River Clyde from his uncle. His income, when father and uncle were both dead, was supposed to be at least £8,000 a year. In other words, by today's standards he was a Getty or Gulbenkian.

It was unfortunate that he was also excessively ugly. Indeed, young Robert Dreghorn was known in Glasgow as Bob Dragon. He had no head for business, no gift for conversation, no ability for drinking, but he did consider himself God's gift to women. Accordingly he would primp and posture along the Plainstanes. If he saw any young girl, no matter what she looked like, he would follow her and, as he made up on her, would ogle her mightily. Unfortunately, any girl in this situation seemed to break into laughter and after a while he would give up the chase.

One day Bob Dragon could stand it no longer, and committed suicide. Henceforth the Dreghorn Mansion was considered a haunted and sinister place. Nevertheless, it was bought by an oil and colour merchant named George

Provand, who used it not only as a dwelling-house but as his place of business. In the year 1822 there was a great deal of talk about the body-snatchers and sack-'em-up men, although the names of Burke and Hare were not yet known. Someone on Clyde Street looked through Provand's basement windows and saw what he thought were rivers of blood. He looked more closely and was almost certain that he could see the severed heads of two children.

He ran up towards the Cross and reported his discoveries. Soon a mob had gathered. They marched down to Clyde Street and first stoned and then attacked the mansion. Before word had reached the magistrates of what was happening at Bob Dragon's house the mob had battered down the door and were occupied in throwing the contents of the mansion into the river – apart from those who were thoughtfully abstracting certain objects with a view to placing them elsewhere to their advantage. If any of the mob had gone down to examine the basement they would have discovered that the rivers of blood were red paint and there were no severed heads of any kind.

However, the pattern of Glasgow riots seemed to be set on that of the Glassford Mansion, which I have already described. In 1822 there was a police force, of course, but even the Master of Police, soon on the scene, could not control the mob. The magistrates called out the military. One of them ran across the bridge at Stockwell to Laurieston and asked the Cavalry Barracks for help. Another ran to the Infantry Barracks in the Gallowgate.

The cavalry and the infantry arrived in double-quick time, the Riot Act was read, the troops charged and the lieges fled. Nobody was hurt. But the next morning the Lord Provost of Glasgow offered a reward of two hundred guineas to any persons who would give information leading to the apprehension and conviction of the leaders of the mob. They didn't have to wait long. Soon they had information of five persons who were in the forefront of the sacking of the mansion.

All were tried and convicted. The only one who concerns us is the man who was judged to be the ringleader – an ex-police officer named Richard Campbell. And he concerns us because he was the last man to be whipped through Glasgow by the last Glasgow hangman. The hangman was an elderly chap named Thomas Young and he was so worried about the nature of his occupation that he never left his home except on business. In other words, he never used The Hangman's Rest at the back of the Trongate.

On 8 May 1823, Richard Campbell was brought out of the jail and lashed to a cart. Surrounded by a strong detachment of the 4th Dragoon Guards, the cart proceeded to south of the jail, where Thomas Young produced the cat o' nine tails, laid bare the prisoner's back and gave him his first twenty lashes. The procession then moved to the foot of Stockwell Street, where the next twenty lashes were administered. And then to the top of Stockwell Street for the same procedure. Finally, the cart, with its groaning and lamenting prisoner, was taken to Glasgow Cross and the last of the eighty lashes was given by Mr Young, who then disappeared rapidly towards his home in the jail. Richard Campbell, having made history unknown to himself, went to the jail as well and then was transported beyond the seas for life.

All this seems very hard, but it must be remembered that some gold and silver was stolen and, even more important, the riot took place just as the kirks were skailing and the whole city was put into a ferment.

Near this china warehouse, which conceals such a story of shame and sin, stands the Roman Catholic Cathedral of Glasgow, St Andrew's, built in 1816. Beside it is Ropework Lane, where there was actually once a ropework. The whole aspect of this district was changed completely when the railway was driven through it, just as I have described in the Saltmarket and Stockwell Street. If you are investigating Old Glasgow in this airt you come, time after time, up against literally a blank wall.

Clyde Street has changed on the river side from a rather dismal view of sheds into a park-like waterway. It decorates the two bridges – the pretty Suspension Bridge, opened in 1853 and costing a halfpenny to cross; secondly, Glasgow Bridge, which didn't take over that name from the Stockwell Street Bridge until 1899.

This bridge, by far the best known in Glasgow and the busiest for traffic, is the third on the site. It was first the Broomielaw Bridge, opened in 1768. Then Thomas Telford built a new bridge at the same place in 1836. The present bridge is a copy of Telford's work and, as I say, it was opened in 1899. There's also the railway bridge from Central Station and the King George V Bridge on the other side of it. But bridges are losing fashion. The great thing nowadays are the Clyde tunnels.

The cross-river ferries have gone now. They follow the fate of the Cluthas, the water-buses built by Thomas Seath at his shipyard in Rutherglen. Seath was a tiny but very energetic man. Once, when he met an English shipbuilder, the Sassenach said: 'So you're Thomas Seath? Why, I could put you in my pocket.' To which Tam Seath replied, 'In that case ye'd have mair in your pocket than you have in yer heid!'

The Cluthas were little screw-steamers and they carried passengers from one river pier to another at a penny a time. They started in 1884 and ran until 1903, when the inordinate success of the famous Glasgow tramway system finished them off. All the same, in 1896 the dozen Cluthas carried two and a half million passengers. Most of these passengers agreed on one point – that the River Clyde was the smelliest river in the world. I hasten to say that today there is no smell at all, not even what we euphemistically call ozone.

9
SATURNALIA

When I was a small boy you could always tell when it was Saturday in Glasgow because of the number of drunks about in the streets. Today you still see the occasional drunk, but perhaps more often on a Friday than a Saturday, because Friday is pay day in a great many Glasgow works and factories. But then the Saturday drunks would come reeling out as far as our prim suburb of Dennistoun, where each stuck out like a sore thumb.

This was considered a bit of a liberty (though such a common phrase was never used in Dennistoun) because drunks were expected to stay in the area where they got drunk – and, as everybody knew, that was Argyle Street. If you heard anyone refer to 'Argyle Street on a Saturday night' you knew he was talking about the wild and disgusting Saturnalia which went on there.

Presumably the drunks chose to celebrate in Argyle Street because of the number of pubs up the side streets there. They were also, however unknowingly, carrying out a tradition that Argyle Street was the place where one paraded in Glasgow. The first pavement in the city was the one which I have already mentioned, the Plainstanes in the Trongate. But the Tobacco Lords and other merchants decided that only they were fit to walk on a pavement and kept everybody else off.

But in 1777 a second pavement was laid, along the Westergait, later to become Argyle Street. It was described as 'Handsome flagged trottoirs, with curb-stones', and the people who had been kept off the Plainstanes hurried to have the pleasure of sauntering up and down the trottoirs. To this day Argyle Street is a place for a promenade, and the biggest crowds you will see in any of the city thoroughfares are here.

As I have already suggested, the promenaders today will go right on into the Trongate, with most of them not realising in the least that the trottoirs have given place to the Plainstanes. Nowadays Argyle Street starts at the junction of the Trongate, Stockwell Street and Glassford Street. This means that the Trongate has lost a little of its original length, because it went on to the West Port and the Westergait for the whole frontage of the Shawfield Mansion. That is to say, the Trongate reached almost to where Virginia Street is today. There was a famous well here, and then the country road called Westergait which, when it became a proper street, was named after the 4th Duke of Argyll.

Perhaps, by the way, it would be a good thing to get this spelling anomaly cleared up. The street is spelled Argyle, but the notable shopping arcade, just before Buchanan Street, is spelled Argyll. Nowadays Argyll is considered correct, but in the 19th century people spelled names any way they chose. On the maps and charts of those days you will find just as many Argyles as Argylls.

From the Shawfield Mansion to the west there were several estates and houses to the north of the Trongate and the Westergait. The pattern of Glasgow at this point was that streets came up from the River Clyde but were stopped from extending north by private property. But this private property, again starting with the Shawfield Mansion, was sold off at a very considerable profit.

On the north side of the now lost bit of the Trongate was Glasgow's banking centre. Three banks were established here, including the famous Ship Bank, then run by Robin Carrick, a little miserly runt of a man who treated most of his clients as if they were trying to steal money from him. Judging by descriptions which have come down to us, the atmosphere in these banks was much the same as that which obtained in Mr Scrooge's establishment in Charles Dickens's *A Christmas Carol*.

Next to the banks was a renowned inn, the Black Bull Hotel. In my young days this part of Argyle Street was occupied by a famous farm which was the object of a favourite riddle of my father's. He would ask, 'Where will you find Glasgow's slave-traders?' And the answer was 'Mann, Byars in Argyle Street.' To get the full flavour of this conundrum, and its answer, you must speak both aloud.

On the Argyle Street wall of Mann, Byars was a plaque which stated that this was the site of the Black Bull Hotel, much frequented by Robert Burns. The plaque existed up until the early days of the Second World War, when it suddenly disappeared. My own theory is that the authorities feared that a Nazi parachutist might be dropped on Argyle Street. If he happened to pass this plaque on his way down he might well guess where he was – and that was something the authorities were trying to avoid at all costs.

At any rate, the plaque was taken down and only four small holes in the wall showed where it had been. It was not seen again until some time after the war, when it was found to be decorating the door of a lavatory in a Civil Defence Station on the south side of Glasgow. I am glad to say that it was rescued and is now in the possession of The Scottish Burns Club (the largest teetotal Burns club in the world). The Mann, Byars building has been replaced by Marks and Spencer and they have put up a much superior plaque recording the association of Robert Burns with the site of the Black Bull.

The Black Bull Hotel was built by John Glassford, whose name is commemorated in Glassford Street. It became the most fashionable hostelry in Glasgow, usurping the position of the Saracen's Head in the Gallowgate. Robert Burns was certainly a constant visitor to the Black Bull. He stayed there on visits to Glasgow or on his way to or from Edinburgh. From the Black Bull he wrote several lovesick letters to 'Clarinda', using his pen name of 'Sylvander'. Burns thought that Clarinda, otherwise Mrs McLehose, was an Edinburgh lady, whereas actually she was a Glasgow woman. She had, however, lived long enough in Edinburgh to become convinced that the only hope for the Scots was to imitate the English, and she was one of several people who tried to influence Burns to write in English instead of in his own natural tongue.

Robert Burns was very fond of Glasgow. He regarded it as a sort of Bohemian place to visit, and he had some very good friends who would forgather with him at the Black Bull. One of them was a young printer named Reid, and the story goes that when Burns first thought of having his poems published he rode up to Glasgow and showed them to Reid, asking his opinion of their possibilities in print. Reid pointed out that the Glasgow publishers did not go in for such frivolities as poems. They concentrated on books of psalms and sermons, editions of the Holy Bible and commentaries on the Scriptures. (It's interesting to note that the world's biggest publisher of the Bible today is Collins of Cathedral Street, Glasgow.) He recommended Burns to take his wallet of poetry to Edinburgh, where the publishers were more inclined to lightness.

But Burns did not have the time to continue his journey to Edinburgh, and he turned his horse's head and made back for home at Mauchline. On the way back he was riding through the town of Kilmarnock when he saw a board advertising that these were the premises of John Wilson, printer. On an impulse he stopped his horse, went in to see John Wilson and had soon arranged for a volume of his work to be published on a subscription basis. And that is said to be why the first publication of Robert Burns is the Kilmarnock edition. If young Reid had taken a chance it might have been the Glasgow edition that would be so much in demand at such a high price in the years to come.

And, talking of money, when the Edinburgh edition of his work came out Burns arranged that the Glasgow firm of John Smith (the oldest booksellers' business in the city) should handle it in their area. When it came to settling up accounts Burns discovered that John Smith was charging him a commission of a mere five per cent. 'Faith!' he said, 'you seem a very decent set o' folk, you Glasgow booksellers. But, eh, they're sair birkies in Edinburgh!'

As it was, some of the Glasgow publishers were sair birkies too, for some of them didn't hesitate to put out pirate editions of Burns's works once he had become famous. Even Reid was affected. He was one of the partners of Brash and Reid and he brought out a four-volume edition of *Poetry; Original and Selected*, which included *Tam o' Shanter* and a number of other

Burns's poems. Still, it can be said that he waited until Burns had died and he included in one of the volumes a poem of Burns and an account of his funeral at Dumfries.

Robert Burns knew not only the booksellers but other shops in Glasgow. Next to the Black Bull Hotel was Virginia Street, named after the plantations of the Tobacco Lords. When he was getting married to Jean Armour (for the second, or official, time) Burns wrote to Robert McIndoe, silk merchant in Horn's Land, Virginia Street.

Mauchline, 5th August, 1788

My dear sir,

I am vexed for nothing more that I have not been to Glasgow than not meeting with you. I have seldom found my friend, Andrew McCulloch, wrong in his ideas of mankind; but respecting your worship he was as true as Holy Writ.

This is the night of our Fair, and I, as you can see, cannot keep well in a line; but if you will send me by the bearer, John Ronald, carrier between Glasgow and Mauchline, fifteen yards of black silk, the same kind as that of which I bought a gown and a petticoat of you formerly – Lutestring, I think, is its name – I shall send you the money and a more coherent letter when he goes again to your good town.

To be brief, send me fifteen yards black Lutestring silk, such as they use to make gowns and petticoats of, and I shall chuse some sober morning before breakfast, and write you a sober answer, with a sober sum which will then be due you from, Dear sir, fu' or fasting,

Yours sincerely,
Robert Burns

Since Lutestring was five shillings and ninepence a yard, the sober sum which Mr Burns eventually sent to Mr McIndoe came to £4 6s 3d, and that was the cost of Bonnie Jean's wedding dress.

Most of the streets on the north side of Argyle Street in this airt run right up to Ingram Street or farther. Virginia Street stops at where a Tobacco Lord's mansion once stood. Alexander Spiers of Elderslie sold the ground between his house and Argyle Street for a new thoroughfare, but, it is said, just to show his power he stopped the thoroughfare at his front door. Part of his mansion still exists inside the present building which blocks the way to Ingram Street. This was Lanarkshire House, the home of Lanarkshire County Council until they moved out to their new skyscraper at Hamilton. It has now been taken over by Glasgow Sheriff Court.

Not much of the old Virginia Street remains. On the right stood the City of Glasgow Bank – its other entrance was in Glassford Street – but Marks and Spencer has taken its place. Glasgow has had two bank failures – the Western in 1857, and the City of Glasgow Bank in 1878. The first was due to bad management. The second was not only mismanagement but fraud as well, and several of the directors went to prison. The loss to the shareholders was £6,000,000, and many people were completely ruined. Some of them went mad, and one white-haired old man was seen prowling round Virginia Street with a loaded rifle, ready to shoot any bank director he came across.

Several of the shareholders committed suicide. People with a few hundred pounds invested were now being asked to pay up thousands. One effect this did have was to impel the Government to press on with the Companies Act of 1879, which allowed established banks to adopt limited liability for their shareholders. To this day one peculiar result of the failure of the City of Glasgow Bank is still seen. In many of our older suburbs you will notice tenement buildings which seem to have suddenly stopped halfway. That's the extent to which they had been built when the crash came in 1878, and the owners couldn't afford to finish them. From where I am writing at this moment I can see three such buildings.

Some of the buildings at the north end of Virginia Street are old by Glasgow standards. One worth seeing is at No 33. This is the Crown Arcade, a pleasant little place of pillars and galleries. Most people on Virginia Street will tell you that sugar sales took place here, but it seems that there were tobacco auctions before that, so that it may well go back to the 18th century.

Diagonally across from Virginia Street, on the other side of Argyle Street, is Dunlop Street and here stood another famous Glasgow inn of days gone by, the Buck's Head, kept by a Mrs Jardine who was renowned for her hospitality. Dunlop Street was another victim of the pushing railway and a bridge was built over into St Enoch Station where Glasgow's first real theatre stood. There isn't a single theatre in or near Argyle Street now, and yet it was around the trottoirs that the Glasgow theatre grew up.

The first theatre in Glasgow was a wooden one, built in 1752 where Cathedral Square is now. I shall tell its story later. The theatre was burned down by religious fanatics. Such was the feeling against it, this Temple of Satan, Home of Belial, that twelve years later Glasgow Town Council turned down a request from a small group of well-off Glaswegians who wanted to build a playhouse in the city. They had gone to the more civilised and sophisticated city of Edinburgh and had fallen in love with the celebrated London actress Mrs Bellamy. So deep was their love that they promised to build a theatre for her if she would only consent to appear in Glasgow.

Mrs Bellamy graciously consented. But, as Glasgow Town Council refused *their* consent, the theatre builders had to look outside the city. Glasgow then ended at the point where Union Street joins Argyle Street today. Just across the road was the village of Grahamston, outside the city boundary. So here, on Alston Street (now among the foundations of the Central Station), Mrs Bellamy's theatre was built. Technically it can't be called Glasgow's second theatre, but to all intents and purposes it was.

Mrs Bellamy's costumes, scenery and company arrived. All was ready for Mrs George Ann Bellamy herself. And then history repeated itself. A Methodist preacher down by the Clydeside denounced the new theatre as the work of the Devil. Once again the Glasgow mob marched. They set fire to the theatre in Grahamston, and, though the building itself was saved, the scenery and costumes were burned to ashes.

As Mrs Bellamy drove in a coach-and-four from Edinburgh she was met by one of her actors, white-faced and trembling.

He told her the sad story. Now Mrs Bellamy, although a fragile, beautiful woman, had the steel-like core which all famous actresses seem to possess. She drove into Glasgow and had an announcement shouted at the Cross that she would appear that night. She was staying at the Black Bull Hotel, so the actors were summoned there for rehearsals. (Incidentally, the Black Bull became *the* hotel for actors for many years after that.)

Rich Glasgow ladies, learning of Mrs Bellamy's predicament, at once called and offered her their wardrobes for any sort of costume she wanted. Carpenters were sent to rebuild the stage and restore the singed part of the auditorium. When Mrs Bellamy revealed that she was hard-up, merchants assured her that she had unlimited credit. And when the news got round Glasgow many citizens decided that they must attend the new theatre that night.

It was a great success. Mrs Bellamy appeared in a comedy entitled *The Citizen*, and a farce called *The Mock Doctor*. She had a wonderful reception. And when the show was over the Town Guard and several prominent Glaswegians escorted her sedan chair back into Glasgow to the Black Bull.

As the season progressed, there was a demand for stronger fare than *The Mock Doctor*. Mrs Bellamy agreed to appear in *Macbeth*. In those days the part of Lady Macbeth was always played in black velvet and there wasn't a suitable black velvet gown in the whole of Glasgow. But a Glasgow merchant's wife, from the Highlands possibly, assured Mrs Bellamy that the ghost of Lady Macbeth appeared on the ramparts of Dunsinane Castle every midnight, dressed in white satin. So, as far as we know, Mrs Bellamy was the first Lady Macbeth ever to appear in white satin.

The theatre was eventually taken over by an actor from Edinburgh, John Jackson. In May 1780 it met the fate of so many Glasgow theatres – it was burned down. By this time, however, John Jackson had decided that it was too far out of the city. He had his eye on ground called St Enoch's Croft. This ground belonged to Provost Colin Dunlop and later the street built over it was called after the Provost. Mr Jackson had some trouble with the church, but at last he opened his

Dunlop Street Playhouse in January 1782. It cost just over £3,000 to build, and was not regarded as one of Glasgow's outstanding pieces of architecture.

All the great actors and actresses of the day appeared in the Dunlop Street Theatre, but, although Mrs Siddons was regarded as the brightest star of all, the greatest ovations were given to the Infant Roscius, Master Henry West Betty of Belfast. This boy appeared in Glasgow in 1804, before he took London by storm. He took the part of Young Norval in Home's tragedy of *Douglas* and he got £100 a night.

The theatre was packed and many ladies fainted. Next day Glasgow rang with plaudits for Master Betty, with the single exception of a newspaper critic who doubted that the Infant Roscius was the greatest actor of all time. Popular feeling was so much against him that it's said that he left the city and got a job with a newspaper somewhere in the Deep South. In my time Glaswegians have demonstrated their love for Tom Mix, Laurel and Hardy, Carl Brisson, Bill Haley, Cliff Richard, Francie and Josie, Larry Marshall, the Beatles and so on. In terms of local excitement compared with the population of Glasgow, I should say that Master Henry West Betty outdid them all. Every time I see Glasgow teenagers (a horrid term, which I use under protest!) making fools of themselves over some newly publicised name I think of the day when their ancestors, and middle-aged ancestors at that, made fools of themselves over the Infant Roscius. Master Betty, by the way, lasted only two years, which seems to be the average lifetime of a 'discovery' today.

In 1805 a new theatre was opened in Queen Street, just across Argyle Street from Dunlop Street. It became *the* theatre of Glasgow and until this new house went the way of all Glasgow theatres of these days, Dunlop Street was in the shadows. Part of it was converted into a warehouse, and the rest was let out to anyone who wanted to put on a show. So Glasgow saw a number of second-rate pantomimes and a procession of elderly pugilists, among them the great Tom Cribb, and variety programmes which could include an address by William Cobbett on the Repeal of the Corn Laws or some other outstanding problem of the day.

At one of these performances a grave Glasgow philosopher rose in the stalls and said, 'I hope, sir, the time may come when the poor man, after the labour of the day, may refresh himself by reading Bacon.'

The silver-haired Cobbett, in his blue coat, white vest and drab breeches, replied, 'Much more to the purpose, my dear sir, if the time could come when the poor man, after the labour of the day, might refresh himself by *eating* Bacon.'

You can tell how far the Dunlop Street Theatre fell when you read this notice: 'Circus, Dunlop Street. On Friday and Saturday, 28th and 29th December, 1821, the performances will commence with the admired ballet dance, called *Hurry-Scurry*, after which the very favourite Melodrama, called *Frederick the Great*, and Horsemanship. The whole to conclude with the admired Melodramatic Burlette, called *The Mill of Glamis*, Splendid New Year's Harlequinade Pantomime will be produced at the Circus. Mr Simpson (from Manchester) with his wonderful performing dogs and sagacious bear are engaged, and will shortly appear in a new grand historical bruno-canine quadrupedical melodrama.'

But in 1825 the Dunlop Street Theatre came back into the public eye in a very big way, owing to the activities of a gentleman I have already mentioned – JH Alexander. There have been several remarkable theatre managers and proprietors in Glasgow, but none quite so remarkable as JH Alexander. He was born in Dunbar, educated in Edinburgh and came to Glasgow to learn the job of hosier from his uncle in the Candleriggs. But he saw a play and determined to be an actor. He did become an actor and, by saving every penny he could, became a manager as well.

He ran companies in Carlisle and Dumfries and decided to add the Caledonian Theatre on Dunlop Street, Glasgow, to his circuit. But a chap called Seymour, who was on the spot, heard of this and got there first. By the time Alexander arrived in Glasgow the theatre part of the building belonged to Seymour. Alexander surveyed what was left, and found a huge coal cellar beneath the theatre. The cellar was occupied by a potato salesman and a cotton dealer, who were agreeable to sell out. So two days later Alexander opened the coal cellar as a theatre called 'The Dominion of Fancy'.

So Glasgow audiences who went to see Seymour's company play *Macbeth* in the new Caledonian Theatre had the remarkable experience of hearing Shakespeare's words spoken against the accompaniment of *The Battle of the Inch* being performed simultaneously in the cellar below. This battle was not only a very noisy one but every now and then the fumes of 'blue fire' rose through the chinks in the stage from the nether world. Big audiences turned out for *Macbeth* as long as *The Battle of the Inch* was accompanying it.

Both Seymour and Alexander complained to the magistrates and it was eventually decided that Seymour's company would perform from Tuesday to Friday, and Alexander's on Saturday and Monday – rather like the splitting up of commercial television programmes in the London area. Seymour didn't like this, because Saturday and Monday were the best theatre-going nights of the week. So, when the 'Dominion of Fancy' opened on its first Saturday night nobody in the audience could hear a word because of the brass band which Seymour had engaged to play upstairs.

Alexander protested again, but Seymour's next step was to make holes in the stage and pour water over the unfortunate audience at the 'Dominion of Fancy'. To this Alexander responded by staging whatever Seymour announced that *he* was going to stage. Seymour advertised a new production of *Der Freischutz* for the following Tuesday. Alexander put it on in the 'Dominion of Fancy' on the previous Saturday. This time Seymour's company used the holes in the stage to such good purpose that they completely wrecked the show.

All this was greatly to the liking of the Glaswegians, who loved a barney. Seymour announced *Tom and Jerry* for four nights. Alexander announced *Tom and Jerry* for two nights. Such crowds flocked to see both productions that they ran for a month together and took so many people away from the Queen Street Theatre that the manager there gave up and sold out to Seymour. As soon as Seymour could get the Queen Street Theatre in order he gave up the Caledonian and Alexander moved up from the cellar to the stage proper.

Although the Dunlop Street Theatre was now his, Alexander continued to put on shows with as little expense as possible. He became more and more eccentric. Here is an account of a performance of *Rob Roy* in 1844, written by one of the critics of the Glasgow *Dramatic Review*:

'The whole time Mr Alexander was on the stage, he was directing everybody, players, scene-shifters, and gas men; saying for instance, audibly, and heard by the whole house – "Come down here, sir"; "Stand you there, sir"; "McStuart, that's not your place, sir"; "Beat your feet, sir"; "Keep time with the soldiers, sir, as I do"; "Hold up your hand, sir"; "Speak out". Never for a moment did he allow the audience to forget he was manager. He beat time to the orchestra, he spoke to the musicians, he sang the music for other people, and he spoke their words. In theatrical parlance, his greatest delight was to "show the company up".'

Audiences began to fall off at Dunlop Street, and so Alexander imported 'attractions' from London. Among them was the famous Davenport and his daughter, whom Charles Dickens had immortalised in *Nicholas Nickleby* as Crummles and the Infant Phenomenon. It was decided to include *Romeo and Juliet* in the programme, but Alexander didn't like the idea of Davenport, who was old and very fat, playing Romeo, so he arranged that he would play the part himself, opposite the Infant Phenomenon as Juliet.

But the Dunlop Street audience just wouldn't have Alexander as Romeo. His every appearance was greeted with ironical cheers. The climax came when the Friar called on Romeo, 'Come forth, thou *fearful* man.' The uproar was so great that a lesser man might have called for the curtain to fall. But not Alexander.

Let me quote from *The Glasgow Stage* by Walter Baynham (a book, unfortunately, long out of print): 'When Mr Alexander had fallen on the ground, "taking the measure of an unmade grave", the uproar became so great that quite unmindful of his being supposed to be lying unconscious, Mr Alexander suddenly raised his head from the stage, and thus addressed his adversaries: "I know", said he, "you think I can't play Romeo. I know I'm not so young as I was. But I have played it all over the world, and with the best actresses, and, thank God, I can play it *still* when there is a necessity. I have been called an egotist. I *am* an egotist, but I know my profession and can play on it, like Paganini on the one string of his violin, and to that you are indebted for the proper management of the theatre. Now!" Then throwing himself once more on the ground he resumed his dialogue with the nurse – "Speakest thou of Juliet? How is't with her?"'

The audience kept up a running fight with Alexander but bore with the Infant Phenomenon. *Romeo and Juliet* being over, Miss Davenport appeared in a song-and-dance act. Among those who decorated the background was her father, 'Mr Crummles' himself. When the Phenomenon sang her first song her father applauded loudly and cried: 'Beautiful! Beautiful!' But the audience were not quite as enthusiastic and in a heavy aside Davenport said, 'I wonder she could sing at all after playing tragedy in the way she has done, and Juliet too.'

The audience didn't rise to this, but then, when a partner came on and danced the polka with the Infant Phenomenon, they shouted: 'Encore! Encore!' This was more than her father could bear. He stepped forward and addressed the crowd. 'Encore!' he exclaimed. 'I am astonished! I am shocked! You call for a repetition of the polka! Are you aware from whom you demand that dance? Do you not recognise the fact that Miss Davenport is a tragedy actress? That she has tonight sustained one of the heaviest tragedy parts – '

'Order! Order!' shouted the gallery.

The outraged parent got his eye fixed on one unfortunate boy in the gods. 'Sir,' he shouted, pointing directly at the boy, 'if *you* had done as much as she has done – yes, YOU, sir! – permit me to remark, *you* would not have been able to move.'

This was too much for the gallery, who started hissing. Mr Crummles's well-trained eyebrows nearly shot off his head. 'These are sounds,' he cried, 'which I am not accustomed to! I have travelled, allow me to inform you, and, as your journals of the universe have testified, all over Europe and America with Miss Davenport, but have never before been treated in this way. I appeal to that justice which has ever, did ever and will, I venture to hope, continue to characterise the British public.'

He then retired from the scene and left the Infant Phenomenon to carry on. Dickens couldn't have done better.

The history of the theatre in Glasgow is one blaze after another but the Dunlop Street Theatre, when it finally perished in the flames, was the scene of a terrible tragedy which arose out of a false alarm of fire. On a Saturday night, 17 February 1849, JH Alexander was presenting his company in *The Siege of Calais*, followed by a pantomime. On the following Monday he was presenting the great new Irish comedian Hudson, direct from Covent Garden, and Hudson had arrived in Glasgow that day. The melodrama was just over and Alexander, still in his armour from *The Siege of Calais*, was talking in the wings with Hudson about the burning of JH Anderson's theatre on Glasgow Green.

'They all, sir,' said Alexander to Hudson, 'come to the ground. No theatre seems exempt from fire, but mine. I've been manager now for twenty years – '

At that moment there came a shout from the auditorium of 'Fire!' It was traced to the gallery, where the price of admission was threepence and the place was packed. There was a little smoke coming from the front of the gallery and then a few sparks. A man took his cap off and stuffed it into the outlet and the fire was extinguished. The band, which had stopped playing, started up again and there was a general shout of 'All's right!' One enthusiastic galleryite called for three cheers. But before the third cheer was given a fireman appeared. Immediately there were renewed shouts of 'Fire!' and a panic started.

Some eight hundred men, women and children pressed towards one stairway and soon they were piling up one on top of another. Led by Alexander, the actors and the theatre staff did their best to rescue people from the trampling, suffocating mass. But, at the end of it all there were seventy dead. Most of them were young men, but there were also six girls and a child of three.

Just eighty years later I spent Hogmanay as a young reporter at the Glen Cinema, Paisley, where fifty children were killed in a false alarm of fire.

Alexander never recovered from the Dunlop Street Theatre tragedy. He gradually lost interest in his theatre and three years later he was dead.

Edmund Glover, already a well-known theatre manager in Glasgow, took over at Dunlop Street and started in great style with Italian opera. He went on to productions where the average cast would number a hundred. His biggest production was *The Battle of Alma*, in which, as well as an enormous cast, three hundred and fifty soldiers and a military band appeared. He wrote his own plays, usually from the works of other playwrights. A typical one was in 1860 – *The Indian Revolt, or the Relief of Lucknow*, which was announced as 'written by many authors'. Some two hundred actors appeared in this production, along with elephants, camels, bulls and Mr Henry Irving.

This is supposed to have been Henry Irving's first appearance in Glasgow. He was twenty-two and had been specially engaged by Mr Glover to play the part of Prince Jung Badahour in *The Indian Revolt*. But it was actually his second appearance. He wrote himself: 'When I came to Glasgow (which I did from Dublin) to attend the rehearsals for *The Indian Revolt*, I was surprised and indignant to find myself cast for some character in *The Warlock of the Glen*, which was to be played as a Saturday night attraction prior to the Revolt on the Monday. As I had made my mark as an actor in Dublin, where I had been a great favourite, you can imagine what I felt when I found myself announced merely as a Mr Irwin – they couldn't even spell my name correctly – but I played the part nevertheless.'

Perhaps Henry Irving was mollified by the success of *The Indian Revolt*, which ran for a whole month. At any rate he stayed on for the season as principal light comedian, except when he was Macduff in Mr Glover's production of *Macbeth*.

Three years after Henry Irving's first appearance in Glasgow the Dunlop Street Theatre met the customary fate of Glasgow theatres. On the night of 31 January 1863, *Married Life* was presented, followed by the pantomime *Bluebeard*. That was the last performance on Dunlop Street. About one o'clock in the morning the alarm was given but by the time the Fire Brigade got to Dunlop Street the whole theatre was in flames, and they had to concentrate on preventing the fire from spreading to nearby buildings.

On Argyle Street, on the other side of Dunlop Street, stood one of Glasgow's biggest shops, Lewis's Store, once John Anderson's Royal Polytechnic. Was this Britain's first department store? There's a good claim to that distinction in John Anderson's own words: 'In 1845 I introduced the idea of universal trading (the idea was original) in the drapery trade.' John Anderson was a great buyer. He went all over Europe buying goods in big quantities. Then he brought them to Glasgow, advertised them on a huge scale and sold them at low profits. He was not just a huckster. He was a man of dignity and some culture. When he included a waxworks in one of his shops he renamed it a 'hall of science'.

Like all innovators, he had his opponents. When he proposed to take Anderson's Royal Polytechnic into the book business in 1849 the Glasgow booksellers reacted violently. They announced that they would not deal with any publisher who dealt with John Anderson. His reply was quite simple. He went to the Religious Tract Society and proposed to buy *seven tons* of books. When the RTS weighed up this order against what they would lose by a booksellers' boycott in Glasgow, they decided to sell their books to John Anderson.

I remember his son, Sir John Anderson. He was a great man for the Boy Scouts in Glasgow, and I can still see him, small, moustached and wearing his kilt much too long, leading his Scout brass band (the only one in the city and paid for entirely by himself) at the head of parades. Sir John sold out to Lewis's in 1925 and gradually the old Poly was rebuilt into the huge store you see today.

Directly across is Queen Street. It leads to George Square and it merits a chapter of its own. So we'll just glance up Queen Street to where Sir Walter Scott stands on his tall column, looking steadfastly to the south, where he made his money.

When I was a small boy this was the part of Argyle Street that I knew best. My father did the main shopping for our household (eight children, of whom I was the eldest) on a Saturday afternoon and early evening and sometimes, as a treat, I was invited to travel in the tramcar from Dennistoun into the centre of the city and wander round the shops with him. I found Glasgow completely enchanting, not least because, every now and then, my father would meet a man he knew – usually one of the workers from Blochairn Steelworks, where he was cashier. This man would pat me on the head and tell me what a fine wee chap I was, and then fish in his pocket and produce money – for me!

This always seemed to happen in or near the part of Argyle Street between Queen Street and the Hielandman's Umbrella, so I grew to look on this bit of Argyle Street as something special. Most of the street salesmen had their stances along the pavement here. My own favourite was 'All the latest pantomime songs, one penny!' I was mad about the theatre (as you may have noticed), and pantomime principally represented the theatre to me then.

But I also liked the men who demonstrated mechanical toys – 'On the table, on the chair, on the palm of the *hand*! Just the toy for a girl or boy!' There was the occasional escapologist, too, but he was a rare bird in my time. And I was too young to have seen Old Malabar, one of the great Glasgow characters, who appeared in a vaguely Eastern costume and bound a hefty cup by a leather band to his brow. He then demonstrated that the leaden ball he carried was very heavy indeed. And when the crowd was big enough he would toss the ball into the air and catch it in the cup on his brow. He deserved the money.

The Argyle Street turn I remember best was the Masked Singer, often called the Scottish Nightingale. I still recollect, one early winter's evening, with a cold wind and a darkling sky, but the illuminations of Argyle Street burning bright, pushing through the pavement crowds with my father. All of a sudden we heard a woman singing. There wasn't a great deal of street traffic on Argyle Street then and the song, from a side street, was quite clear. There was a huge crowd, and they were standing in a semicircle round a woman wearing poor clothes and a black mask. She was singing *My love is like a red, red rose* in a voice that would melt your heart.

When she ended her song there was a shower of money on the pavement and roadway. Even though I was a small boy, I was gleg in the uptak', and I understood from the conversations round about me that this girl had been an opera singer, had come down in the world through no fault of her own and was reduced to singing in the streets. This did not surprise me in the least because I was quite accustomed to hearing, in the back garden (some people called it 'back court', but in Dennistoun we said 'back garden') of 7 Kennyhill Square, women of various sizes and shapes and voices of all kinds singing for money. It seemed to me then that the ones who chose hymns and psalms did the best.

Years later, when I was investigating the past for a BBC series, I came across the truth about the Masked Singer or the Scottish Nightingale. Possibly there was originally a singer who was down on her luck and chose this way of making a little money. But I know now that one or two enterprising music-hall managers cashed in on the idea. They would choose a good female singer and send her out, with an appropriate escort, and a mask of course, to sing on Argyle Street, Renfield Street or Sauchiehall Street. Then they would advertise that next week they would present the Scottish Nightingale, direct from singing in the streets. This didn't last long, naturally. After the public had been fed with six or seven Scottish Nightingales the novelty wore off and the comics had to take over once again.

But, going back to my boyhood days, I had another reason for liking this part of Argyle Street. It included the Argyll Arcade. (Note the difference in the spelling.) The Argyll Arcade was built in 1828 and it runs in a dog-leg from Argyle Street into Buchanan Street. When John Reid built the place it was a work of faith, because Buchanan Street then was little more than a country road leading up to Port Dundas on the Forth and Clyde Canal. In a way, the Argyll Arcade made Buchanan Street, as I shall demonstrate later.

The shape of the Arcade was conditioned by a place already built on the west side of the entrance. This is Morison's Court, built in 1797 and still fairly similar to its original outlines, with the circular staircase which seems to have been so popular in Glasgow in the 18th century. The Court was built by Bailie John Morison, and wise folk around Glasgow Cross thought that he was daft to build so far out of the centre of the city. However, John Morison included a coffee house in his courtyard, and he also ran cockfighting mains there. There were sometimes bets up to a thousand guineas wagered in Morison's Court.

When, more than thirty years later, the Argyll Arcade was built, the coffee room was pushed through into the arcade, so that there was an entrance from both sides. The bigger building was called Sloan's Arcade Cafe, and it exists to this day. Because of its origin in the coffee house of Morison's Court in 1797, it claims to be the oldest restaurant in Glasgow. And, although it has been modernised here and there, there is still enough of an Early Victorian atmosphere about it to remind you of the old days when, according to its own 'Bill o' Fare', cockie leekie soup could be had for a penny, broon troot (trout) for tuppence and sheep's heid for fourpence. You can still get all these dishes today, but they cost a bit more. As far as I know, Sloan's is the only restaurant in Glasgow which continues to serve sheep's head every Wednesday. If you have never tasted this dish, try it. Almost everyone who has a shot at sheep's heid becomes a convert.

The Argyll Arcade itself has always been a place for small shops. It was built by John Reid, a man who toured the Continent studying arcades there before he made up his mind about the kind of arcade he would give to Glasgow. John Reid was another Glaswegian who wanted culture as well as trade. In 1829 he was running exhibitions of the Fine Arts by 'living British artists'. He also presented 'refined entertainment', including that accomplished magician Signor Blitz, who was the darling of Glasgow for a time.

Soon after it was opened the Argyll Arcade got into the news because a silly young cavalry officer, riding with his troop along Argyle Street, suddenly decided to ride his horse through the Arcade. This caused great consternation among 'the toy-shop keepers' and the public, and later the officer was severely dealt with by his commanding officer. Now the cavalry have long since gone, and jewellers have replaced the toy-shop keepers.

Argyle Street has Buchanan Street to its north and St Enoch Square to its south. We shall leave Buchanan Street a chapter by itself. St Enoch is a corruption of St Thenew, the mother of St Mungo, and long before the city of Glasgow got as far as this there was a little church known as St Thenew's Chapel, down by the River Clyde, approximately where the Customs House stands now.

St Enoch Square was built as Glasgow extended westwards, and it was originally a square of mansion houses with a grass plot in the middle. Round the railings stood the sedan chairmen, ready for hire. St Enoch Square was one of their special stations and their hiring charges were usually calculated from there. Later a church was built in the centre of the square. Later still St Enoch Station was made, with St Enoch Hotel up on ramparts overlooking the Square. Then the Glasgow Subway was laid underneath the Square and the strange pseudo-Gothic station put in front of the church. No wonder the residents left and the Square became a place of shops and warehouses.

The Subway, or Underground as it's called now, follows the line of the St Enoch's Burn down Buchanan Street and below the Square towards the Customs House, and it was on the banks of this burn that St Thenew's Chapel was built, just as her son, St Mungo, built his chapel on the banks of the Molendinar.

One of Argyle Street's biggest stores, Arnott Simpson, wiped out two well-known caravanserai hereabouts. One was His Lordship's Larder in St Enoch Square, and the other the Queen Anne Restaurant on Argyle Street. The proprietors of His Lordship's Larder would point proudly to a ring attached to the wall at the side of the entrance to the restaurant. This was for a man to tether his horse while he went inside for refreshment. For long enough His Lordship's Larder had an argument with Sloan's Arcade Cafe as to which was the older. Now there is no argument, for His Lordship's Larder was pulled down when the new store was built.

I was sorry to see it go. But I was even sorrier when the Queen Anne Restaurant went on fire and disappeared from the Glasgow scene. This was an eating house with a special flavour. The Bells, who ran it, kept up an old reputation for oysters, beautiful steaks, Welsh rarebits (they claimed to have introduced the Welsh rarebit to Glasgow and served a ton of it at the opening of the City Chambers in George Square) and good beer. It was Gilbert Harding's favourite restaurant in Glasgow – a fact which I know because I took him there after we had made our recordings of the 'Round Britain Quiz' at Broadcasting House, Glasgow.

In my young days the Argyle Street-Union Street-Jamaica Street corner was really regarded as the heart of Glasgow. The majestic tramcars clashed across it. The lorries, horse-drawn cabs and a motor car or two rattled round it. Huge crowds of pedestrians crossed and re-crossed this junction. I have witnessed the same size of crowds in only two other places in the world – New York and Moscow.

The buildings were not distinguished, nor are they much better now that the Victorian examples have come down and some rather unfortunate modern ones have taken their place. The first change was when the Adelphi Hotel was built at the eastern corner of Argyle Street and Union Street (it has since been replaced). I remember it mainly because I took part in a broadcast programme about Glasgow and the highlight was the sound of the traffic and the crowds at this famous corner, obtained by holding a microphone out of a first-storey window of the hotel.

I remember the Adelphi also because a broadcasting friend of mine was refused a drink in The Odd Spot, the hotel's cocktail bar, because it was considered that he had already had enough. 'All right,' he said, 'if I'm to be treated like a dog, I'll behave like a dog,' and he got down on all fours and crawled out of the bar and down the flight of stairs to Argyle Street.

Jamaica Street, running south from Argyle Street, is much older than Union Street, which runs north to join Renfield Street and the great shopping centre of Sauchiehall Street. The corner was known about 1807 as Union Place, but there was no Union Street, merely a cart road running north in the direction of the important Port Dundas, the Glasgow end of the Forth and Clyde Canal. The carts came up Jamaica Street from the Broomielaw, bearing goods to the Canal, and brought other goods from the Canal back to the Clyde.

By 1812 a Unitarian Chapel was built on the cart road, and gradually stores and shops were set up along it. There was a Horse Bazaar and a posting establishment, and this pattern was followed higher up in the part of the road which became Renfield Street. Indeed, at one time the people living in this area complained bitterly about the huge amount of horse manure which was left lying in the middle of Renfield Street.

The buildings at first were mainly on the east side of the cart road, but about the middle of the 19th century the Laurie brothers developed the west side and Union Street came into being. The one outstanding building in Union Street is the Egyptian Halls, now shops and offices between Nos 84 and 100. The Egyptian Halls, once an entertainment centre, were built by Alexander Thomson, known as 'Greek' Thomson because of his architectural predilections.

Jamaica Street was an important thoroughfare in Glasgow before Union Street was thought of. It was natural, of course, that a street should grow up from the bridge across the Clyde and the port of the Broomielaw alongside. In most old prints of Glasgow you will see the unmistakable shape of the bottle works, which were started in 1730 in approximately the same place that one of Glasgow's newer hotels now stands – the corner of Jamaica and Clyde Streets.

The street was officially opened in 1763 and it was named Jamaica after the great trade between Glasgow and the West Indian island, especially in sugar and rum. About one hundred years ago Jamaica Street was famous for its warehouses, and the greatest concentration of the drapery trade was in this area. By the 1960s not many of the original firms were left. Arnott Simpson became part of the great Hugh Fraser empire. Likewise, the Colosseum no longer belongs to the Wilson family, although Walter Wilson at one time seemed likely to outdo all the other warehousemen in the city, even including the redoubtable John Anderson of the Polytechnic.

The premises of two old firms remain in Jamaica Street. One was the furnishing firm of A Gardner and Son Ltd, and it is noteworthy because its building was, as anybody can discover, the first cast iron edifice to be erected anywhere in this country. This was in 1856, and today it seems a very good advertisement for a way of building that does not seem to have been much used. The Ca'doro Restaurant building at the top of Union Street is also cast-iron, but, as far as I know, these are the only two buildings of their type in Glasgow.

I have a special affection for Paisley's Ltd, part of which remains at the foot of Jamaica Street. I remember it because, until I was making enough money to buy my own clothes, I was taken to Paisley's by my father, who led the way to the juvenile department and said to the shopwalker sternly, 'A suit for this boy!'

From there you can walk across Glasgow Bridge and admire the elegant Suspension Bridge and Carlton Place. But if you look westwards your view is spoiled by the railway bridge which takes the trains leaving Central Station.

The Central Station is built on top of what was once a village called Grahamston. I have already told of the attempt to have the first theatre in these airts in Grahamston. To this day, if you go down into the bowels of the Central Station, you can see the pavement kerbs and sometimes even the suggestion of a shop front which existed in the days of Grahamston.

Argyle Street, just past the Union Street-Jamaica Street junction, is crossed by another railway bridge, which supports some of the Central Station platforms. This is the famous Hielandman's or Highlandman's Umbrella, which I have already described.

Argyle Street goes on its rather humdrum way through what were once the villages of Anderston and Finnieston until it joins Sauchiehall Street where the Kelvingrove Art Galleries stand. But the whole scene has been changed by redevelopment in building and a great swirling complex of motorways where the old Anderston Cross once stood. Elderly Glasgow people find difficulty in remembering what the old place looked like. Of all the changes in the Glasgow scene, this is one of the most radical.

In the 18th century this was a pleasant country road, and it led to a particularly snug little inn at Anderston. Some of the professors at Glasgow University in the High Street and a group of convivial merchants in the Trongate formed the Anderston Club, and every Saturday morning they walked all the way from Glasgow Cross to Anderston for dinner. The great dish on the menu was how-towdie, a broth made from three hens. This was followed by a saddle of lamb. The members of the Anderston Club drank claret and a rum punch of their own invention. Not long ago the members of the All Saints Club (which is divided between Glasgow and Edinburgh) met in an inn at Anderston and had precisely the same menu and the same drinks. But they didn't walk from Glasgow Cross.

An outstanding member of the Anderston Club was Dr Robert Simson, Professor of Mathematics at Glasgow University. He had a habit, not quite as uncommon as it might seem, of counting his steps as he walked. Even though he walked every Saturday to Anderston he still counted his steps. If he was stopped he kept repeating the number he had just come to, so that he could restart counting immediately.

One Saturday he was stopped by an earnest gentleman who said, 'Dr Simson, I believe?'

'The same,' replied the Professor. 'Five hundred and seventy-three.'

'I beg your pardon – one word with you, if you please.'

'Most happy – five hundred and seventy-three,' the Professor said.

'Nay, merely *one* question.'

'Well?' asked the Professor. 'Five hundred and seventy-three.'

'You are really too polite, but from your known acquaintance with the late Dr Brown, and for the purpose of deciding a bet, I have taken the liberty of inquiring whether I am right in saying that the Doctor left £500 to each of his nieces.'

'Precisely – five hundred and seventy-three,' said the Professor.

'And there were only four nieces, were there not?'

'Exactly – five hundred and seventy-three!' And the Professor went on his way happily, counting his steps to the inn at Anderston.

As far as I can make out, the nearest hostelry to that famous inn was the Shandon Buttery. I am delighted to know that although most of Anderston is being swept away, this inn, and the old building above it, remains by a special dispensation of Glasgow City Council. Instead of standing in the middle of a busy street, it's now in a cul-de-sac, for the famous Argyle Street has been cut in two.

The tenement above the Shandon Buttery is an example of the kind of building which was popular in Victorian days. Workmen got together and ran their own building. They put up tenements and then occupied them. There was an even finer tenement next door to the Shandon Buttery, but it has since been demolished. However, in the public bar of the inn you can see photographs of Anderson as it used to be. And it's up to you to decide whether it has been improved or not!

10
THE SHEPHERD'S PATH

Now we must retrace our path to where the Trongate met the Westergate. On the north of Argyle Street is Queen Street, running up to the third centre of Glasgow, George Square. The Cathedral was the first, Glasgow Cross was the second, and who knows where the fourth will be?

According to some Glasgow stories, this city gave the world its first tearoom. At the east corner of Argyle Street and Queen Street stood a shop which specialised in selling tea. It was run by Stuart Cranston, a name to become famous in Glasgow temperance circles and even places in London where tea was drunk. Victorian ladies dropped into Cranston's to see what new tea had arrived, and Mr Cranston developed the idea of allowing them to taste each new infusion.

But this caused some confusion in the shop, and Mr Cranston decided to give the ladies their tea in another room. Accordingly, he opened up a room on the floor above, put in some tables and chairs and, when his customers wanted to taste a new tea, he conducted them there so that they could sip in comfort.

After a while it seemed to him that many of the ladies were using this tea-tasting room as a, so to speak, convenience! And so he got the idea of charging them money for a cup of tea, whether they were trying it or not. The ladies did not object in the least. Indeed, they flocked to Cranston's for tea. And behold! the tearoom was born.

Queen Street today is mainly Victorian, with a few modern excrescences. But although it does not come into the roll of honour of the eight original streets of Glasgow, it is a very old thoroughfare indeed. It was the old Cow-loan, and the city shepherd drove the city cows up this track to the pastures of the Cowcaddens. As the cattle went up the Cow-loan they might be joined by other cattle coming along the Back Cow-loan, which corresponds approximately to Ingram Street today. Opposite was a little farmhouse where The Gallery of Modern Art now stands. Then the Cow-loan took a turn to the west, past what is now George Square, and up the line of Dundas Street, then a track between the Crackling House Quarry (Queen Street Station) and Provenside Quarry (towards Buchanan Street).

You can follow the shepherd's path still, although the geography of the city has changed so much. When you come to a tearoom in Dundas Lane you'll see a plaque which states that the Old Thorn Tree once stood there. This was the point where the Rottenrow joined the Cow-loan.

The last town herd of Glasgow lived in Picken's Land, Rottenrow. His name was John Anderson, and he wore the kilt and carried a cow's horn slung round his neck. This was to call the cattle home from the Cowcaddens. Many people imagine that the name of the Cowcaddens refers to the fact that the Glasgow town cattle were pastured there. Parts of the Cowcaddens here and there, small, once bien buildings, add to this effect. But the authorities say that the name is derived from Gaelic, which means that it is in much dispute. The Gaelic derivation which I prefer is 'the ridge of the little people', meaning the brownies, or fairies or maybe even the Picts. Even today, despite the prominence of the old Theatre Royal in Hope Street, now turned into the Scottish Opera House and the new Scottish Television studios on Cowcaddens, you can see the ridge quite plainly. And there are plenty of little people about too. But most of the old Cowcaddens has disappeared, and it will end as a completely modern thoroughfare.

Now if you take the way that John Anderson, town herd of Glasgow, took about the year 1790, you walk up a one-way street which is, more or less, the centre of the 'rag-trade' in Glasgow. Two or three places are remembered with affection by middle-aged Glaswegians. There's Tam Shepherd's, the trick shop. Here you can buy practical jokes, such as imitation ink blots, false noses and cushions which when sat on produce most embarrassing noises. No, let me make that quite clear – *a* most embarrassing noise!

Next to Tam Shepherd's is a restaurant (now modernised and renamed), formerly the Bank Restaurant, one of the oldest in Glasgow and owned for many years by the renowned Willie Maley, manager of Celtic Football Club in its heyday. At one time it was the sporting centre of Glasgow. On the first occasion I ever entered the bar I was most impressed when a wee bloke came in, nodded to the barmaid and said, 'The Usual, Mary.' She immediately poured him a glass of champagne.

When I frequented it, the Bank had an oyster bar presided over by Willie Craig, who was serving oysters long, long before I was born. Oyster bars were once a great feature of Glasgow life. Over the years Willie Craig's customers were the Top People of the city.

The Bank Restaurant is on the west side of Queen Street. On the east, a little bit up the street, was the oldest music shop in Glasgow, Bayley and Ferguson's. Here you could get the libretti and scores of the cantatas and kinderspiels which were all the rage when I was a small boy in Dennistoun.

These cantatas tended to copy the Gilbert and Sullivan operas. After *The Mikado* came a cantata called *Princess Chrysanthemum*, and following the success of *HMS Pinafore* there was a cantata entitled *The Midshipmite*. Apparently these confections, which enthralled me when I was aged eleven, are still being performed.

Queen Street is a short thoroughfare and soon you see one of the minor glories of Glasgow, Royal Exchange Square. Glasgow's finest statue, the Duke of Wellington by the Baron Marochetti, stands in front of a pillared mansion which once housed Stirling's and the Commercial Libraries, and is now a modern art gallery. It has a noble appearance, marred only by so many bird droppings that the wits of the day renamed it Starling's Library! Fortunately, the starlings have been evacuated, so to speak – though some nature lovers still miss their shrill occupation of the city as dusk was falling.

JM Reid, who wrote of the architecture of Glasgow in his book *Glasgow*, described how the city had the equivalent of the 'New Town' of Edinburgh, but most of it was swept away or allowed to fall into a sad state of neglect. But, he added: 'One finely planned public place remains – Royal Exchange Square, with its entrance arches from Buchanan Street and in the centre David Hamilton's high-windowed, temple-like Exchange ... The Square, which makes a frame for David Hamilton's Exchange, is by Archibald Elliot of Edinburgh. The two men's work makes a composition (pre-Victorian) that is one of the finest things in the city.'

Yes, Royal Exchange Square is fine, but it owes its existence, primarily, to one of the Tobacco Lords of Glasgow. He was William Cuninghame of Lainshaw, and he might be described as by far the smartest of the nicotine millionaires. When the American War of Independence broke out, supplies were cut and the situation seemed dire. Cuninghame and his partners held the largest stocks of tobacco in the whole of Britain, probably in the whole of Europe. With the anticipated shortage of tobacco, the price rose from threepence to sixpence a pound. The partners, fearful of the future, decided to sell.

But the tobacco never came on the market. William Cuninghame bought the entire stock from his own partners at sixpence a pound. He held it until it reached three shillings and sixpence a pound, and then he sold out at an immense profit. He was the only Tobacco Lord who remained a millionaire after the American War – although it's true that most of the others didn't have to worry about where their next penny was coming from.

In 1778 William Cuninghame thought he should have a house in the country. He had been for country walks up the Cow-loan from Westergate and had noted two small cottages standing among marshland which was popular among city sportsmen for shooting game. That marshland is today Royal Exchange Square and George Square. Cuninghame bought the cottages and the marsh. The cottages were removed and the marsh was drained, and the sportsmen had to move up the road a bit. It wasn't until 1780 that Cuninghame's country mansion was completed. It cost him £10,000, an immense sum of money in those days, and most of this had gone to the draining of the marsh. However, he had his satisfaction in a contemporaneous report that 'It was universally allowed to be the most splendid urban mansion in Scotland'.

The use of the word 'urban' here shows that within a couple of years Glasgow was already moving west – although Buchanan Street, just a track then, was considered out of this world. It's a mere step from Royal Exchange Square into Buchanan Street, but it seems to have been a long way for Glaswegians then.

William Cuninghame occupied his fine new house for a mere nine years, and then it was sold to John Stirling, who got a bargain of it for £5,000. But John Stirling didn't have it for long. It was next sold to the Royal Bank of Scotland, who wanted to make the mansion their Glasgow offices. They changed their minds and decided to build an entirely new bank, with one face to the square and the other to Buchanan Street.

So now the mansion was sold by the Bank to the Glasgow Royal Exchange. David Hamilton was given the job of making it a suitable building for such an important organisation and it was he who put the Palladian pillars on the front and built the great hall at the back. Archibald Elliot had to plan the Royal Bank and if you go into the main hall of The Gallery of Modern Art today and look through the windows at the façade of what was the Royal Bank you will see how perfectly he worked in harmony with David Hamilton.

You can still see the old mansion of William Cuninghame's quite clearly, between the pillars and the hall. Some of the rooms and ceilings are much the same as in his day, and it will give you a good idea of how the Tobacco Lords lived in their heyday.

And now if you cross from the Duke of Wellington to the bank building at the corner of Queen Street and Ingram Street you find yourself facing a part of Queen Street which once housed the oldest wine merchants' premises in Glasgow. Above, on the front of the building you will see a number of pillars, now built into the façade. These are all that remain of the Queen Street Theatre, once Glasgow's leading theatrical ornament. The inside was gutted and rebuilt, but, in my time, I visited the wine merchant's cellars and saw the place where the orchestra rested between appearances, and the stage 'trap', which would take the Demon King from the bowels of the earth up on to the stage, to the accompaniment of thunder and lightning and any other effects the stage manager could devise.

At the beginning of the 19th century the merchants of Glasgow were theatre-minded to a degree which, alas, they are not now. While they had a strong affection for the old Theatre Royal on Dunlop Street, they felt that it had declined considerably and that the city needed a new theatre. So a group of the merchants founded a company and in 1805 they built the theatre in Queen Street at a cost of £18,500. It was considered by the experts of the day to be the finest in Britain. It was seated for nearly 1,500 of an audience. The only trouble was that the owners had spent so much money on the theatre itself that they couldn't afford to engage the big stars from London.

However, they managed to rub along with ordinary actors until June 1807 when it was announced that 'an engagement had been made, for a few nights only, with the greatest living actor of the day – George Frederick Cooke'. He was to open as Richard III, the part with which he made his name at Covent Garden. John Philip Kemble, the leading Richard at that time, gave up the part after seeing Cooke play it. As an actor, Cooke was described by Edmund Kean as 'the finest in the world'.

The only trouble was that George Frederick Cooke kept on getting drunk, and was frequently drunk on the stage. Once, when a young officer in a box remonstrated with Cooke for being drunk, the actor went as close to the box as he could get and, in a stage whisper heard by the whole audience, said: 'Damn you, sir, you an ensign! Sir, the King (God bless him!) can make any fool an officer, but it is only the great God Almighty that can make an actor.'

Glasgow audiences counted themselves lucky, however, when they did see Cooke. Many a night the announcement had to be made from the Queen Street stage that Mr Cooke could not appear because of 'a sudden and serious indisposition'. On the following evening, when he did appear, there would be shouts of 'Apology! Apology!' Then

Cooke would step solemnly forward, shake his head, bow low, put his hand on his heart and say, 'Ladies and gentlemen, I have had an attack of my old complaint!'

On the other hand, he once dried up in the middle of a scene. When he came off the stage he said: 'I knew how it would be. This comes of playing when I am *sober!*'

In time the order of things was reversed, and the Queen Street Theatre in Glasgow gave stars to London. One of them was the celebrated 'Child of Nature', Fanny Kelly. She was beautiful, shy and sensitive. When she made her first appearance at the age of seventeen in the Queen Street Theatre she suffered so much from stage fright that the audience could hardly hear a word she said. But she improved so much that she eventually became the leading lady of the Haymarket Theatre in London. There the 'Child of Nature's' main trouble was keeping adorers at arm's length. Love letters arrived every day. Fanny was a polite girl and always answered her letters. One gentleman received the customary letter of rejection and turned up at the Haymarket the same night. While Fanny was acting he fired a pistol at her. Luckily he only hit the scenery.

All the great actors of the day appeared in the Queen Street Theatre, but the most popular man there was Harry Johnstone, who was manager in 1814. His claim to fame was that he had thrashed HRH the Prince of Wales, and this appealed greatly to Glaswegians. Harry's wife was an actress – not a very good one, but a great beauty. When she was appearing at Drury Lane, the Prince (later George IV) forced himself into her dressingroom. But Harry Johnstone had followed him with a whip and gave him a thrashing in the dressingroom.

He was arrested, but escaped and hid himself in Lambeth. Then he disguised himself as an old soldier and went to the North of England, where nobody in London would think of looking for him. Johnstone managed several theatres before he arrived in Glasgow. His fame had come before him and many a Glasgow man boasted that he had shaken the hand which had actually horse-whipped the Prince of Wales.

Johnstone was the man who brought the great Edmund Kean to Glasgow. I've already mentioned Master Betty and some others who made a sensation in the city. Kean was not behind them. According to Walter Baynham: 'The boxes had all been taken weeks before, and even temporary boxes were erected on the stage. All the professors of the University and the literati of Edinburgh, including Francis Jeffrey, were present. Glasgow was in an uproar of excitement. Crowds from all the surrounding districts flooded the city. Not a bed in a house, private or public, was to be obtained. The theatre doors were besieged for hours before they were opened. Queen Street was literally blocked by the mass of people eager for admittance. When at last the portals were opened, a crush, which was mingled with shouts, cheers and shrieks, ensued. Men fought, women fainted, and were carried fainting in some instances into the theatre, unable to get out of the dense multitude.'

Perhaps the only comparative audience for size ever seen again in the Queen Street Theatre was when, on 18 September 1818, it was announced that the auditorium would be 'Illuminated with Sparkling Gas'. According to the advertisements at the time, this was to be the very first theatre in Britain so lit up. The place was packed when the band played the National Anthem. When the audience had sung it they resumed their seats, the gas was turned on and the effect, said a writer of the time, was such as to leave 'some of them to fancy that they had been ushered into a new world'.

The Queen Street Theatre had another claim to fame. The very first production of 'Scotland's national drama', in other words *Rob Roy*, took place there in June 1818, nine months before it was presented in Edinburgh, the home of the author Sir Walter Scott.

The last presentation in the theatre was Andrew Ducrow's equestrian spectacle *A Stag Hunt*. For this production Mr Ducrow had a cast of one hundred, a stud of forty horses, a pack of hounds and a stag. The back of the theatre had to be opened up to let the hunt thunder through. When the last horse had trotted off, the stage was cleared for rehearsals for *Bluebeard*.

But, on the morning of 10 January 1829, some workmen who were engaged on the front of the Royal Exchange, which

The Bridgegate in 1834, with the Merchant's Steeple on the left.

Looking up High Street, 1868.

Stockwell Street from a drawing of 1871.

Glasgow's second bridge on Stockwell Street, 1846.

The Trongate in 1855, with the Tron Steeple on the right.

The Trongate in 1821, showing the Tollbooth and Tontine buildings, with the statue of William of Orange on Argyle Street.

© Roy Firth

The Tollbooth Steeple built in 1626 as it is today.

Looking towards the city from Glasgow Green in 1830.

Glasgow Cathedral as it is today.

was then being built, saw smoke coming from the roof of the theatre. They called the Fire Brigade, but by the time the fire engines arrived the whole building was alight, and the firemen had to concentrate on making sure the new Royal Exchange did not catch fire.

In the days of the Lainshaw mansion, however, there was another big house north of the marshlands. It was built some years later than William Cuninghame's, but both were occupied at the same time. This was Bailie George Crawford's Lodging. When Queen Street came into being it was known as Queen Street Park. It was, as they say, an imposing mansion, with a lawn in front of it and tall trees round it. James Ewing of Strathleven, later MP for Glasgow, bought it in 1815 for £6,000. Because of the crows which nested in his trees he was known generally as 'Craw Ewing'. You can depend on the Glaswegians to cut the wealthiest down to size.

Crawford's Lodging looked out on to what was, on the map, George Square. But it was a square on paper only. In 1745 it was a marsh and, although the Square was laid out in 1781, it was described as a 'hollow, filled with green-water, and a favourite resort for drowning puppies and cats and dogs, while the banks of this suburban pool were the slaughtering place of horses.'

By the end of the 18th century people were starting to build round the Square, and a Glasgow historian wrote in 1804 that 'the buildings here are very elegant, particularly those upon the north, which for the beauty of the design and taste displayed in the execution, surpass by far any other either in this city or Scotland'.

Well, as I write, the buildings on the north of George Square still display beauty of design and taste but they are dwarfed completely by a skyscraper on the hill above, a skyscraper which has the most curious collection of bric-à-brac I have ever seen on any roof.

George Square has been much criticised over the years. I have always defended it, but I have to admit that now it is being ruined. There may be architectural plans to save its face, but the proportions of the Square will never be the same.

Most criticisms of George Square are based on the fact that a dozen statues are placed in it. Once there were thirteen, but Glasgow City Council removed the statue of David Livingstone to Cathedral Square and thoughtfully put up a sort of pre-fab which they called an Information Office. Many Glasgow city councillors would like to see the statues removed, and if it were not for the cost of removal this might have been done some time ago. My own theory for the Glasgow town councillors' dislike of the statues is that they are jealous of the intelligent look on the statues' faces.

Our Victorian ancestors liked the statues and described George Square grandiloquently as Glasgow's Valhalla. A rather different description was given by Neil Munro, in his *Erchie, my Droll Friend*. Erchie, the Glasgow waiter, tells of the visit of King Edward VII to Glasgow at the beginning of the 20th century. The king travelled from Edinburgh by train and when he came out of Queen Street Station and saw George Square he said (according to Erchie), 'Whit'na graveyaird's ... this?'

The statue in the middle of the Square is Sir Walter Scott, on a pedestal eighty feet high. You might have expected him to be looking east, where he lived, but he has been put facing the south, where he made his money. The great Glasgow story about Scott's statue is that there is a mistake in it, and when he discovered this the sculptor committed suicide. Similar stories are told of statues all over Scotland and the death rate among sculptors must have been very high in Victorian days.

That's to say, if the stories are true. The Glasgow one is not. John Greenshields, the sculptor of the George Square Scott, died in his bed. Indeed, he died in 1835, two years before the statue was erected and the mistake was discovered. And the mistake? Scott is wearing a plaid over his right shoulder, and the plaid is normally worn over the left shoulder. Defenders of the sculptor point out that the left shoulder is Highland practice. Scott is supposed to be wearing a shepherd's plaid and in the Borders it was the practice to wear it over the right shoulder.

Greenshields was a Lesmahagow man who was apprenticed to a mason at Crossford in the orchard country of the River

Clyde. He was self-taught but he set up as a sculptor in a thatched cottage on the banks of the river and soon made a reputation for himself. Scott visited him once or twice and the young sculptor never took his eyes from the great man's face. As he said to Sir Walter, 'I've a devilish greedy e'e!'

Sir Walter's last visit to Greenshields was on the day before the Shirra died. That was in 1831, and three years later Greenshields was asked to design a model of Scott for erection in George Square. Two other sculptors were also asked to submit designs. When Greenshields was on his deathbed he learned that his design had been chosen.

The first statue to be erected in George Square was that of Sir John Moore, the Glasgow-born soldier hero immortalised in that poem you must have learned at school:

> Not a drum was heard, not a funeral note
> As his corpse to the ramparts we hurried ...

This statue was appropriately made from brass cannons, and that's maybe just as well, for it received some hard treatment in its early days. It was put up, on an eight-foot-tall plinth of granite, in 1819. In a sketch from the *Northern Looking Glass*, published in the summer of 1825, the artist shows some juvenile delinquents (possibly future city councillors?) attacking the statue. Two of them are throwing stones at it, while two others have got a rope round an arm of the statue and are trying to pull it down.

There were railings round George Square then and a fifth boy is shown tearing the railings down. At one side is a battered and broken lamppost. In the middle of the open ground of the Square three ladies are shaking dust from a carpet. Not far from them, another lady is hanging out clothes, while a friend nearby has her skirts kilted to well above the knees while she tramples out the 'wash' in a byne. In the background are the houses to the north of the Square.

Since Glasgow is claimed to be the finest Victorian city in the world, you expect to see the statues of Victoria and Albert. They are equestrian, and by the Baron Marochetti, sculptor of the Duke of Wellington just down the street. I have already mentioned this statue as the finest in Glasgow. If you want to see the worst go to Kelvingrove Park. There a really wicked statue of Thomas Carlyle was thoughtfully placed outside a gentlemen's lavatory. Wits say that this was so that you could see it at your own convenience. But the lavatory has been removed and half the joke is lost.

Victoria and Albert are on either side of the Information Point. Originally the statue of the Queen stood in St Vincent Place, where it was erected in 1854. It was removed to George Square in 1865, and the statue of Prince Albert was put up in the following year.

James Watt came after Sir John Moore. This statue was erected in 1832. Watt was born in Greenock, but when he was twenty he was given the job of repairing instruments at Glasgow University, at that time in the High Street. He had a shop there with the sign 'Mathematical Instrument Maker to the University'. Several university professors encouraged him in reading and he was allowed to use the College Library. This was the foundation of his great success, and when he became famous he loved to return to Glasgow to visit his old haunts and walk across Glasgow Green.

You may wonder that Sir Robert Peel and William Ewart Gladstone are represented in effigy in George Square. Both were Rectors of Glasgow University, and both were Free Traders. Glasgow took the repeal of the Corn Laws very seriously indeed. When Peel was installed in 1837 as Rector, the chief citizens of Glasgow gave him a dinner, described afterwards by the *Spectator* as 'one of the greatest political marvels of the time'.

A great wooden pavilion was built in a garden on Buchanan Street for the dinner. It was 127 feet long and 126 feet broad, lined with cloth of crimson, blue, white and gold, with pillars and woodcarvings of Greek design. The number of those present was more than four thousand and they 'sat down to a dinner of the most sumptuous character', which must have been something very special in those days.

One of the speakers was Peel's pupil Gladstone. His statue is typically Victorian in what is concealed. Gladstone was out shooting in September 1842 when his gun burst. The forefinger of his left hand was so badly shattered that it had to be removed. However, the sculptor got over this by supplying the statue with a book, held in the left hand and seeming to show that the forefinger is hidden by the leaves. Gladstone's rectorial address, incidentally, was delivered in the Kibble Palace, a glass structure in the Botanic Gardens. One can only assume that Glasgow University students were much better behaved in those days than they are now, when the City Council threatened them with expulsion from Glasgow Corporation halls.

The statue of Lord Clyde is very much a 'local boy makes good' one. He was born Colin McLiver in a tenement in George Street, not so very far away from where the statue stands. He went to Glasgow High School, but was taken under the care of his uncle, Colonel John Campbell, to be trained for the Army. He received his commission when he was fifteen years of age and was still a McLiver until he was introduced by his uncle to the Duke of York, Commander-in-Chief of the British Army. The Duke cried out, 'What! Another of the clan?' and his name was noted down as Colin Campbell.

It remained Colin Campbell for the rest of his life. He served under Sir John Moore and fought in many a battle. His most famous was the Battle of Balaclava, where he commanded the 93rd Highlanders, and drew them up in a line two deep to face the Russian cavalry, six times their number. His instruction to the Highlanders was for them to stand firm, but when the Russian cavalry charged there was a grave breach of discipline. Some of the Scots infantrymen rushed forward to meet them.

'Confound your enthusiasm,' shouted Sir Colin Campbell. 'Ninety-third, come back to your line!'

So they came back, repelled the Russians with great slaughter and have their niche in military fame today as 'The Thin Red Line'.

When the Indian Mutiny broke out, Sir Colin Campbell was given the post of Commander-in-Chief of the Indian Army. It was because of his victories there that he was made Lord Clyde.

Visitors to George Square knit their brows a bit over two of the statues – those to Thomas Graham and James Oswald. They've heard of everybody else in the Square, but who were *they*?

Thomas Graham was a great chemist and physicist and became Master of the Mint in London. He was born in Glasgow and went to the High School and the University, where his close friend was David Livingstone. He was a scientist who was known mainly to scientists. To the ordinary Glaswegian he's merely another statue in George Square.

James Oswald is better known to ordinary Glaswegians because he is the statue holding out his hat in an inviting position. At various times birds have built nests in this topper. Small boys have also used it for target practice with chuckies, or wee stones. And there was one occasion, recorded by George Blake, when Joseph Conrad was taken from dining in the North British Hotel by Neil Munro to throw a stone into James Oswald's hat. Munro explained that this would make Conrad an 'honorary Glaswegian'. So Conrad kept trying until a stone landed in the hat, and they all went back to dinner in the hotel.

Neil Munro was quite capable of inventing ancient Glasgow superstitions at a moment's notice. It's difficult today to know whether some of the stories he told in print are true or not. For instance, he wrote of an artist who was so in love with George Square that he went there every day for a year and painted a different picture of the Square. At the end of that time he exhibited the three hundred and sixty-five paintings in the North British Hotel, and sold most of them. That's Neil Munro's story, anyway.

Back to James Oswald, whose statue, 'Erected by a Few Friends', stood originally at Charing Cross. He was another Liberal and he took a great interest in the Reform Bill of 1832. When seventy thousand Glaswegians demonstrated on Glasgow Green in favour of the Reform Bill it was James Oswald who was called upon to preside. Glasgow at this time had a population of a hundred and fifty thousand and shared a single Member of Parliament with Rutherglen, Renfrew and Dumbarton!

When the news of the passing of the Reform Bill reached Glasgow the city went daft with delight. The bells were rung, flags put out and at night candles lit in every window. Rich citizens provided transparencies in front of their houses. Provost Dalglish's house in West George Street was lit with three thousand jets – 'the centre piece being "Let Glasgow Flourish", surrounded by splendid representations of Trade, Commerce and Manufactures saluting a figure of Reform'. When the news of the Battle of Waterloo reached Glasgow in 1815 the *Glasgow Herald* sold two thousand one hundred and twenty-two copies. When the news of the passing of the Reform Bill reached Glasgow in 1832 the *Reformer's Gazette* sold over thirty thousand copies.

James Oswald was elected as one of the Glasgow Members in the first Reform Parliament. He served from 1832 until 1837, and then from 1839 to 1847, and was regarded as 'one of the most influential of Scottish members in the House of Commons'. So perhaps he is entitled to his place in George Square, after all.

Two statues are left in George Square, and they represent Scottish poets. One was so famous that he was buried in the Poets' Corner in Westminster Abbey. Yet he is little remembered today. The other never got as far as London in life, let alone in death. Yet he is everywhere remembered. The first is Thomas Campbell, the second Robert Burns.

Although Thomas Campbell's name is not much remembered today, several of his works are. He is the Glasgow man who wrote *Ye Mariners of England*. He also wrote *Hohenlinden* and *Lochiel's Warning*, and he is remembered in the textbooks for *The Pleasures of Hope*. To me he will always be the man who wrote:

> Delightful Wyoming! beneath thy skies
> The happy shepherd swains had nought to do
> But feed their flocks on green declivities
> Or skim perchance thy lake with light canoe.

I just can't understand why it was that *Oklahoma* achieved stage fame when there was this for theatrical entrepreneurs to cull.

Thomas Campbell was born in the High Street of Glasgow, opposite the old University. He attended it and later was elected Rector of Glasgow University on three successive occasions, a tribute unique in the University's history. It is claimed that Campbell was the inspirer of London University.

Campbell died in 1844. The George Square statue was unveiled on the centenary of his birth, in 1877.

The statue of Robert Burns might be called the most democratic in the Square. It was built from the shillings of ordinary people who wanted to see a statue of their poet. When a shilling subscription was started more than forty thousand people contributed. The statue was unveiled on the poet's birthday, 25 January, in the same year as Thomas Campbell's was erected. The Campbell unveiling was a small affair.

For the Burns unveiling the societies and trades of the city gathered in Glasgow Green and marched in procession to George Square for the ceremony. Some thirty thousand people were waiting in the Square for them. No other statue in George Square ever had such a reception, and the only bigger number of people was for the unveiling of the Cenotaph in front of the City Chambers.

Even today, on every 25 January, the Burns Clubs line up to lay their wreaths at the foot of the Burns statue.

Behind the Cenotaph are the City Chambers, a great Italianate block with a council hall, a banqueting suite, various salons, committee rooms, a restaurant, offices, loggias, mosaics and, of course, the City Council. They were opened by Queen Victoria on 22 August 1888, and she must have felt thoroughly at home.

The job of designing the City Chambers was made the subject of a competition, and it was won by William Young, a Paisley buddy who had been trained in Glasgow and now worked in London (a familiar progression to architects even today!). If you would like to see the design which came second all you have to do is to go out to Paisley Road West and have a look at the main building of the Scottish Co-operative Wholesale Society. What will, perhaps, strike you is how similar it is to the winning building in George Square.

Naturally, the City Chambers in Glasgow are the finest in Scotland. The All Saints Club, which I have already mentioned, had a dinner there in one of the committee rooms. Afterwards the Edinburgh Saints accompanied the Glasgow Saints on a tour of the principal rooms. They were properly impressed, because the City Chambers in Edinburgh are a far-out second to Glasgow. One magnificent room followed another, until eventually the visitors were conducted to the great Banqueting Hall, where murals by distinguished artists portray some of the history of the city. In the Banqueting Hall a reception was being held, and the awed Edinburghers beheld young inhabitants of Glasgow dancing the Twist. What intrigued them most was that the girls had taken off their shoes and were dancing in their stocking soles. The Edinburghers realised that they were seeing the real Glasgow.

Before the City Chambers were built the eastern side of George Square was occupied by mansions, and one of them was the town house of the Alexanders of Ballochmyle. It was to a daughter of the house, Wilhelmina Alexander, that Robert Burns had addressed his song *The Bonnie Lass o' Ballochmyle*. Miss Alexander was most indignant when she was told that a common peasant had dared to make up a song about her. She did not reply to Burns.

But years later, when Robert Burns was dead and famous, Miss Wilhelmina, still a spinster, was inclined to be rather coy when the song was mentioned. I can imagine her listening to someone singing *The Bonnie Lass o' Ballochmyle* in that house in George Square, and letting it be known that she had not been unaware of the admiration of (as they called him then) the Poet Ploughman.

Round the corner from that part of the City Chambers where Wilhelmina Alexander once lived are the buildings of the new University of Strathclyde. They are partly the red structures of the old Technical College, and partly new and somewhat frightening architectural feats.

The Technical College, known in Glasgow for years as 'The Tech', became the Royal College of Science and Technology, and then the University of Strathclyde. Wherever 'Jolly Jack

Phosphorus' is now he'll be chuckling heartily. 'Jolly Jack Phosphorus' was Professor John Anderson, an 18th-century character who disliked his fellow professors intensely. He was always inveighing against the way the College in the High Street was run. He started the first known night classes for artisans in Glasgow and they gave him the name of 'Jolly Jack Phosphorus' because he so delighted in explosive demonstrations.

Professor Anderson left a will in which he instructed his trustees to use his fortune to found a new university in Glasgow, and he laid down the lines on which this university should be run, and the four faculties which it should have. The only trouble was that the trustees found that his fortune amounted to little more than £1,000. Even in the 18th century you could hardly found a university on that. However, they didn't give up and, one way or another, they eventually had enough money to found the Anderson Institution. And it was from the Anderson Institution that the Technical College was started. So 'Jolly Jack Phosphorus' got his university, after all.

While you are still able to, admire the buildings on the north side of George Square. One of them is the North British Hotel. The other was an hotel too. Indeed, George Square was famous for its hotels at one time, and the North British is, in fact, three hotels joined together. The west side of the Square was another row of hotels, but it was rebuilt as the Merchants' House and the Bank of Scotland, with offices in between.

The Glasgow Chamber of Commerce, the second oldest in the world (the first was founded in New York), meets in the Merchants' House. There are one or two interesting old plaques and tablets from the original Merchants' House, which I described in my chapter on the Briggait.

On the south of George Square there was the General Post Office, and the building which once housed what some rude people called the leading opposition to Glasgow City Council, the Scottish Gas Board.

Queen Street Station, beloved of John Betjeman, has changed completely. At one time the citizens of Glasgow regarded it as Glasgow's answer to the Crystal Palace in London. But now the wonderful glass façade is hidden by an extension to the North British Hotel. Between the extension and Dundas Street stood a kirk which was much older than Queen Street Station or the North British Hotel. The station is the oldest in Glasgow and was opened in 1842. The kirk was built for the congregation of the Reverend Ralph Wardlaw in 1818, but it has been a railway building since 1826.

The old Cow-loan followed the line of Dundas Street up to the Cowcaddens. But now Dundas Street has been cut in two by the joining of Buchanan Street Underground Station with Queen Street Rail Station. There are some parts of Glasgow where you can fancy for a moment or two that you are back in the past. If you look at the place now you cannot imagine that the town shepherd ever drove his cattle this way.

11

GLASGOW'S GOLDEN WEST

B uchanan Street is the one thoroughfare in Glasgow which impresses the Sassenachs, and this is especially so since it became our first pedestrian precinct. Sauchiehall Street has a name famous throughout the world, and it is now partly a pedestrian precinct too, but suffered badly in a rebuilding programme. The Sassenachs have probably heard of Argyle Street on a Saturday night, and are disappointed because they don't see a single man looking like Will Fyffe singing *I Belong to Glasgow*. The city, generally, falls in their estimation because they don't see any gangsters wielding razors or bicycle chains.

Glasgow is depressingly like any big place in England to the Sassenach. But when they view Buchanan Street – at least from St Vincent Place down to St Enoch Square – they say, especially on a fine day, 'This is delightful!' Even Glaswegians have a vague idea that, though they laud Sauchiehall and Argyle Streets, Buchanan Street is their greatest pride.

As I have shown you, Buchanan Street is a mere stripling compared with Argyle Street and the Trongate. But it is a great deal older than Sauchiehall Street, and it was the first indication that the town was moving west. The Wise Men of the East laughed to scorn the idea of a street so far west of Glasgow Cross. You were out of Glasgow altogether when you were in Buchanan Street. Besides, it was started by a Tobacco Lord who was bankrupted by the American Revolution. What good could come of it?

This sort of speculation is sprinkled through a Glasgow book which is one of the scarcest of our incunabula. In 1885 the famous Glasgow chemist Daniel Frazer wrote a piece about the making of Buchanan Street. He had it finely printed by James Frazer on Drury Street. Daniel wasn't old enough to see the beginnings of Buchanan Street, but he was one of the first men to live and work on it.

He was a great patriot for his native city, and he writes of Buchanan Street as though it were the Golden Road to Samarkand – as, indeed, it was in a fair way of being to him. The bromide has it 'an expert is a man who knows more and more about less and less'. This is certainly true of our Daniel. His lions' den is Buchanan Street and Buchanan Street only – except for small excursions into Argyle Street, Mitchell Street, Royal Exchange Square and St Vincent Place.

The birthday of Buchanan Street was on 15 February 1763. On that date a Mr Andrew Buchanan acquired the first portion of 'five acres or thereby of ground in the Burgh of Glasgow, in the part called Palezeon's Croft, on the North side of Argyle Street, with plots or steadings for building on each side thereof'.

Andrew Buchanan was the son of an ancient Glasgow family which had made its money out of malt. Andrew liked the malt well enough, but he was out to make bigger money than his ancestors had ever known. So he became one of the Tobacco Lords and walked the Plainstanes in style. Where he differed from his fellow merchants was that he had a vision of the town spreading to the west, and at the height of his prosperity he didn't mind speculating on ground so far from Glasgow as his proposed Buchanan Street.

In the year 1777 this pioneer advertised as follows: 'Andrew Buchanan, Merchant, has made improvement on his former plan, and now proposes to take down his house in Argyle Street to make the entry to his intended Street correspond exactly with the opposite entry leading into St Enoch's Square. The Lots are laid off sixty-five feet in front, with sufficient room backwards for garden plots. The situation is very pleasant and convenient, and affords a prospect rural and agreeable.'

But Andrew got exactly nowhere with his plans. The American colonies revolted that very same year, and the fortunes of the Tobacco Lords crumbled into something like tobacco dust. Mr Buchanan's two great firms trading between Glasgow and Virginia were wound up and his idea of a street was handed over to some Glasgow bankers. He lost his money but he gave his name to a street. The bankers started to sell the steadings in Buchanan Street the very next year. Two years later, in 1780, the street was opened as far as Gordon Street. And, from Gordon Street up, it was opened in 1804.

One of the first people to live on Buchanan Street was a William Glen, merchant son of a well-known Glasgow merchant. Glen, Junior, was a makar as well as a merchant. He wrote some verse which started, 'A wee bird cam' tae oor ha' door', that is sung everywhere in Scotland to this present day. The interesting point is that Mr Glen was anything but a Jacobite and yet the song is a lament for Bonnie Prince Charlie. The answer is that, when he wrote it, Mr Glen knew that there was a new demand for Jacobite songs, so he supplied one!

In the early days of the 19th century Buchanan Street was a thoroughfare mainly of villas and farms and an occasional workshop. The first great building on the street was St George's Church. The foundation stone was laid in 1807, and the congregation moved in somewhere about 1809. There is some dubiety about the actual year in which this event took place. The trouble is that the great chronicler of Glasgow about that time was Dr James Cleland. Dr Cleland was an eminent statistician, but he was so used to blinding others with science that he didn't always take care of his facts. He was careless in several volumes, and his mistakes have been perpetuated by those who thought that LLD after a man's name meant he knew.

The kirk was designed by a William Stark, already celebrated for having built the Lunatic Asylum on Parliamentary Road and the jail on Glasgow Green. The great Glasgow historian Senex wrote: 'When St George's Church was built in 1807, and the congregation removed from the Wynd Church to this, the then suburban locality, it was considered it would assuredly form the Western terminus of Glasgow, and yet already [1855] we have a magnificent city pressing farther west still.'

The fact that the city was moving west, indeed, was proved in 1823 when the first plate-glass windows ever seen in the town were put in a shop on Argyle Street, just about the Buchanan Street entry. And an enterprising showman found it worth while to build a diorama of the Battle of Waterloo, which was not pulled down until 1826.

This diorama stood about the foot of Buchanan Street, on the west side, and there was a school nearby. In those days the weans could run up Buchanan Street a bit and ploiter in the St Enoch Burn.

Buchanan Street didn't become at all commercial until 1828 when, as I have said, the Argyll Arcade was built from Argyle Street. John M Leighton, writing in *Swan's Select Views of Glasgow*, said in the same year: 'Buchanan Street is the approach to Glasgow, from the north-west, and is decidedly the finest it possesses; but it is to be regretted that, with the exception of the strangers arriving by the passage boats on the great canal, the district with which it communicates affords little intercourse with the city.'

This great canal was the Forth and Clyde, built partly out of the money raised by selling the forfeited estates of the Jacobite lairds after the 'Forty-Five'. In 1828 the canal was the main artery between Glasgow, Edinburgh and Falkirk.

Daniel Frazer was brought up as a boy on Buchanan Street. He started work in his brother's shop there soon after it was opened in 1830. A Mr Green joined the elder Frazer, hence Frazer and Green. The day the blind was first drawn up in NB Frazer's shop was the day that King William IV was proclaimed at Glasgow Cross.

The rent of this shop on Buchanan Street was £25 a year – but this small rent was because all the leading shops of this city of two hundred thousand were situated east of Buchanan Street. In fact, the grass was still growing luxuriantly in the upper part of the street. 'Some of the older druggists', wrote Daniel, 'laughed at my brother's boldness in beginning business in such an outlandish street, and at first it looked as if they were right and he was wrong.'

The daily sales varied from three shillings and sixpence to £3 9s – but it should be added that on only two days during the first six months did the day's sales amount to more than £2. For the whole of July 1830 the sales were under £17. And business increased to such an extent that for the whole of December 1830 the sales were under £25.

In the back shop the Frazer brothers spent the time reading and playing at birkie or catch-the-ten, two popular card games of the time. If someone came in to buy something in the middle of a game the senior brother sent a junior to get rid of the intruder. 'But', says Daniel, in one of the finest Irishisms ever perpetrated by a Scotsman, 'the business grew apace, though slowly.'

But all this time a reagent was working through the rich blood of Argyle Street into Buchanan Street. It was the Argyll Arcade. I have already described its start and its success. The people who entered the Arcade from Argyle Street and found themselves in Buchanan Street must have had an effect.

Exactly where the building known as 'The Lighthouse' now stands there was a building known as the New Town Market. This market was built as a square. Low-roofed shops for the sale of fish, meat, poultry and other food were built round a large pond. This pond was stocked with fish and you could go and pick your fish, watch it being caught and carry it off still wriggling. The New Town Market did well because more and more Glasgow people were recognising that Buchanan Street was a pleasant suburb to the city.

But the fact that the street was doing so well killed the New Town Market. The value of the land went up to such an extent that the proprietor felt bound to sell about 1866. A new building went up on the site of the market, and in December 1868 the *Glasgow Herald* moved in.

Just opposite the Buchanan Street entrance to the Argyll Arcade a venturesome chap opened the Buchanan Street Hotel. It had a walled garden with apple and pear trees, and a big conservatory where they grew their own grapes.

The Frazers, while they appreciated their surroundings and their growing aptitude at cards, liked to think occasionally of the Works of God.

Daniel writes with a certain relish: 'The outbreak of Asiatic cholera in Glasgow in the Spring of 1832 led to a rapid and considerable augmentation of business. ... The development of the business at this time was also helped by the reputation acquired by my brother for making a pitch plaster (then worn as a preventive of cholera) of a special pattern, received by him from Germany, through the kindness of Mr Frederick Zoller, long the highly esteemed Consul for that country in Glasgow.'

162

Perhaps because it was so out of the way this chemists' shop in Buchanan Street began to make quite a reputation. The Frazers set up a soda-water manufactory in the cellar. Very soon indeed they became known as hangover curers, as, in the 1830s, the great hangover cure was soda water. Every morning there was a procession of pale young gentlemen to Buchanan Street. Once they'd had some soda water they said they felt much better.

There were elderly, purple-faced gentlemen too. One of them swore, each morning he arrived, that he had to take the soda water because he'd put too much salt on his egg that morning.

The soda-water business was only equalled by the laudanum business. The Frazers had one regular customer who was in the habit of swallowing an undiluted wineglassful of laudanum at the counter. Then he'd get his two-pint flask filled and take it away. Apparently this poor chap had got the taste for laudanum when a doctor had recommended it to cure 'rheumatism in the head'. He tried to get rid of the habit by putting a lump of putty in his glass, and increasing the size of that lump day by day. But the day came when the putty was nearly at the top of the glass, and then the rheumatism returned to the head and the putty left the wineglass.

Young Daniel Frazer could dispense the soda water, but the laudanum was a bit too much for him. In any case, he was fully occupied with the leech department. Leeches were so popular in Glasgow that Daniel would order two or three thousand at a time. On one occasion he put in an order for five thousand. Even in 1885, when he wrote his book about Buchanan Street, Daniel was putting in a regular order for twenty-five leeches. He thought the reduction in numbers was 'a change for the better'.

Buchanan Street, about the 1830s, was a very popular thoroughfare for a procession. The processionists could muster in the fields to the north, get into their ranks on the green grass at the top of the street and march solemnly down Buchanan Street, turning left onto Argyle Street and impressing the populace as they stamped through the Trongate to Glasgow Cross.

Daniel Frazer saw the Reform Bill procession of 1832, which I mentioned in my last chapter. By this time the Western Club, at the corner of Buchanan Street and St Vincent Street, had come into being. It was originally on the south-west of the crossing, but in 1841 it was transferred to the north-west. Today the 1841 frontage still stands, but the interior has been completely changed into offices. The Western Club, Glasgow's oldest existing sodality with a habitation, sold its premises and moved into Royal Exchange Square. Many people are sad about this, particularly those who remember the days when one Western clubman approached another who was standing looking out of the big windows into St Vincent Street.

'What are you doing, Alan?' he inquired.

'Just watching the rain falling on the damn' people,' was the reply.

It's ironic, in a way, that the Western Club should move. Most members were quite undisturbed when they saw the Eastern Club disappear. The Eastern Club was Jimmy Cairns' pub, at the north-east corner of Buchanan Street and St Vincent Place. It had to give way to a financial company, and such companies abound here, because just north of the Western Club is the Glasgow Stock Exchange, a pink, fancy building that gives no indication of the solid dealings behind its façade. Like the Western Club, the frontage of the Stock Exchange has been preserved in its Italianate state while the inside has been completely remodelled. I'm glad to say that more and more of these fine frontages (the St Andrew's Hall front on Granville Street is another example) are being retained by Glasgow City Council instructions.

Just beside the Stock Exchange is St George's Church, the only one I know in Scotland which had electric signs saying 'Ladies' and 'Gents'. This, for a church built in 1807, is very enterprising. Dr James Cleland, whom I have already mentioned, put forward a proposal at one time that this kirk should be made the Glasgow City Chambers by a few judicious additions, but his idea was turned down. All the same, in 1834, by which time Buchanan Street was becoming a business and shopping centre instead of a mere lane to the great canal, a group of representatives of 'this wondrous city' – an English professor's description of Glasgow at the time – met to discuss some way of honouring Dr James Cleland.

They agreed on a building to commemorate Dr Cleland, and if you stand at the corner and look up to the top of the building opposite, you will see inscribed 'The Cleland Testimonial'.

On the other side of Nelson Mandela Place from the Stock Exchange is a group of buildings which once included the Athenaeum Club and the Liberal Club. They now house the Royal Scottish Academy of Music and its very successful off-shoot, the College of Drama. Within the building is the one-time Athenaeum Theatre, now used by the Academy and the College, but once the home of amateur drama in Glasgow, and the starting place of the Citizens' Theatre during World War II.

But I am moving too fast up Buchanan Street and into regions which Daniel Frazer never knew. He remembered when the firm of Sturrock the hairdressers opened a new shop at 19 Buchanan Street in 1847 (they are on Bath Street now). To celebrate the opening they brought the carcass of a bear they had slaughtered in Edinburgh, and put it on public view. The crowds were so great that the police had to be called in.

In the following year Daniel Frazer saw another procession marching down Buchanan Street. They were the 'ill-fed, ill-clad' Chartists. Just before they got onto Buchanan Street one or two of them had broken into a gunsmith's shop in Royal Exchange Square and stolen some guns and shot. So elated were these dangerous Chartists that they actually fired a couple of shots in the air as they marched down Buchanan Street. A Glasgow doctor was watching the procession. He immediately dashed into the mob and disarmed the men who had fired the shots. That sort of thing might have been very well for the Gallowgate but it would not do for Buchanan Street.

In the same year as the Chartist riot the first professional photographer in Scotland came to Buchanan Street. He was a Mr J Bernard, either a Canadian or an American, and he described himself as a 'photographic artist (Daguerrotype)'. He took pictures of most of the leading Glaswegians and was considered to be distinctly high-class.

Bernard's success led other photographers to Buchanan Street and soon it became the camera street of Glasgow. In 1854 there were nine photographic artists in the city, and six of them had establishments on Buchanan Street. But by this time the street was no longer regarded as west, though it was still golden. The rents went up and exactly thirty years after the photographers had settled on Buchanan Street the high rents had almost driven them out. In 1884 there were fifty-eight photographers in the Glasgow Directory, and only four of them were on Buchanan Street.

By 1870 Buchanan Street was regarded as one of the great thoroughfares of the city. But by that time its importance as the roadway from the great canal had declined considerably. Nowadays you have difficulty in finding any remnants of the Great Canal at all. If you go north up Buchanan Street you leave the familiar buildings around Sauchiehall Street (and even these may not be there for much longer) and enter a new and, to my mind, somewhat arid part of Glasgow. The old Buchanan Street Railway Station, with its Wild West aspect, looking as though a sheriff's posse might emerge at any moment, has gone. A great new headquarters building for British Rail occupies part of the site and new buildings are still going up in the background.

Not so very long ago you reached a grass-grown flight of stone stairs protected by a railing. This was the way to the Port Dundas terminus of the Forth and Clyde Canal.

At one time this harbour was more important than the Broomielaw. Goods from the west came in by Bowling on the River Clyde and were transported by barges to Port Dundas, or across Scotland to Falkirk, Grangemouth and Edinburgh. From the other side of Scotland goods also flowed in, and there were passenger barges which were used before the railways came into being. Indeed, if you were a young couple eloping from Edinburgh the way to do it was to join a fast barge at the Edinburgh terminus of the Union Canal, proceed to Lock 16 on the Forth and Clyde Canal near

Falkirk, change over to a *Swift* barge, and get to Glasgow long before the girl's father could follow you by coach on the tortuous road between the two cities. The *Swift* was drawn by horses ridden by men in livery, to denote that this was a Royal Mail boat. The captain wore a top hat, a sky-blue coat and black trousers. And aboard the *Swift* were a library, a ladies' retiring room and a bar.

Now the glory has departed. A bewildering complex of motorway, flyover and new roads faces you. When you do get to where Port Dundas once stood, all you see is a little bit of the canal in front of what was the grain distillery, the White Horse blending and bottling plant and the whisky cask menders. In fact, the Forth and Clyde Canal still exists to the west of the traffic-way but it is virtually derelict. The diesels run between Glasgow and Edinburgh in 45 minutes.

12
THE BELL O' THE BRAE

When you consider that the High Street of Glasgow was the spine of the city in Daniel Defoe's day, linking the Cathedral with Glasgow Cross and the River Clyde, you wonder that later inhabitants of this town should have treated it with such disdain. It was the educational centre, a place of fine houses and the site of the Battle of the Bell o' the Brae, a notable victory over the English by Sir William Wallace. And today it is drab and dirty until you reach the environs of the Cathedral. Another neglected thoroughfare, also once famous, is the Gallowgate, which goes east at the point of Glasgow Cross where the High Street goes north. But the Gallowgate has still a raffish air that takes away its drabness.

For a time the High Street was threatened by a new inner-ring road, which could have destroyed what few old buildings remain and actually separated Glasgow Cathedral from the rest of the city. But, praise be, the planners' idea seems to have been lost.

As I have said, the High Street is the way which led down from the Cathedral to the Clyde. But, as we pick Glasgow Cross as our centre, we shall follow the High Street up from the Tolbooth towards and beyond the Cathedral. Almost as soon as you leave the Tolbooth you come across the site (11 High Street) of David Dale's shop, one of the many in this part of the thoroughfare. It was a 17th-century building known as Hopkirk's Land, and it was removed just before the Great War started. David Dale had the sign of the woolpack over his door. His yearly rent was £5, but he sublet half of the shop to a watchmaker for £2 10s.

When David Dale was appointed Glasgow agent for the Royal Bank of Scotland in 1783 under circumstances which I have already detailed, he put the watchmaker out and turned his half of the shop into the Bank. The Old Glasgow Club, founded in the year 1900, had a farewell meeting in David Dale's shop in 1913. In those days the Club rather specialised in farewell meetings, and they got plenty of opportunities!

There is nothing to show nowadays where David Dale's shop stood and, indeed, you walk up the High Street and realise that its purpose nowadays is merely to provide an artery, an important artery, towards the heart of the city. Here and there are remnants of former grandeur. There is a building, with fading religious texts painted on it, that goes back to the Adam brothers, but almost everything has gone. On the front of the College Street Goods Station a plaque states that Glasgow University, founded in 1451, stood here. The plaque is on the site approximately where the gate to the old College stood. After the University was removed to Gilmorehill, the gate was taken down in 1887 at the expense of Sir William Pearce, shipbuilder, and re-erected at the north-west entrance to the new University on University Avenue. It is preserved as the doorway of Pearce Lodge and was, of course, named after Sir William.

The railway goods station site on the High Street was not the original home of Glasgow University. The first classes of the old College were started in Glasgow Cathedral, just up the road. Then the College moved to the house of the Laird of Luss in Rottenrow which, I am sorry to say, we shall be visiting as we walk north up the High Street. Then the University moved to the place where the station stands now and remained there for four hundred years.

It was a handsome building, made round a courtyard, with gardens and an orchard behind it and the Molendinar Burn purling through it. But in Victorian days the worst slums in Glasgow (and that was certainly saying something) were just outside the university walls to the north, where Duke Street leads off the High Street now. There were two streets, the Havannah and the New Vennel, and they were reckoned by experts to be the filthiest places in the city. Lord Kelvin's brother was on the staff at Glasgow University and he contracted typhus and died. Lord Kelvin always swore that the infection had come over the wall from the Havannah and the New Vennel, and he was one of the large body who wanted the University moved from the dirty High Street to the pure air of Gilmorehill.

As we see it now, of course, the destruction of the old College was a crime. The Victorians should have destroyed the slums round about it and kept the University, though undoubtedly they would have had to build extensions elsewhere. Glasgow is full of missed opportunities like that. All we can do now is look at the plaque, which was put up only in comparatively recent years, and try to imagine what this pleasant Glasgow University looked like.

I have quoted the Glasgow poet, John Mayne, on Glasgow Green. In the same set of verses he writes about the old University:

> Here great Buchanan learnt to scan
> The verse that mak's him mair than man;
> Cullen and Hunter here began
> Their first probations;
> And Smith, frae Glasgow, formed his plan –
> 'The Wealth o' Nations'.

This is a very patriotic Glasgow stanza, but it must be admitted that all these gentlemen came from outside the city. 'Smith, frae Glasgow', for example, was Adam Smith, and he was born in Kirkcaldy. Still, he taught in Glasgow. Among those who studied in the University were John Knox, Tobias Smollett, John Gibson Lockhart (son-in-law and biographer of Sir Walter Scott) and Archibald Campbell Tait, who became Archbishop of Canterbury.

On the opposite side of High Street from the University was the Glasgow Grammar School, now the High School of Glasgow. It was started in the Cathedral and may go back to the 12th century, although evidence on paper shows only its existence in the early 14th century. So the High School existed before the University was founded, and indeed it is one of the oldest schools in Britain.

It stood near the junction of the High Street and Ingram Street as you see it today. Ingram Street is an old loan and probably was a track leading to the Cow-loan, or Queen Street. I have mentioned it already, but it comes into the story of High Street because the Ramshorn lands were connected with the University. If you walk along Ingram Street to St David's Ramshorn kirk you will see inscribed on the pavement in front of the kirkyard a cross with the initials RF and AF.

This marks the grave of the Foulis Brothers, the famous printers who were called 'the Elzevirs of Glasgow'. The kirkyard once covered the ground right to the other side of Ingram Street. The Foulis Brothers went to the University in the High Street and later started a bookshop. Then they became printers, and it was their object to present the finest printing in Europe. When they were appointed printers to the University of Glasgow they decided in 1743 to publish an 'immaculate' edition of Horace. They engaged six of the best proof-readers they could find, so that there should be no mistakes on the typographical side.

This wasn't enough for the Foulis Brothers. After the proof-readers were finished, each page of Horace was put up on a board in the quadrangle of the University and a reward of £50 was offered to any person who could detect a printer's error. You can imagine that professors, lecturers, students and anyone, in fact, who could read studied each page carefully. The page was left on the board for two weeks, so there was plenty of time to discover mistakes. At last the great work, vetted so carefully, was published. And then the pundits and the pedants discovered that there were 'at least as many errors as the number of proof-readers who had been employed; one of which errors was in the very first line of the first page!' (I am quoting Robert Alison's *Anecdotage of Glasgow*.)

Robert Foulis was also interested in art. In 1753 he worked out a plan to establish an Academy of Arts in Glasgow. He made a collection of several hundred paintings and invited Continental artists to come to the city to act as instructors in drawing, painting and modelling. The University co-operated with Foulis. They had just built a new library and they gave him part of it for the Foulis Academy. And so we had, in 1754, an Academy of Arts fourteen years before

London had the Royal Academy of Arts. Indeed, it's suggested that London took the idea from Glasgow, and it wouldn't be the first time.

The Foulis brothers are without the Ramshorn kirkyard, but there are plenty of good Glasgow characters within the railings. This graveyard is second only to the Glasgow Necropolis, which we shall visit soon, and it is second mainly in size. It contains, under the tombstone labelled 'Kennedy', the grave of Pierre Emile L'Angelier, poisoned by Madeleine Smith in Blythswood Square in 1858. True, Madeleine was acquitted by the Edinburgh jury, who returned a verdict of 'Not Proven', a peculiar Scottish verdict which means, according to the experts, 'Go away and don't do it again'. But all the best criminologists agree that Madeleine administered arsenic in the cocoa she handed out to L'Angelier through her bedroom window. This didn't worry her. She went from Glasgow to London, dispensed cocoa to George Bernard Shaw, married a pupil of William Morris and was the first hostess in this country to introduce table mats on a bare table instead of the customary tablecloth.

Some of the graves in the Ramshorn kirkyard (and in the ground round Glasgow Cathedral, as we shall see later) have heavy stones laid on top of them, or elaborate railings round them. This was an attempt to prevent the resurrectionists, the 'sack-'em-up boys', from stealing corpses. The Medical Faculty of Glasgow University had this in common with all other medical faculties in Britain – that they could not get enough 'subjects'. The *cause célèbre* was that of the association of Dr Knox of Edinburgh with the murderers Burke and Hare. These two Irishmen started quite respectably in robbing graves, but they found it easier to murder people and present their bodies to the anatomists.

Glasgow was not one whit behind Edinburgh. The surgeons and the students took what bodies they could get from local graveyards, but they also imported corpses from Ireland. Indeed, one of the scandals of those days was the big consignment of well-filled sacks which arrived from Belfast and was stowed away in a shed. Somehow or other this was forgotten, and it was only when a powerful and awful smell arose from the sacks that they were investigated. It was then found that they were filled with dead bodies and bits of bodies. They were intended for the anatomists, but something had gone wrong in the system of communication.

Graves were constantly harried in the Ramshorn kirkyard. Guards were brought in, relatives stood watch all night, alarm wires were placed round the new graves and heavy stones were placed over them. But still the 'sack-'em-up boys' succeeded in removing corpses. The great Glasgow scandal was in December 1813. By this time the amateurs – in other words, the medical students – were competing with the professional body-snatchers. The professionals had worked out a method. The students believed in smash-and-grab.

One night a policeman coming along Ingram Street from the west heard suspicious noises around the Ramshorn kirk. He gave the alarm, but by the time the police had closed in the resurrectionists had disappeared. There were plenty of witnesses, however, to say that they were all young men and that they had disappeared in the direction of the University.

The word went round Glasgow quickly, and soon there was a procession of relatives to the Ramshorn to examine the graves of their most recent nearest and dearest. Right away a man found an empty grave. There should have been a Mrs McAllister in it, but the body had gone. There was a mob hanging around the Ramshorn, waiting for the latest news. When they heard it they rushed to the house of the Professor of Anatomy at Glasgow University, Dr James Jeffrey, and broke all his windows.

Public opinion was so strong that the Glasgow magistrates, for once, had to act without delay. They empowered officers to enter any suspected place, by force if necessary. To help these officers they added to the band two of Mrs McAllister's intimate friends and a surgeon-dentist named James Alexander, who had actually attended Mrs McAllister on the very day that she died.

The investigators concentrated on the area round Ingram Street and the High Street. One of the places they visited was on College Street, where Dr Granville Sharp Pattison had his rooms. Dr Pattison was the perfect host and showed the investigators all over the house. They could see nothing untoward. It was only after they had left that the surgeon-dentist suddenly suggested that they should have examined a tub full of water in the middle of one of the rooms.

So back the investigators went. They emptied the water from the tub, and found a jawbone with several teeth attached, some fingers and other parts of a human body. Mr Alexander examined the jawbone and announced that these were the very teeth of Mrs McAllister. He had been working on them right up to the time of her death. And one of the relatives picked out a finger which, he said, was undoubtedly the one on which Mrs McAllister had worn her wedding ring. The officers immediately arrested Dr Pattison, his lecturer on surgery, Andrew Russell, and two of his students who were on the premises at the time, Robert Munro and John McLean.

Once again the word had gone round Glasgow by the mysterious grapevine which seemed to operate in those days. By the time the officers were ready to move the accused men to the jail, a crowd had collected. They screamed abuse, they threw whatever was handy and they threatened to lynch the doctor and his students. The four of them were glad to get into the jail.

The officers went back once again to Dr Pattison's rooms and examined them carefully. When they dug up the floors they found the remains of several bodies, including bits of what was said to be Mrs McAllister's corpse. These remains were carefully sealed in bottles and put up to the High Court of Justiciary in Edinburgh.

The trial of Dr Pattison and Messrs Russell, Munro and McLean took place in Edinburgh in June 1814. They were charged under an indictment which alleged that the grave of Mrs McAllister in the Ramshorn kirkyard 'had been ruthlessly or feloniously violated by the prisoners, and her body taken to their dissecting rooms, where it was found and identified'.

By the time the Crown witnesses had finished their evidence it seemed an open-and-shut case. But the defence were able to prove to the satisfaction of the court that the portions of the body produced as belonging in her lifetime to Mrs McAllister could not possibly be hers. Mrs McAllister was married and had several children. It was shown that these were portions of a woman who had never had a child. And so the doctor, the lecturer and the students were set free.

But public opinion was so strong against Dr Granville Sharp Pattison that he soon left Glasgow and emigrated to America. Many years later, when he was an eminent professor in that country, he wrote about his unfortunate experiences in his rooms off the High Street and indicated that the Glasgow people were rude savages to behave in such a way to a sincere seeker after knowledge.

Before we leave the Ramshorn kirkyard I should mention that David Dale of glorious memory lies here, alongside William Glen, who wrote *Wae's me for Prince Charlie*.

Back on the High Street we near its junction with George Street on the west and Duke Street to the east. Just before you reach that cross you may see, on buildings on the west side of the High Street, plaques to the memory of two poets who were born on this thoroughfare. I say 'may see' because plaques have a habit of disappearing in this city, or buildings disappear and the plaques with them. At any rate, the poets born in this part of the High Street are Thomas Campbell, whom I've already mentioned, and William Motherwell, a delightful versifier who was regarded as a great man in his day.

There are big changes in this part of Glasgow. It's not so long ago that I heard a committee of experts in a Glasgow pub argue about which was the worst street, from every aspect, in Glasgow. Eventually they settled on George Street. They said that every crime in the book was committed on George Street and that it looked like it too. But now many of the old buildings have gone and are replaced by skyscraper offices and the many flamboyant new colleges of the University of Strathclyde. One of these days, and quite soon too, George Street may be a completely new thoroughfare, with the exception of the City Chambers and similar buildings at the western end of it.

Duke Street, on the other side, was famous for its prison – first of all the main jail of Glasgow and then the women's prison for the West of Scotland. It was a great, gaunt, grey building with a clock that didn't go in my time and a flagpole on which the black flag was hoisted when someone was hanged there. I can remember to this day travelling along Duke Street in a tramcar and seeing the black flag flying.

In my father's day Duke Street Prison was also famous because it was used as an address by the 'mashers' down the Firth of Clyde. When some girl you had picked up wanted to get your name and address and you didn't want her to know, you gave a fictitious name and added the address – 77 Duke Street. This, of course, was the main entrance to the prison, though it was later bricked up when the entrance was transferred to Cathedral Square. The whole front wall of the prison was removed after the Corporation had built one of the pleasantest and most modern housing developments in the city. The flats rise at various levels right up to Cathedral Square. But there is still a macabre touch on the western side of the scheme, where a prison wall remains. You will see the various initials inscribed on that wall. These are not modern graffiti. They are the initials of murderers who were hanged in Duke Street Prison and were buried there.

But Duke Street has yet another claim to fame. It is regarded by Glasgow experts as the longest street in the whole of Britain (they except Watling Street, because they say that isn't really a street as we know it today). The story is that there was a dispute between Glasgow and London as to which city had the longer street. The Londoners said Oxford Street was the longest in Britain – although, when pushed, they added New Oxford Street to it. The Glaswegians stuck by Duke Street and at last a measuring team was sent up from London to determine the exact length of Duke Street. They knew already, of course, the exact length of Oxford Street. Well, now, it would be wonderful if I could tell you the length of these respective streets, but all I can say is that the London measurers discovered to their chagrin that Duke Street beat Oxford Street by several yards.

Perhaps I should add that I have walked the entire length of both of these streets and I would vote unhesitatingly for Duke Street. Mind you, there's not much more to be said for

Duke Street. It had a charming Victorian school, a working man's caravanserai known as the Great Eastern Hotel, outside of which big American cars stopped momentarily (they knew nothing of Glasgow and, coming from the Edinburgh side, imagined this was a typical Glasgow hotel), an enormous brewery, the meat market, the entrance to a greyhound race-track and a gambling casino, and adjacent pubs called the Uneeda Bar and the Shuna Bar.

If we resist the temptation to go either right or left we cross the junction and come to the steepest part of the High Street, the Bell o' the Brae. There have not been many 'official' battles in Glasgow, though there have been plenty of unofficial ones. The Battle of the Bell o' the Brae is an official one.

In the days of Sir William Wallace, about the end of the 13th century, there was an English garrison in the Bishop's Castle at the top of the High Street. The Royal Infirmary occupies the site of the Bishop's Castle today. The Castle itself was administered by Bishop Beck of Durham and he was one of those fighting bishops who kept the countryside in subjection. Wallace made a direct attack on the Castle and the English sallied forth. They chased him down the High Street. But, just at this point, the Scots suddenly turned to fight. At the same time another Scottish force came up the Drygait. It was led by Wallace's uncle, Auchinleck, and it came in behind the English troops and attacked them from the rear. Not surprisingly, this was a small Scottish victory.

Just over six hundred years later there was another Battle o' the Brae and it took place perhaps a little north of Wallace's one. After the Great War there was considerable Sinn Fein activity in Glasgow. Like Liverpool, it was a natural place for Sinn Feiners to arrive and leave. A number of them were caught and sentenced to imprisonment. One day they were being taken by Black Maria from the Sheriff Court to Duke Street Prison. Although, as I have said, the old entrance was on Duke Street it had been changed to, as it were, the back door, which was near the junction of the High Street and the Drygait.

The Black Maria was proceeding on its lawful purposes up the High Street when Sinn Feiners suddenly opened fire on it. We actually heard the shots in Whitehill School, where I was a pupil, and the story was that they killed an inspector of police and wounded the driver. Then the Sinn Feiners burst open the door of the Black Maria and the imprisoned men escaped. Naturally, I have believed this story for years. But since I published it last, I've heard from the son of one of the policemen involved, and he reports that no-one was killed, and no prisoners escaped. It must have been Sinn Fein propaganda, but there's no doubt that there was an actual attack.

A number of bullets bit into the wall of Duke Street Prison. When I was taking visitors round Glasgow I always took them up the High Street, told them this story and showed them the bullet holes in the wall. I invited them to put a finger into a bullet hole. At the end of the day, when I had shown them the wonders of this wonderful city, I would ask them what had impressed them most. Almost invariably each would reply, 'Putting my finger into a bullet hole in the wall of Duke Street Prison.'

Well, as I have said, Duke Street Prison is no more. But part of the wall in the High Street has been preserved, merely as a screen between the new houses and the busy thoroughfare. I am glad to say that the Sinn Fein bullet holes are still there. Just the other day I put my finger into one of the bullet holes and felt I was in tune with history.

On the other side of the High Street you will see a Glasgow Corporation hydraulic station. There is no plaque to show it, but here was the drugstore of Dr Thomas Lyle, the author of the song *Kelvingrove*, which is used constantly as a theme song by the BBC in Scotland. It starts:

Will ye gang to Kelvingrove, bonnie lassie-O?

And the part of Kelvingrove in Dr Lyle's song is just where the present Broadcasting House stands.

Farther up on the left of the High Street is the entrance to the Rottenrow. This, I may have to remind you, was one of the eight great streets of Glasgow. I have already explained that its name has nothing whatever to do with the Rotten

178

Row in Hyde Park. Like so many Glasgow names, it comes from the Gaelic and means 'the way of the king'.

Rottenrow is a sad sight nowadays, especially to one who has lived in Glasgow for the last seventy years. When the Bishop was in his castle beside the Cathedral, and for a long time after, Rottenrow was a place where clerics and schoolmasters dwelt. Glasgow University stood here before it moved to the High Street. Now Rottenrow has been carved into bits by the University of Strathclyde, and you can walk along only the beginning of it and the end of it and there is practically nothing left to show the ancient way and nobody will have a thought for the sweet place that Rottenrow once was.

Going up from the High Street you see a piece of wasteland (at the moment of writing) where stood one of the earliest efforts to build decent houses for what were then known as the working classes. It was considered to be a model tenement and had an air about it. Alongside was a rather sombre-looking home for old men and old women. It is now the Balmano Building, a student's residence for Strathclyde University. Next to the building stood Balmano Street, known as Balmano Brae, which was considered the steepest street in Glasgow. In my young days, before automobiles had the power they have now, it was used as a test for cars. Any car which could get up Balmano Brae was considered a good one.

Before that the district, owned by a family named Balmano, was famous for its orchards and gardens. The last garden, the few trees left and Balmano Brae itself have all been swept away by the extensions to the University of Strathclyde. But I remember when there was still a garden on the other side of the walls of the home, and trees still flourished in the wasteland that was Rottenrow.

Across from the home is Weaver Street, which became a thoroughfare in 1792. In Rottenrow, on the east side of Weaver Street, the 'Auld Pedagogy' stood – otherwise, the original Glasgow University. Students studied there for ten years before they moved to the High Street.

On the west side of Weaver Street stood the Cross Keys Inn, built from the stones of the Manse of Eddleston, which stood nearby, in the late 18th century. The Incorporation of Weavers managed to preserve two old sculptured stones from the Manse and these were built into the back wall of the Cross Keys. One of them was dated 1573.

Thomas de Quincey lived in Rottenrow for a time, although the plaque which records his stay in Glasgow is on a building in Renfield Street. So did David Livingstone, and the renowned preacher Dr Chalmers. One of the last of the old buildings to disappear was Dean Place, and here de Quincey had his lodging. The Place and Deanside Lane on the other side (also now gone) were named after the Dean of the Cathedral who had his house here.

Angel Close has gone from Rottenrow. It was erected on the site of a building belonging to the Prebendary of Roxburgh in 1512 and was originally known as the Manse of Roxburgh. It got the name of Angel Close because of an effigy above the entrance, showing a cherub's head with a pair of wings. This cherub was said to be all that remained of the Manse of Roxburgh.

It's slightly sad to read James Cowan, in his excellent *From Glasgow's Treasure Chest*, saying: 'I have been assured on good authority, however, that the "angel" has no such romantic history, but that it was merely a fragment from an old tombstone placed in its present position at the whim of one of the workmen engaged in the erection of the existing tenement. Well, there it is, and there it is likely to remain for long enough, whatever the truth may be.'

Mr Cowan wrote that in August 1932, so 'long enough' lasted less than thirty years. The John Anderson Building of Strathclyde University straddles Rottenrow at this point and has blotted out the past. You have to cross through or go round the John Anderson Building to get back to what remains of Rottenrow. It's with a wry smile that you see that the ancient buildings have been replaced, first by the Department of Architecture and then by the Centre for Industrial Innovation.

Rottenrow ends in darkness, in the shadow of the bulk of the Maternity Hospital, where newspaper reporters held vigil every New Year's Eve so that they could tell an anxiously waiting world the name of the mother who bore the first child of the New Year. The Glasgow newspapers still publish this entrancing information, but, since there are no Scottish newspapers on New Year's Day, there's no need to hold a vigil.

The University of Strathclyde stretches up John Street and has almost blotted out Love Loan, which was once a strange little continuation of the Rottenrow.

It still had an air about it when I first walked through it, but it went down and down in the world and only its name gave it any atmosphere. Yet less than a hundred years ago there was an advertisement in a Glasgow paper offering 'Summer quarters to be let at the West end of Rottenrow, in the Common Gardens'. And Love Loan was the pleasant wee lane that wandered through the Common Gardens.

While we are weeping the salt tears for the days that are past, let us return to the High Street and weep some more. Straight across from the Rottenrow is the Drygait, and you will maybe recall that these two streets were once a Roman road. Duke Street Prison dominated the Drygait for many years. Now there is the great new housing complex, and its pillared entrance, with the green Cathedral Square opposite, which gives a very different aspect to the Drygait as I knew it.

And when you cross John Knox Street, you find that the rest of the Drygait, which led over the Molendinar Burn to the Lady's Well, has been reduced to a short cul-de-sac, for the gigantic Tennent's Brewery has reached out over the Molendinar and swallowed up part of the ancient history of Glasgow.

The Drygait was the place where such great lords as the Dukes of Montrose had their town houses. Some people have suggested that the Drygait got its name because one of the first bridges in Glasgow was built over the Molendinar Burn here and so people were able to get across the water without wetting their feet, but I doubt this ingenious story. I have yet to hear a derivation of Drygait which impresses me. I knew this place mainly as a slum and so don't regret the disappearance of the buildings. I do regret the covering over of that little bit of the Molendinar, even though it had been turned into a sewer. Owing, presumably, to a lack of communication, a party of boys from the High School of Glasgow were allowed to clean up the Molendinar at this point, and a very good job they made of it. But the refurbished Molendinar didn't last for long, though at least it was looking cleaner than usual until the brewery covered it over.

One relic of the past that has also gone in the Drygait was a rather ramshackle single-storey building used as a garage when I saw it last. It stood on the other side of the Molendinar and was Glasgow's first Penny School, where the pupils took a penny to the master each time they went to school. In winter he was prepared to accept a piece of coal or some good wood instead of the penny. Apart from that memory, the building had no value and its days were numbered too.

We go back to Cathedral Square, which is rather attractive with its trees, its seven statues (vying with George Square), its churches, the towering Royal Infirmary, the Cathedral and the extraordinary skyline of the Necropolis. The statues are not up to the George Square standard – with the exceptions of David Livingstone, which was brought up from George Square, and King William of Orange, otherwise King Billy, which once stood at Glasgow Cross. I have told the story of King Billy already and how it is the statue with a moveable part. The tail is attached by a swivel arrangement and sways in a strong wind. A fence has been put round King Billy by the authorities because a couple of merry gentlemen were trying to see if my story was true.

Apart from Queen Victoria, who sits solidly in front of the Royal Infirmary, the other statues are of earnest and worthy men, of whom only the Reverend Norman MacLeod is well known today. He is looking at the 'new' Barony Church. But he was minister of the 'old' Barony, supposed to be the ugliest church building in Scotland, which stood on the statue's side of the High Street. It was removed when Cathedral Square was being laid out and the new kirk was built opposite.

Near the Barony Church is Provand's Lordship, the oldest house in Glasgow. It's a museum now, with rather restricted opening hours, and it is run by the Provand's Lordship Society. It is one of the few 'rescued' buildings in Glasgow. Old men can remember when it was a tumbledown tenement with a barber's shop occupying part of the ground floor.

Provand's Lordship was built some twenty years after the University of Glasgow was founded – in or about 1471. Bishop Andrew Muirhead gave it to the priest in charge of St Nicholas Hospital. It got the name of Provand's Lordship because it was the town house of the Canon of Barlanark and his rectory was known as the Lordship of Provan. (It is connected with Provan Hall, a 15th-century building which stands in the middle of the Easterhouse housing scheme of Glasgow Corporation, some four miles to the east. It, too, is worth visiting.)

Among the lay canons of Barlanark were King James II and King James IV of Scotland and they are supposed to have slept here. So did Mary Queen of Scots. She came to Glasgow in 1566 to see her sick husband Lord Darnley. If she did write the famous 'Casket Letters', which were supposed to implicate her in the murder of Darnley, she wrote them in Provand's Lordship.

Not far to the north-east of Provand's Lordship stood the Bishop's Castle. Its site was roughly on the corner of the Royal Infirmary grounds nearest the High Street. By early Victorian days it was a ruin and there was one Glasgow worthy who would never go near the remaining high wall. He had been told that that wall would fall some day on the best man in Glasgow, so he was taking no chances.

The first Royal Infirmary, of which little if anything remains today, was built in 1792 to a design by Robert Adam. It replaced the ruins of the Bishop's Castle and was much admired. By the beginning of the 20th century it was not nearly big enough and in 1907 the new building was started. Today there is a plaque on the infirmary wall on Castle Street, the continuation of the High Street, recording the fact that this was the site of the Lister Ward, where Sir Joseph Lister turned the medical world of the 1860s upside down with his demonstrations of antiseptic surgery.

Glasgow's well-known official vandalism came to the fore at the Royal Infirmary, first by removing the Adam building and second by tearing down the Lister Ward for more rebuilding. Protests flowed in from all over the world when it was known that the Lister Ward was to be demolished. The appeals were ignored. Glasgow was to be satisfied with a plaque. But in the University of Rochester, New York, a single brick from the Lister Ward was given a special position on permanent show. And the Wellcome Medical Museum sent emissaries to the demolishers' scrap-heap in Glasgow in order to pick up any bits of the ward building that they could. These were built into a replica of the ward which is a permanent London memorial to Lister.

The Royal Infirmary towers over Glasgow Cathedral and makes it look almost insignificant. The first view of the Cathedral is a disappointment to most visitors. They are amazed when they get inside. But if you want to appreciate the size and shape of the Cathedral you should cross the Bridge of Sighs into the Necropolis, walk some way up the hill and look at the High Kirk from there. You will then see that it is a cathedral with a crypt which is above ground.

The Victorians did not help the appearance of the Cathedral when they removed a square tower and the Consistory Court from the front. They thought they were improving this ecclesiastical edifice, as it undoubtedly would be called then. But, of course, they were improving the Royal Infirmary too, and you can appreciate all their improvements today.

No one knows when the first cathedral was built in Glasgow, but in the presence of King David I, the 'Sair Sanct for the Croon', a church was consecrated on the present site by Bishop Achaius in 1136. This church was destroyed and it's thought that Bishop Jocelyn started the building of a new one. When Glaswegians talk about the Cathedral 'going back to the 12th century' they mean that part of Bishop Jocelyn's building is incorporated in the present one. The choir and crypt, however, were not finished until the following century, and the building was completed by Robert Blacader, first Archbishop of Glasgow, in the 15th century.

Glasgow Cathedral is the only complete example of pre-Reformation Gothic church architecture on the mainland of

Scotland (in Kirkwall, Orkney, there is St Magnus Cathedral). Why did our cathedral survive while the reformers were dinging doon cathedrals and kirks all over the country? The story is that when the reformers were planning to attack the Cathedral word came to members of the Incorporated Trades of Glasgow of their plot. The Trades decided that the Cathedral must be saved. They took up arms and Hammermen, Weavers, Bakers, Gardeners, Wrights and all marched to the Cathedral. Somehow or other, word had reached the Royal Burgh of Rutherglen, Glasgow's great rival, that the Cathedral was in danger. Rutherglen men had been working on repairing the cathedral roof, and they too took up arms and joined the Glasgow Trades.

This valiant body of men then posted themselves in a great ring right round the church, and when the reformers arrived told them that not a man would get though that ring. There was a parley and eventually the Trades agreed that the reformers would be allowed to enter the Cathedral and tear down the statues and other signs of Popery, as long as they did not touch the fabric of the building. Thus Glasgow Cathedral was saved for posterity.

As it was, a great library was totally destroyed, with valuable vestments, jewellery and altars. Some of the precious things, however, had been saved by Archbishop Beaton, who took them with him when he fled to France.

Many kings and queens have visited the Cathedral. Edward I, the 'Hammer of the Scots', made offerings at the high altar of the shrine in the 13th century. Some years later the man who defeated Edward's son at Bannockburn, Robert the Bruce, stood at that same altar and was absolved by Bishop Wishart for the killing of the Red Comyn at Dumfries.

Charles I might be said to have lost his head because of Glasgow Cathedral. The General Assembly of 1638 met in the Cathedral nave and abolished Episcopacy in Scotland. By defying Charles I they set in train a series of events which ended in his downfall. Oliver Cromwell worshipped in the Cathedral in 1650. He was very suspicious about his reception in Glasgow. He'd been told that gunpowder was stored in the Bishop's Castle to blow him up when he came down Castle Street to the Cathedral. So he entered Glasgow by the Cowcaddens. On Sunday he went to the Cathedral and heard the famous Dr Zachary Boyd preach.

Zachary Boyd feared no man. He didn't care a docken about Cromwell or his Ironsides. He preached a fiery sermon in which he made it very clear that he disapproved of Cromwell and all his works. The denunciation got to such a pitch that one of Cromwell's aides whispered in his leader's ear, 'Shall I pistol the fellow now?' Cromwell shook his head.

That night he invited Zachary Boyd to dinner. The dinner was a very frugal one and after it Cromwell put up a prayer. This prayer lasted a good three hours and the intention was to make Zachary Boyd suffer. But it is said that Zachary enjoyed every moment of it, and his opinion of Cromwell went up as a result.

Besides being a great preacher, Zachary Boyd was a poet – in his own estimation. When he died he left his poems to his Alma Mater, the University of Glasgow, and a large sum of money to publish them. The University took the money, but, somehow or other, the poems have never been published. I have had the opportunity to see some of the poems and I must say that the University could put the money to a better use.

I am not going to describe the interior of Glasgow Cathedral. More expert hands than mine have already done so. There are official guides who take parties round and sometimes baffle foreign visitors with their use of the Glasgow accent. Foreign visitors should not worry overmuch, though. They, at least, can say that they have seen the inside of Glasgow Cathedral, which is more than most Glaswegians can say.

To me, the best moment of a visit to the Cathedral is when I go down into the crypt and see St Mungo's tomb. Under the fan vaulting a lamp is kept burning and I find it impressive to think that the first Glasgow Man is sleeping there.

There are other Glasgow men sleeping in the graveyard outside, and still more of them in the Necropolis on the Fir Park Hill. The entrance to the Necropolis is just beside the entrance to the Cathedral. It has a gatehouse and when I first visited it the man at the gate was an uncle of the late 'King'

John MacCormick, the Scottish National leader. The uncle was not only a Gaelic speaker but a Gaelic writer, and he had translated all the principal plays of Shakespeare into the Gaelic.

He also subscribed to the theory that the Lost Tribes of Israel had settled down in the Highlands. That, he told me, explained why so many of the Highlanders were small dark men with big noses. He added that it also explained the name MacIsaac, meaning 'Son of Isaac'. There is, as I have said, a body of opinion in the Highlands that the Garden of Eden was situated there and that the tongue which Adam and Eve spoke was Gaelic.

The Bridge of Sighs crosses over Wishart Street and the buried Molendinar Burn to the Necropolis, the graveyard of the Glasgow merchants. The Merchants' House opened it in the Fir Park in 1832, but the statue of John Knox which crowns the hill was put there in 1825. If you climb up to John Knox you can see by his expression what he thought of Glasgow. He scowls over the scene and seems to be calling down the Wrath of God on the city spread before him.

The first person to be buried in the Necropolis was a Jew. If you take the low path to the left as you enter the Necropolis you will come to the tiny and now overgrown Jewish burial ground. The Necropolis itself was laid out in the style of the Père la Chaise Cemetery in Paris. It is said to contain almost every kind of architecture in the world, for the various merchants who have been buried there arranged that their memorials should be built in Indian, Burmese, Chinese or whatever was the architectural style of the place where they made their money.

I have a penchant for cemeteries myself and walk through the Necropolis whenever I get the opportunity. A walk through the cemetery is, or maybe was, the right way to spend a Sabbath afternoon in Scotland. But I was rather surprised when I was in Helsinki some summers ago to find that a walk though the cemetery there was listed as one of the attractions in the official guide book.

Two things to look out for in the Necropolis are the memorial to William Miller, the man who wrote *Wee Willie*

Winkie, and the Egyptian Vaults. The Egyptian Vaults can be recognised by their elaborate gate in front of an entrance into the hillside. Originally this was used for keeping coffins until the burial was due to take place, but now it is just a somewhat melancholy curio.

When we return to the High Street we can go up its extension, Castle Street, to see the last remnant of history hereabouts. We walk up the side of the Royal Infirmary. As you reach Alexandra Parade, you find a complete change in the Townhead scene. A motorway, with all its attendant flyovers and side thoroughfares, has taken over. Gone is the entrance to the Monkland Canal, even in my day a busy place with its barges queuing up to unload. There was a link with the Forth and Clyde canal too, but it has been bulldozed away.

In Castle Street, in front of the canal, there was a picture-house. In its wall was the Martyrs' Memorial fountain, a memorial to three Covenanters who were executed on this spot in the bad old 'killing times' of the 17th century. Both cinema and fountain have gone, and the martyrs memorial stones now lie in Martyrs Church, Townhead.

Glasgow had many martyrs for the Covenant. There is another memorial to nine of them in the Cathedral kirkyard. But only one Roman Catholic was ever martyred in this city. Despite all you may have heard of us, we are a most tolerant lot of people.

13
THE WEE MAN'S WAY

Now we come to the last of the eight original streets of Glasgow – the Gallowgate. It runs to the east from Glasgow Cross and most writers on Glasgow have said that its name means 'the way to the gallows'. A former historian of Glasgow, George Eyre-Todd, has disagreed. He pointed out that if this were the way to the gallows the thoroughfare should be called Gallowsgate. But I don't think our forefathers were quite as pernickety as this. Perhaps Mr Eyre-Todd made a better point when he said that there were no gallows in the Gallowgate. According to him, the gallows were housed within the yard of the Bishop's Castle in the High Street.

He suggests that, 'like the Gallowgate at Aberdeen, it may have been the *gait*, or way, to the *gia lia*, or sacred stone of early pagan times. If so, it is probably one of the oldest thoroughfares in the country, older even than Roman roads and Roman walls.' This is a very interesting theory, but no archaeologist so far has discovered any traces of a sacred stone along the route of the Gallowgate.

The Gallowgate is one of the Glasgow streets which has had a bad reputation for years. I should add an undeserved bad reputation, for it has become a somewhat drab motorway in recent years and the old excitement of the days when a colonel could call on his Glasgow soldiers facing the enemy to 'Charge them down the Gallowgate, lads!' has long since gone. But in my time there were sixty pubs in the Gallowgate and I never ventured there without an occasional *frisson* disturbing me. Clifford Hanley, the Glasgow novelist and author of *Dancing in the Streets*, has described his early boyhood in the Gallowgate and it held few terrors for him.

In Victorian days the Gallowgate was a notorious place. There was a famous roving reporter, who called himself simply 'Shadow', and in 1858 he brought out a book graphically entitled *Midnight Scenes and Social Photographs, Glasgow*. He describes how (with a couple of friends for reasons of safety) he followed an evil-looking woman from Glasgow Cross along the Gallowgate. She was 'helping' along a young man who was half drunk. 'Shadow' and his friends followed them into a court off the Gallowgate and entered a two-roomed house with an earthen floor. There were four beds in the two rooms and two 'loathsome women' in each bed.

'As we smell the whisky,' writes 'Shadow', 'and pass it round, a feeling of disappointment is evidently felt. "I doot you dinna like the whisky," says Jenny. "It's real gude by what we get maist times at this time o'night." "I daresay it is," we remark, "it can't be expected good at so late an hour." A proposal is made to form a circle round the fire, and enjoy ourselves. However, giving a significant look to the young man, who by this time is again beginning to be a little elevated, we make our way towards the door, but find it locked. A trifle of money to the doorkeeper, who remonstrates against our leaving, and we forthwith take our departure, congratulating ourselves on an escape from a very dangerous den of the worst of thieves and prostitutes.'

Great stuff, eh? 'Shadow' certainly earned his money, taking his life into his hands in that Bond-like manner. All the same, you can see how the Gallowgate got its reputation.

Perhaps the great affair of the Black Boy Tavern in the Gallowgate in 1837 helped too. Once again I must quote; otherwise you would not get the full Victorian flavour. There have been several accounts of the Black Boy Tavern stramash, but my own favourite is the one recounted in *The Anecdotage of Glasgow*, written by Robert Alison and published in 1892. Mr Alison, as far as I can discover, was no relation of the courageous Sheriff Alison of this story. He wrote as follows:

'During the commercial crisis and panic of 1837 which swept over the country, Glasgow, as a great mercantile and industrious centre, suffered severely. Prices of all kinds of manufactured goods sunk to nearly one half; many workers were thrown idle, and the wages of those still employed were reduced, which reduction again led to general and foolish strikes, at the instance of their trades unions; first, of the operative cotton-spinners in and around Glasgow, and soon after of the whole colliers and iron miners in Lanarkshire.

'The effect of these two strikes was to let loose, upon an already over-distressed community, above eighty thousand persons, all in a state of utter destitution, and yielding implicit obedience to their trade leaders. To cope with this formidable and well-organised body there was, in and around Glasgow, a police force of only two hundred and eighty men. Bands of eight hundred to one thousand men traversed the streets, with banners flying and drums beating; and the colliers assembled in such numbers as to render any attempt to disperse them, except by military force, out of the question. Many violent assaults were made on the nobs or new hands, who took the place of the men out on strike, and at length, on the 22 July of that year, a new hand was shot dead on one of the streets of Glasgow.

'The masters met and offered a reward of £500 for the discovery of the persons implicated in the murder; and three days afterwards two informers met Sheriff Alison by appointment in a vault under the old college, to which the informers were admitted by a back door though the college green. They disclosed to the sheriff a plot "to assassinate the new hands and master-manufacturers in Glasgow, one after another, till the demands of the combined workmen were complied with", that the man shot three days before had been selected as the first victim, and that Mr Arthur, master-manufacturer, was to be the next victim. The informers told the sheriff that the next meeting of committee would be held on the evening of Saturday, 29 July, in the Black Boy Tavern, Gallowgate, Glasgow.

'At nine o'clock at night the sheriff left his office, with no arms but his walking stick, accompanied by Mr Salmond, the procurator-fiscal, and Mr Nish, the principal sheriff-officer. They met Captain Miller of the police force, with twenty constables, at the mouth of the Black Boy Close, a vile den in the Gallowgate, near to the Cross. Four constables were stationed at the entrance to the close, with instructions to let no one out or in; twelve of the others were stationed round the tavern at the front, and four at the back, with orders to seize anyone attempting to escape.

'Sheriff Alison, Mr Salmond, Captain Miller and Mr Nish then entered the tavern. They at once passed by a trap-door, in the chief room, and to which they ascended by a moveable wooden stair or ladder, into the room above, Captain Miller first, the sheriff second, Mr Salmond and Mr Nish following in rotation. They found the whole committee, sixteen in number, seated round a table in consultation, with a lot of money spread out before them, and only one light, from a gas pendant descending from the roof, lighting the apartment.

'The sheriff brought up eight of the police, whom he stationed in the room below, re-entered the upper room, and took up his position under the gas-light to prevent it from being put out. He then looked round and saw that the committee were so panic-struck that no resistance would be offered, though they were in the room four to one. Captain Miller next called out the name of each member of the committee, and as each was named, beckoned him to go out, and they were thus one by one secured by the police in the room below. Not a blow was struck, so coolly, quietly, and firmly did the sheriff and other officials go about their work.

'On Monday following (31 July) the cotton-spinners met on Glasgow Green, and by a great majority resolved to resume their work on the masters' terms; and on Tuesday the courageous sheriff had the delight of seeing the whole of the tall chimneys in Calton and Bridgeton sending forth their wonted smoke, after a stoppage of three months. The trial of the cotton-spinners came on at Edinburgh on 8 January, 1838; and resulted in the whole of the would-be assassins receiving sentence of transportation for seven years.'

I have not the heart to comment on this ineffable stuff. Let's go along the Gallowgate. Like the Saltmarket, the street has hardly started ere it is brought up against a railway bridge. During the Second World War a troop train was held up on this bridge. It was full of American soldiers and they amused themselves by throwing packets of chewing gum and sweets and cigarettes out of the train windows to a huge crowd which gathered in the Gallowgate below.

Just before the bridge, to the left, is a short street in which a truly Glasgow theatre was situated until it met the customary Glasgow theatre fate and was burned down some years ago. It was the Queen's Theatre. It had been the Star and the People's Palace and several other names before that. But it became really famous just before, during and after the Second World War. This was due to a series of pantomimes produced at the Queen's. All Glasgow went to them. They were what is politely called 'earthy' and they were very, very funny. The stars were Doris Droy, who might have been the Gracie Fields of Glasgow, and Sam Murray, who always appeared as a dame named Fanny Cartwright, whatever the subject of the pantomime was.

Soon the Queen's had such a reputation that it was the done thing for the young bloods of Glasgow to have an early dinner and go to the second house of the pantomime. The management were not happy about this. They felt that patrons in dinner-jackets were not right for the Queen's. Invariably when there was a row of young swells there would be a couple of bouncers standing ready to deal with them.

Word of the nature of this pantomime reached the police, whose headquarters were only a couple of hundred yards away. They investigated and found that much of the comedy was rude and also that the script had never been passed by the Lord Chamberlain. So it was officially ordered that the script should be sent to London. Now each year the script was written by Doris Droy's husband Frank, who also appeared in the show. He wrote the entire pantomime in what we call in Glasgow a B2 – in other words, a small school jotter. Moreover, he wrote it in pencil and didn't worry a great deal about the spelling. He didn't worry about other things either. He always called his principal boy Colin, so that you'd go to see *Robinson Crusoe* (called *Robertson Crusoe* by Doris Droy) at the Queen's and find no Crusoe in the cast. Colin was the one who was wrecked on the desert island and found a Man Friday.

All the comedy scenes were written in the strongest of Glasgow dialect. Dear knows what the Lord Chamberlain made of this B2 jotter with its pencil scribblings in a strange tongue. Each year he passed the pantomime script, and each year the show got ruder and ruder. The audience roared and the police turned puce in the background.

I had a great affection for the Queen's Theatre, for it was there that I achieved one of my great ambitions. I appeared as the hind legs of a horse in the pantomime. I can't for the life of me remember the name of the pantomime, but it was one in which Doris Droy appeared as a woman carter who had taken over her husband's job during the war. Naturally, she had to have a horse with her. The horse was played by a married couple named Carr and Vonnie (Vonnie was Mrs Carr), who appeared on Scottish music-hall stages for many years after.

The management of the Queen's agreed that I should appear as the hind legs (Vonnie's part) for one performance only. So I went along to the Gallowgate to rehearse. You may not realise it, but pantomime horses are customarily performed by either acrobats or tap-dancers. Carr and Vonnie were tap-dancers, and the whole routine was built on tap-dancing. I am neither an acrobat nor a tap-dancer, and the routine had to be simplified extremely for me. Fortunately, when you are appearing as the hind legs of a pantomime horse, you can see the front legs through a sort of window in the soft under-belly of the horse. The theory is that whatever the front legs are doing you will do the same.

We rehearsed for a whole afternoon. I found that the front legs wore a heavy belt so that, as the hind legs, I bent over and grasped this belt. That kept us in cohesion. Mr Carr said to me: 'See that bit where we fall down on the stage? For heaven's sake don't get the body of the horse twisted. If you do, you won't be able to get up on your feet again and I'll have to drag you off.'

I promised to do my best, but I can tell you that I felt very worried and excited as I got into the horse's costume in the wings. The entire cast of the Queen's Theatre pantomime were there to see me make my debut. Came the cue, and on we trotted. All went well. We fell down but the body wasn't twisted. We got up again and finished by carrying Doris Droy off on my back. Then we took off the top part of the costume and went on to the stage to take our bow and show that we were really men all the time.

I don't suppose I am the only person who misses the Queen's pantomime when Christmas comes round, but I have my personal reason for remembering it, and we shall never look upon its like again.

Just behind the Queen's Theatre was a blacksmith's shop. When I visited it the smiddy was rather quiet. There wasn't much for the smith to do in the way of horses. But this smith specialised in singeing sheep's heads for hotels and restaurants in Glasgow. Sheep's head, or sheep's heid as we know it, has been a popular dish for years in this city. It was regular fare in city restaurants every Wednesday, which was Market Day in Glasgow and consequently the town filled with country people. The best sheep's heads are singed before they are cooked, and most restaurants sent the heads along to this smiddy. Alas, it perished in the same fire which burnt down the Queen's Theatre. But in any case, the blacksmith would soon have found his occupation gone. Someone discovered that sheep's heads are the ideal food for mink, which are bred in a big way in Scotland. Therefore, most of the sheep's heads go to the mink farms and butchers and restaurants never see them.

You go under the railway bridge and there to the right is the quaintly named Schipka Pass. At one time it ran from the Gallowgate into London Road and was under cover, a sort of one-sided arcade, in fact. But now, although the Gallowgate end still goes up the Pass, entrance into London Road is blocked by brick. The wee shops have all vanished. The name of the pass came from a battle between the Russians and the Turks, in which the Russian Gatling guns left mounds of Turkish bodies lying on the field. A Glasgow cynic has suggested that the name was originally given to the pass because there were so many bodies lying about in Victorian days.

Across from the Schipka Pass, on the north side of the Gallowgate, are the Spoutmouth and Molendinar Street. The Molendinar Burn runs under the street of its name. The Spoutmouth is called after a spout of stone through which the burn water flowed. Some steps were carved below it, so that people who wanted the fine fresh water from the Molendinar need only descend a little to catch it in their vessels from the spout's mouth.

On the same side of the Gallowgate are the Little Dovehill and the Great Dovehill, known to Glaswegians as the 'Doohills'. St Mungo used to take the air on the Little Dovehill after bathing in the Molendinar. The Great Dovehill was one of St Mungo's miracles. He was speaking to the Glaswegians from the Wee Doohill when some of his audience objected that they could not see him. So he immediately commanded the adjoining ground to rise. Obediently it rose and that is now the Big Doohill. It is said that it was this miracle which gave Glasgow its motto – 'Lord, let Glasgow flourish by the preaching of the Word'. We are so materialistic nowadays that we just say 'Let Glasgow flourish'.

Here you see a rather shabby pub called the Saracen's Head. Adorning its frontage are panels showing the famous Saracen Head Inn, Glasgow's first real hotel, and the implication is that this pub is the site of the Saracen's Head Inn. But that is not the case. The site of the renowned hostelry was occupied by a red sandstone tenement on which you could see inscribed 'Saracen's Head Buildings'. But apart from the pavement-level shops, this has gone.

Until 1754 there was no such thing as an hotel in the city. There were plenty of inns, but a traveller took his chance with them. The best accommodation was supplied by stablers, who hung out signs saying 'Entertainment for man and beast'. The Magistrates and Council of Glasgow decided to encourage a gardener and vintner, Robert Tennent, in his proposal to build an hotel in 1754. Robert Tennent was the founder of the famous brewing family of Tennent, whose beer is still made in Glasgow. The old Bishop's Castle in the High Street was now a ruin, and Glasgow Town Council gave Mr Tennent permission to build his hotel from the stones of it.

He called his hotel the Saracen's Head after the famous Saracen's Head of London, which was named in honour of St Thomas of Canterbury, whose maternal grandfather was a

Saracen. The Glasgow Saracen's Head was considered a wonderful place by the Glaswegians. It had a ballroom which could hold one hundred dancers. The stables could take sixty horses and many carriages. The Lords of Justiciary from Edinburgh stayed there when the circuit brought them to Glasgow, and walked in procession down the Gallowgate to the Court Hall at Glasgow Cross. At night they would entertain the bailies and the town councillors to a 'poor man', which meant shoulder of mutton and oceans of claret.

When a 'poor man' was being served two town officers stood guard on the fine staircase of the Saracen's Head, wearing scarlet coats and carrying halberds. The waiters wore powdered wigs, embroidered coats and red plush breeches. All stage-coaches stopped at the Saracen's Head and one of the sights of the city was the appearance of the two tall porters, also bewigged, powdered, embroidered and breeched, to take in the guests' luggage.

The kitchen had such a reputation that well-to-do people in and near Glasgow sometimes sent their daughters there for instruction. In 1770, when a 'county' dinner was served at the Saracen's Head, all the waitresses were 'county' too.

In October 1773 Dr Samuel Johnson and Mr James Boswell returned to Glasgow from their tour to the Hebrides. They put up at the Saracen's Head and this is what Boswell wrote:

'On our arrival at the Saracen's Head Inn, at Glasgow, I was made happy by good accounts from home; and Dr Johnson, who had not received a single letter since we left Aberdeen, found here a great many, the perusal of which entertained him much. He enjoyed in imagination the comforts which we could now command, and seemed to be in high glee. I remember he put a leg up on each side of the grate, and said, with a mock solemnity, by way of soliloquy, but loud enough for me to hear it:

"'Here am I, an Englishman, sitting by a *coal* fire."

'On Friday, October 29, the professors of the University being informed of our arrival, Dr Stevenson, Dr Reid, and Mr Anderson breakfasted with us. Mr Anderson accompanied us while Dr Johnson viewed this beautiful city.

He told me, that one day in London when Dr Adam Smith was boasting of it, he turned to him and said: "'Pray, sir, have you ever seen Brentford?" This was surely a strong instance of his impatience and spirit of contradiction. I put him in mind of it today, while he expressed his admiration of the elegant buildings, and whispered to him, "Don't you feel some remorse?" ...

'Professors Reid and Anderson and the two Messieurs Foulis, "the Elzevirs of Glasgow", dined and drank tea with us at our inn, after which the professors went away; and I, having a letter to write, left my fellow traveller with Messieurs Foulis. Though good and ingenious men, they have that unsettled speculative mode of conversation which is offensive to a man regularly taught at an English school and university. I found that instead of listening to the dictates of the sage, they had teased him with questions and doubtful lisputations. He came in a flutter to me and desired I might come back again, for he could not bear these men.

"'O ho! sir," said I, "you are flying to me for refuge!" He never, any situation, was at a loss for a ready repartee. He answered with a quick vivacity:

"'It is of two evils choosing the least!" I was delighted at this flash bursting from the cloud which hung upon his mind, closed my letter directly, and joined the company.'

Boswell's picture gladdens my heart. To think of two loquacious Glaswegians confounding the Grand Cham himself! True, they were rather unusual Glaswegians, but it's typical of any citizen of Glasgow that he refuses to be put down by pontifical statements.

Boswell and Johnson left the Saracen's Head the following day, and went to Ayrshire. There is a story that Dr Johnson and Adam Smith had a night's drinking at the Saracen's Head and their discussion ended in a swearing match. But I cannot trace this episode, although the very bowl from which they drank their punch at the Saracen's Head was produced at a meeting of the Old Glasgow Club in October 1904.

Any notables who visited the city stayed at the Saracen's Head. Robert Burns and John Wesley, two rather different types, took rooms there. In the summer of 1803 William

Wordsworth and his sister Dorothy arrived, along with Samuel Coleridge. They stayed for two days and admired Glasgow greatly. The hackney coach in which they travelled was the first ever seen in the city and when they left to travel westwards a crowd of small boys followed the coach, cheering and shouting, for several miles.

Dougal Graham, the Skellat Bellman of Glasgow, was often seen about the Saracen's Head. He was lame, a hunchback and a poet. He wrote several chapbooks which had a great sale for those days. He was appointed bellman about 1770 after a competition in which dozens of bellmen took part. The magistrates apparently picked Dougal because of his unusual appearance, his peculiar way of ringing the bell and his fine loud voice. For his test he cried in stentorian tones:

'Caller herring at the Broomielaw,
Three a penny, three a penny!'

Then he added:

'Indeed, my friends,
But it's a' blewflum,
For the herring's no' catch'd,
And the boat's no come.'

What Glasgow magistrate could resist such wit?

One day in 1776 some officers newly returned from the American War were looking out of one of the windows of the Saracen's Head. When the humpbacked bellman came along, one officer shouted rudely, 'What's that on your back, Dougal?'

Dougal Graham just looked up and replied: 'It's Bunker Hill. Do you care to mount?'

When other good hotels were built in Glasgow, and the city started moving west, the Saracen's Head fell on evil days. Latterly it was turned into a tenement and became a very seedy building. At last, in 1904, it was sold for demolition. Before it was demolished the Old Glasgow Club met in the Great Dovehill Mission Hall, which, in its palmy days, had been the Assembly Room of the Saracen's Head. The club members were able to make out the 'Fiddlers' Bank', a sort of minstrels' gallery, where the famous Niel Gow, among others, had played.

On display was the great punch-bowl of the Saracen's Head, made to hold five gallons. On the bottom of the bowl is a fancy depiction of Glasgow's coat-of-arms and the inscription 'Success to the Town of Glasgow'. This punch-bowl, which must be about two hundred and sixty-five years old, is now in the People's Palace on Glasgow Green.

The Saracen's Head building was demolished in 1905 and under part of it the workmen came across some skeletons. These were the remains of the kirkyard of Little St Mungo's Chapel, a very ancient church.

It takes considerable imagination to reconstruct in the mind's eye the Saracen's Head where the present red sandstone building stands. Not so long ago you could go into the courtyard behind the building and make some sort of attempt at reconstruction. But the vandals have been there and it's a scene of devastation.

There are, for example, the remains of St Mungo's Well, but you wouldn't know that this huddled piece of stone was important. The top has been closed as long as I've known it, so you couldn't see whether there was water in the well or not. An inscription on the well has disappeared. It said: 'The ancient well of Little St Mungo, restored 1906. Near this spot Christian Converts met St Kentigern on his return from Wales. Near this spot also, his meeting with St Columba is said by some Historians to have taken place.'

Across the yard from the well was a charming iron fountain which, appropriately enough, was made by the Saracen Foundry in Possilpark. Walter MacFarlane started his business in Saracen Lane off the Gallowgate and carried the name with him. It's a pity his descendents hadn't carried the fountain up to Possilpark too, because the vandals reduced it to scrap-iron.

There was another oddity in this yard, an Elizabethan-type building at the back, now demolished. It was put up by one of the Andersons of John Anderson's Royal Polytechnic as a boys' club. It served various functions, including, for a time, that of a film studio.

If you are in the Gallowgate on a Saturday or a Sunday you'll see huge crowds moving steadily towards one place – the Barras, Glasgow's open-air market, considered by Glaswegians to be far superior to Petticoat Lane or any other open-air market anywhere. 'Open-air' is perhaps a misnomer. Much of the market is under cover. Above it is the renowned Barrowland Dance Hall, said to be one of the buildings marked by Lord Haw – Haw for destruction by the Nazi Air Force during the Second World War. The reason was that it was so popular with the American Forces.

Glasgow has had open-air markets for years. I have already mentioned Paddy's Market in the Briggait. There have been others, always near the River Clyde. The present Barras was the invention of a redoubtable woman, Mrs McIver, who was known as the 'Barras Queen'. She and her husband had a single barrow from which they sold all manner of goods. Mrs McIver invested in some extra barrows and hired them out. Then she rented a piece of ground in the Gallowgate and the Barras started there.

It was such a success that the family (Mrs McIver had several sons and daughters) got together and built a dance hall on stilts, leaving space below for the market. This dance hall went on fire some years ago, but was rebuilt by Sam McIver, the 'Barras Prince', in record time. His mother had now retired. She was said to be a millionairess and was living in luxury in a swanky Glasgow suburb. But she missed the Gallowgate. So Sam McIver bought a little shop just opposite Barrowland and installed his mother there. Every day she sat there and did whatever business came her way, and was a satisfied woman.

Eventually the McIvers went into the car business as well as the Barras. I once took Bessie Love, the film star of the thirties, to Barrowland. Sam McIver showed her the veritable automobile in which King George V took his last ride at Bognor Regis. We went up to the dance hall, where Miss Love was 'lifted' (in English, asked to dance) several times. Someone had told her that almost every man there had a razor tucked away somewhere. The Americans, a trusting people, will believe anything.

As we were leaving Barrowland, Miss Love said to Sam McIver, 'Do you ever have any trouble here?'

'Trouble?' said Sam. 'No, there's no trouble here.' He put his hand behind his back and produced a police truncheon. 'See that?' he said, pointing to some indentations in the truncheon. 'That's the teeth of a big Irishman we had to deal with last night.'

As we go down the Gallowgate we come to a railway goods station and a thoroughfare called Barracks Street. The old Infantry Barracks stood here. Glaswegians didn't like troops being billeted on them and so in 1795 the barracks were built. They remained there until 1870, when they were moved to Maryhill. Today the Maryhill Barracks have been replaced by skyscrapers and there are no barracks left in Glasgow.

It was appropriate that the first barracks should be built at this spot in the Gallowgate, because it had been known for hundreds of years as 'The Butts'. It was an open piece of ground where the wappenschaws were held. The wappen-schaw was a 'weapon show', and swordsmen, spearmen, archers and other military types did their training and exercises here. It was the site of two of Glasgow's battles.

Glasgow's most famous battle is the Battle of Langside, where the forces of Mary Queen of Scots were defeated. But much earlier in Mary's career there was the Battle of the Butts. In 1544 the Earl of Lennox garrisoned the Bishop's Castle in the High Street. He was besieged by the Regent Arran. He held out for ten days, and then, being promised quarter by the Regent, he surrendered. But the Regent did not keep his promise. As soon as Lennox's troops left the protection of the Castle they were massacred. Only two escaped.

They took the news of this treachery to the Earl of Glencairn, who immediately raised an army of eight hundred men and met the Regent Arran's army in the Gallowgate at the Butts. The Regent defeated Glencairn after a bloody battle. He had learned that the Provost and citizens of Glasgow were on Glencairn's side, so he gave the town up to plunder. 'The very doors and windows of many dwelling-houses were carried away', said a contemporary report.

The next Battle of the Butts was in Covenanting times. In 1679 Claverhouse was defeated at Drumclog. He retreated to Glasgow, roused the garrison there to join the remnants of his forces and met the victorious Covenanters at the Butts in the Gallowgate. Claverhouse won this battle and showed his contempt for the Covenanters by allowing the dead bodies of his enemies to lie on the field for more than a day, so that they were devoured by the butchers' dogs.

Claverhouse also found that many Glasgow citizens supported the Covenanters and then began Glasgow's own 'Killing Times', remembered by plaques and tablets in the cathedral yard, at Cathcart, and in Castle Street.

I have mentioned the great number of pubs the Gallowgate once had. My own favourite was the Wee Man's, just along the street from the site of the battles. There is still a Wee Man there, but not the one I knew. I'd been in once or twice at lunchtime and had written about the place, so the Wee Man himself (who said he had chosen the title of the pub because he *was* a wee man) asked me to go on the pub's summer outing to Rothesay. Many Glasgow pubs, or those which are the equivalent of the English 'local', run summer outings and the customers pay a small amount each week to build up a kitty for the great day. A committee is appointed to arrange the details.

Pub summer outings are held on a Sunday, naturally. This one started in the gentlemen's lavatory opposite No 13 Platform of the Central Station. Ushers showed you into the lavatory where you received several tickets. Each ticket allowed you either a half of whisky or a bottle of beer, and a trestle table was set up in the lavatory so that you could start right away. Then, much refreshed, we went to the Wemyss Bay train where there were reserved coaches labelled 'The Wee Man'.

There were about fifty of us altogether and we carried with us cases of whisky and beer, two footballs, a wig, a trumpet and a false moustache. When we boarded the steamer at Rothesay the Wee Men started a concert right away. Then I saw the reason for the wig, the trumpet and the false moustache. Incidentally, Sunday steamers are 'dry' and nobody attempted to raid the cases of whisky and beer either on the train or on the steamer. This was a very respectable do.

When we got to Rothesay we went straight to the Victoria Hotel and had lunch. Then two buses took us over to Ettrick Bay, where the more energetic among us played football, ran races and paddled in the Firth of Clyde. A bar was set up so that we could use what tickets we had left. When we were tired and the bar was finished we got back into our buses, returned to the Victoria and had high tea and 'harmony'. And on the steamer back up the Firth the Wee Men started yet another concert, in which most of the other passengers joined. I still remember one beautiful young woman saying to another, 'Aw, Sandra, here a rerr crowd frae Glasga!'

Of course, Glasgow has advanced considerably since then, and we are now allowed singing and music in pubs. In the days of the Wee Man's outing singing in pubs was banned, and the only chance the customers got was the summer outing.

The Wee Man is just on the outskirts of Glasgow's Meat and Cattle Market. The difference, of course, is that the Meat Market is for dead animals and the Cattle Market for the live ones. They are like similar markets all over Britain, but the Cattle Market itself is also used for selling second-hand cars. All that is guaranteed with some of these cars is that they will leave the Cattle Market under their own steam!

Graham Square is the entrance to the Cattle Market and I recommend a visit to the Market Hotel. It still has a 19th-century atmosphere, but I mean a cattleman's 19th-century atmosphere! In my young days you'd still see Feeing Day in Graham Square. All the country boys and girls were there and the farmers moved among them, talking terms and then settling with a clasp of hands.

We travel on east out the Gallowgate and come to Camlachie and Calton. Camlachie House, the home of John Walkinshaw, the man who supported Bonnie Prince Charlie when he was in Glasgow, was at Nos 809 and 811 Gallowgate. It was his daughter Clementina Walkinshaw who left home to follow the Prince into exile on the Continent. Naturally the